The New York Times
ESSENTIAL LIBRARY

Jazz

The New York Times
ESSENTIAL LIBRARY

A Critic's Guide to the
100 Most Important Recordings

BEN RATLIFF

TIMES BOOKS

Henry Holt and Company   New York

Times Books
Henry Holt and Company, LLC
Publishers since 1866
115 West 18th Street
New York, New York 10011

Henry Holt® is a registered trademark of
Henry Holt and Company, LLC.

Some material in the book has appeared, in slightly different
form, in *The New York Times, Slate* magazine, and the *Village Voice*.

Library of Congress Cataloging-in-Publication Data
Ratliff, Ben.
    Jazz, a critic's guide to the 100 most important recordings / Ben Ratliff.
        p.   cm.—(The New York Times essential library)
    ISBN: 0-8050-7068-0 (pbk.)
    1. Jazz—Discography.   I. Title.   II. Series.
ML156.4.J3 R37 2002
016.78165'0266—dc21   2002069551

First Edition 2002

Designed by Paula Russell Szafranski

Printed in the United States of America

1   3   5   7   9   10   8   6   4   2

Contents

Preface

Let me begin a book on the essential recordings of jazz with a strange disclaimer: it's dismaying to me that the story of jazz is retold so often through the medium of recordings. For me, the transcendent experiences of jazz—the ones that make you feel weepy, or uprooted and a little sick, or so beguiled that you feel light for the next few days—are performances.

They don't happen often; in my case, maybe once every two or three months. But that's a decent rate for a thrill seeker; that's a possible six per year. Albums don't often do this to me anymore. That could be for a number of reasons that don't concern you, principal among which are my two young children and the difficulties of hearing jazz records uninterrupted at home (or anywhere in New York City, given how much time New Yorkers must spend working in order to make ends meet). But I've got a portable disc player and a good set of headphones, and I keep listening.

Jazz records have different significances today than they did in 1965 or 1940 or 1927. We must keep this in mind as we consider their importance—and when we wonder why such a high percentage of the ones discussed here were made prior to the Nixon administration.

Forty-three of them were made between 1950 and 1965. When the photographer Lee Friedlander moved to New York and began his life as a professional picture taker in the mid-1950s, he noticed that—by his own rough estimate—80 percent of the photographers in the world were still alive, and most of them were still working. The same was true in jazz (a connection that was apparent to Friedlander). Starting from that observation, it's easy to understand why the music reached its zenith of riches in the 1950s and 1960s and then began to dwindle.

As late as the 1940s, Americans went to record stores that sold only one or two labels; breadth of stock was not an issue. And musicians were touring so much that you could see Duke Ellington in Fargo, North Dakota, or Eddie Vinson, with John Coltrane in the band, in Lumberton, North Carolina. Now, outside of a few exceptions (those by Wynton Marsalis, Marian McPartland, and others with public-radio or -television exposure), jazz concerts are rarely presented in third-tier American cities anymore. I've just heard from a friend in State Center, Iowa, who tells me that the most exciting live musical events in his vicinity this year were the Commodores, sans Lionel Richie, and casino-circuit nostalgia-rock bands like .38 Special and Kansas. He's a jazz-record fiend, with a particular love for late-fifties and early-sixties hard bop—Hank Mobley, Horace Parlan, like that; once in a while, he'll buy something new. He orders from Amazon. com, of course; he probably hasn't seen the inside of a record store in years. He's not retired or anything—he's thirty-five.

That describes many of us these days: forget about live music and the discouragingly high cover charges, we don't even go record shopping. Yet we still adhere to the notion of jazz as a story of recordings, although recordings are only one medium and can present such a different picture of a band from the way it plays live. That goes doubly in the current age of concept albums. If a band always did live what it does on concept albums—routinely play the work of only one composer, for example—they'd get bored. Excuse me: I'd get bored, having to listen to it.

I feel sad that jazz doesn't seem to have it within itself to keep up with the sensual experiences that big-money rock or hip-hop producers have generated in the past ten years. In the rest of popular music, records sound great now—so great that it's easy to be fooled by mediocre talent—whereas jazz records are still pretty much documentary affairs.

This book reflects other sadnesses as well. There's the pain of seeing jazz dismissed or deemed unintelligible by some of the brightest people I know; that problem isn't going to get better any time soon, as the opportunity for journalistic exegesis drops, along with the limited number of new places on record-label rosters. (When I started at *The New York Times* in 1996, there were often critics from four New York–area dailies reviewing the same concerts; now, just as often, there is only one.) There is a sadness in the way musicians get pathologically wired by their formative surroundings, whether that be North Texas State's undergraduate jazz pedagogy or the Lower East Side free-jazz scene, so that they can't partake in whatever aesthetics lie on the other side of the fence. That situation, actually, is slowly improving—due to the different ways in which people now get their information about jazz. (It's not just evenhanded, canonical history books anymore but energetically partisan websites and niche-marketing online record stores.)

In this book, I keep returning to the idea of a mainstream. Mainstreams are the majority truth of art: a few people establish a language, and if they've hit on the right ingredients, it becomes commanding, by a mysterious consensus. Jazz, which still clings to remnants of the popular but in many ways has become an art music, is a particularly interesting test case for this point. If only five thousand people are going to buy a first-rate jazz album (another sad truth), then why would a jazz artist care at all about carrying on a tradition or expanding on an established language? Why wouldn't he just cut loose and play the original baby talk he always knew to be inside him?

But jazz musicians tend to stick within their autoformulation because nearly all of them are reverential toward the past; they're also trainspotters, statisticians, reference hounds. They tend to know which of jazz's many traditions they're coming from; they want to finesse that tradition (even if it's an avant-garde tradition) and, given the right circumstances, add something new to it.

History, mostly, lies in the meat of these traditions. You oughtn't look at jazz only by its corners, its Hot Fives and Sevens, its *Kind of Blue*s and *Love Supreme*s. You have to look at what the corners surround. I don't feel good about fetishization, and I'm interested in albums that say everything that needs to be said about a particular period without having accumulated the crust of myth. Up until the end of writing this book, I had left *Kind of Blue* out, on the theory that modal jazz, in and of itself, was a dead end, a spice rather than a language; that all the best playing of all the musicians on *Kind of Blue* is to be found elsewhere; that the album is, for the most part, rhythmically dull; and so on and so forth. But sometimes theory loses touch with reality. Almost everyone I told about this book assumed that I was *ranking* the top one hundred albums, as opposed to listing them chronologically, and that I would naturally put *Kind of Blue* at number one. Also, it really is a pretty good record, you know?

So I've tried to include both kinds of albums, the sacramental and the useful, sometimes favoring those that were more broadly popular, representative of an artist or his time, or directly influential on the practice of jazz rather than the legendary and one of a kind. I have felt a bit perverse in including Ella Fitzgerald's *Cole Porter Songbook,* for example, rather than some of her other songbook albums with better arrangements. But that was the album that made her famous—the one I first heard, as well—and commerce, every once in a while, really matters in jazz. Why I didn't put in many other top-selling albums on the pop side of jazz is for you to guess. I had to please myself. I couldn't write according to a single criterion, whether sales, mystique, influence on run-of-the-mill tenor players, or famous obscurity. To make my rationale even more nonsensical, I included a few albums that are very hard to find on CD at this writing: *Coisas,* by Moacir Santos, *Dogon A.D.,* by Julius Hemphill, and Jeanne Lee and Ran Blake's *The Newest Sound Around.* Others in the book may well be unavailable a year from now. But good music passes rapidly in and out of print on CD, and the resourceful listener has more ways to access recordings than he did in 1990; it stands to reason that he will have even more five years from now.

I do confess to a bias that favors understanding jazz as it is currently played. There are an awful lot of recordings of pre-1945 jazz—or jazz in a pre-1945 style—that might have been included. But this book is in some way a work of advocacy, and the moment calls for emergency measures: it seems wrong to overstuff a small list with music that can't be reconciled with what you currently hear in clubs. For a differently balanced overview, I recommend the CD box set *The Smithsonian Collection of Classic Jazz* (selected and annotated by Martin Williams), which covers the music—with greater specificity in the prewar years—up to the early eighties.

To counter the abrupt decisions, I've added a list at the back of the book of one hundred more albums you'd have nearly as much reason to own. To the middle-aged men who write huffy letters to jazz critics: read the B-list first, then fire away.

My parents, Marcus and Jennie Ratliff, raised me right, and never dissuaded me from becoming a music critic—a gift that I tend to take for granted. I couldn't have found the time and physical space to do this without Kate Reynolds and our Massachusetts family, but also without the help of Jackie Myers, Annie Hartenstein, and Robert Cox, the reading room at the New York Public Library, and Café Santiago on Fort Washington Avenue in New York.

Thanks to my agent, Zoë Pagnamenta, and to my editors, David Sobel at Henry Holt and Mike Levitas at Times Books. John Parsley, David's assistant, did more photo research on my behalf than I probably deserved. My editors, supervisors, and colleagues at *The New York Times*—principally John Darnton, Jon Pareles, and Fletcher Roberts but also Ben Sisario and Kelefa Sanneh—allowed me forbearance in the winter of 2001. Adina Zion rescued a good amount of this book in a split-second decision on the B train, and I don't want to think about that for another minute except to commend a remarkably selfless act.

I can't imagine contemplating jazz in isolation. My friends and colleagues make the evolving discussion about jazz and music of the New World worthwhile. (They also suggested the inclusion of certain albums.) They include Peter Watrous, Sasha Frere-Jones, Jon Abbey, Jon Munk, Kim Smith, Rob Saffer, Tom Moon, Lewis Porter, Lee Friedlander, Robert Farris Thompson, Sergio Martins, Joshua Weiner, Yuval Taylor, Jack Vartoogian, Harold Bott, John Szwed, Marcus Boon, Don Leavitt, and John Murph (special thanks to the late Albert Abbey). For continual encouragement through their writing of similar and related books, I thank the late Martin Williams, Gary Giddins, Allen Lowe, Whitney Balliett, Gunther Schuller, David Thomson, and Arthur Danto. Thanking musicians gets me into hot water; they don't look well on conflict of interest at the *Times*. But I have learned as much about jazz by talking to musicians after gigs—or calling them the next morning after eleven—as by any other method, and to those musicians who helped me it will probably be apparent that you did.

For assisting me in collecting materials, I thank Cem Kurosman and J. R. Rich at Blue Note, Tom Cording at Sony Legacy, Jenifer Levy and Regina Joskow-Dunton at Verve, Kevin Kennedy at Rhino, Arto Lindsay, Jordi Pujol at Tumbao, Rachelle Schlosser at RCA, Terri Hinte at Fantasy, and Jeff Roth at the *Times* archives.

My wife, Kate, will always be the number-one without-whom; she and my children, Henry and Toby, are my life. (HENRY: THIS IS YOUR NAME IN THE BOOK.)

1. ORIGINAL DIXIELAND JAZZ BAND:

The Creators of Jazz

(AVID 702, 2 CDS)

Nick LaRocca, cornet; Eddie Edwards, Emile Christian, trombone; Larry Shields, Artie Seaberg, clarinet; Don Parker, soprano saxophone; Henry W. Ragas, J. Russel Robinson, Harry Vanicelli, piano; Tony Sbarbaro, drums.

Recorded 1917–1936

The Original Dixieland Jazz Band—and its leader, Nick LaRocca, an Italian-American cornet player from New Orleans—has functioned as a trickster element in jazz history. It has felt the hot wind of both racial and aesthetic shame, and it has been defended as something greater than it was. But its initial records provided the start jazz deserved: something irresolutely poised between art and the low end of popular culture. Its songs have been among the most controversial ever recorded, and they still start disagreements.

"Livery Stable Blues," recorded for Victor on February 26, 1917, was the first jazz record. It was the result of a cult of celebrity set in motion by a successful run by the band at Reisenweber's Café in New York City—a booking made through the suggestion of Al Jolson. LaRocca was a great advance man; he came from New Orleans, where self-mythographers are bred by the thousand, and he was part of the same culture that produced Louis Armstrong and King Oliver and Freddie Keppard. He saw parade bands, opera (while working as an electrician in the opera house), and ragtime bands. He wasn't the first at anything, artistically speaking; he was simply involved in a music that was growing, and he saw a potential trend, with his own band as the trendsetter.

From then on, he sold himself, hard, as a creator, and the newspapers liked the story. Given the poor documentation of New Orleans jazz before the 1920s, as well as the unlikelihood that a black man's word would be taken seriously by a newspaper reporter of any influence, few were around to disprove him. Annotators like Brian Rust—who wrote the liner notes for this reissue of all the ODJB's recordings—have relied on the cream-rises-to-the-top theory to prove that the band was, in fact, the best of all playing in that idiom at the time. Rust is English, and white American scholars since the civil rights era have vociferously claimed the opposite: LaRocca ripped off better musicians who were black (particularly Freddie Keppard, who may have been too proud and paranoid to record his own music) and claimed originator's credit. Then there's the history of objecting to the ODJB on pure aesthetic grounds. In 1924, Paul Whiteman, presenting his minihistory of jazz at Carnegie Hall, which wound up with George Gershwin's *Rhapsody in Blue,* started the evening with "Livery Stable Blues," exaggerating the corn pone in it; he described it to the audience as "an example of the depraved past from which jazz has risen."

More recently, through the work of entirely different kinds of historians—Richard Sudhalter and Allen Lowe are two—the artistic value of the ODJB has been somewhat restored. Partially, they found virtues to the music in and of itself; they also gave secondhand support, citing the fact that Louis Armstrong and Bix Beiderbecke went on record admiring LaRocca's playing. (Sidney Bechet and Rex Stewart, on the other hand, wrote about LaRocca and his band with disdain; their attitude may well have been tempered with ad hominem disgust, for LaRocca was probably the worst racist in the history of jazz, given to blanket condescension toward black musicians.)

Historians born after 1950 have added more fuel: some have drawn parallels between the short histories of the ODJB and the Sex Pistols, a band that was a similarly blinding supernova of self-promotion and questionable (or, rather, questioned) talent.

I believe in the virtues of the ODJB. They hadn't been together very long when they made their first recordings, and in a few years they progressed from crude to streamlined; but I hear the crude state and the smooth state as equally interesting. I find the music itself repetitive and structurally limited, but it was hard-edged and anxious, a marked distinction from what we can assume to be the more soulful black New Orleans jazz of the same period, as exemplified by Kid Ory's first recordings in 1922. There is originality in this weird drive, and clarinetist Larry Shields—who can be heard prominently, benefiting from the practice of placing the cornetist well away from the recording horn—has a pulsating, fervid, nearly out-of-control sound.

"Livery Stable Blues"—originally titled "Barnyard Blues"—is wild, raucous, and pure show business, complete with instruments imitating barnyard sounds. The band advertised itself as "untuneful harmonists playing peppery melodies"; LaRocca didn't read music and used that fact in his publicity. It is squeaky-wheel art, calculated to shock and delight. But it is also smart, and if you subtract Tony Sbarbaro's untasteful brass-band volume, you're left with the kind of lilting New Orleans street rhythm that has ties to Brazilian samba-school drumming.

As with Shields, it can take a while for Sbarbaro, who thumps through these early recordings with little sensitivity, to become palatable; at first he's merely obnoxious (and the precursor of Gene Krupa's kind of bass-drum obnoxiousness). These can be lumpy performances. "Ostrich Walk," to cite another example, begins as rowdily as possible, with Sbarbaro simply gunning out the eighth-note rhythm of the horn introduction rather than presenting any more sophisticated rhythmic idea.

How curious it is that by 1936, when the band re-formed and cut six more songs, Sbarbaro should turn out to be among the most advanced musicians in the group. But such surprises make sense, given the feinting and posturing and japing and, as a matter of fact, art making that pervade these records.

2. KING OLIVER:

The Quintessence

(FREMAUX 220, 2 CDS)

Joe "King" Oliver, cornet; Louis Armstrong, cornet, slide whistle; Tick Gray, cornet; Honore Dutrey, Ed Atkins, Bob Shoffner, Kid Ory, James Archey, trombone; Johnny Dodds, Jimmie Noone, Ernest Elliott, clarinet; Paul "Stump" Evans, C-melody saxophone; Albert Nicholas, Billy Paige, Barney Bigard, Omer Simeon, Arville Harris, saxophones; Charlie Jackson, bass saxophone; Lil Hardin, Luis Russell, Clarence Williams, piano; Arthur "Bud" Scott, Johnny St. Cyr, banjo; Bert Coff, Cyrus St. Clair, tuba;

Eddie Lang, guitar, violin; Alberto Socarras, flute; Warren "Baby" Dodds, Paul Barbarin, drums; Justin Ring, percussion; Richard M. Jones, Georgia Taylor, Lizzie Miles, Texas Alexander, vocals.

Recorded 1923–1928

The mists of jazz history don't really part until the early twenties. So we must accept on faith the information—consistently reiterated by eyewitnesses—that hearing the Joe "King" Oliver band, in the early 1920s, even before it was joined by young Louis Armstrong, was an epiphanic experience, the sort of thing for which a new descriptive vocabulary had to be invented. These recordings start in 1923, when the band had been playing with Armstrong for a year, and, though they are powerful, they suffer from two things: the crude techniques of early record making; and the necessarily disorienting effect of the recording process on a fundamentally "live" working band.

The Oliver band set a new standard for imposing professionalism, tempering its force with great control. Its records show the first significant instance of improvised form—cuing systems, the practice that has developed through eighty years of jazz, like the curriculum of an invisible academy.

King Oliver's groups prided themselves on their breaks, those four-bar lacunae placed toward the ends of tunes, at the height of their emotional crescendos, where the soloists write their signatures in the moving medium. As the recordings in this anthology proceed, the breaks grow more inventive. At the Lincoln Gardens in Chicago, where the band established a much-noticed residency, nobody seemed to figure out how Oliver and Armstrong negotiated what they would play together in these little fissured moments, amid the rush of the music. "I don't know how they knew what was coming up next," said drummer George Wettling, who was just old enough to see the band in the early twenties. "But they would play those breaks and never miss." They couldn't merely have reproduced the exact arrangement of a record; none of the recordings, made for Gennett, OKeh, Columbia, and Vocalion, went beyond three minutes and fifteen seconds, and it was said that the Oliver band would play "High Society Rag" at the Lincoln Gardens for forty minutes, like a proto–Grateful Dead.

Making jazz is a kind of acting. In movies, actors choreograph chases and sex scenes. Musicians often improvise or communicate to one another some preconceived routines; it often seems surprising, especially when there's a good deal of fresh, unpreconceived improvisation going on around it. A great example of this occurs at two moments in this collection's "Snake Rag," where the horns—Oliver, Armstrong, Honore Dutrey, and Johnny Dodds—rage through a collective improvisation. Suddenly there's a two-bar break in unison played by the cornets; they lift out of the tangle with a single hot phrase. Armstrong later talked about how this was done: Oliver would feed him a cue, a little phrase, during his improvisation in the preceding chorus.

Compared to the Duke Ellington recordings made for Columbia a little more than four years later, these are primitive. Armstrong, because of the force of his projection, had to stand alone, separated from the rest of the band by twelve or fifteen feet; he's a faint presence except on the breaks. (These were recorded in one take, of course, long before the advent of postproduction mixing; imagine the difficulty of shuttling quickly up to the recording horn for those eight beats then fading back fifteen feet.)

Clarinetist Johnny Dodds is of particular interest here, too. He is technically as perfect a player as there was in jazz at the time, and his solos are light-toned, floating, and emotional. (Hear him in "Alligator Hop," which features him all the way through: he adds startling tongue-slaps toward the end of his final solo.) He had a pure, unsentimental style, even when surrounded by self-conscious corniness, and his sound counterbalanced the hard punch of the trumpets.

The band represented on the first disc of *The Quintessence* basically holds fast to Oliver's Lincoln Gardens group; on the second disc, there are many variations. Included are some vocal numbers with Lizzie Miles, a "classic blues" (i.e., urbane, not rough-hewn) singer whose archaic style would imminently be blasted out of relevance by Louis Armstrong's first vocal performances. There are some quartet blues with guitarist Eddie Lang; there's also a cornet-piano duet with Jelly Roll Morton, "Tom Cat," where we hear some of Oliver's genius with mutes in the horn's timbral variation.

Starting in 1926, Oliver took up with a group he called the Dixie Syncopaters, and the group sound changed entirely with the addition of a saxophone section; jazz was beginning to change, and Oliver needed to be in the vanguard. It was a way of fattening up the sound without necessarily giving those added saxophonists much that was interesting to do, and as a result the internal balance in the music got thrown off. Yet this new music sounds more present in the improved recording quality, and you can get a better sense of Oliver's trumpet-playing power in his solos in songs such as "Jackass Blues," "Sugar Foot Stomp," and "Wa Wa Wa." During the first two, he continued to dine out on the hard, high, simple riff-phrases of "Dippermouth Blues" from three years before; in the third, Oliver and the nine musicians around him made a masterpiece. The arrangements themselves aren't brilliant—comparing them even to early Ellington is a cruel exercise. But in the variation of timbre and texture from one section to another (this is a piece cut into many sections), an awful lot goes on within two and a half minutes.

Armstrong, by 1927, was long gone, making his own records in Chicago under the name Louis Armstrong's Hot Five. His playing would far outstrip Oliver's. But without Oliver's style and group sound, perhaps there would have been no Armstrong.

3. BESSIE SMITH:

The Essential Bessie Smith

(COLUMBIA LEGACY 64922)

Bessie Smith, vocals; Ernest Elliot, Buster Bailey, Coleman Hawkins, clarinet; Clarence Williams, Irving Johns, Fletcher Henderson, James P. Johnson, Porter Grainger, Steve Stevens, Buck Washington, piano; Fred Longshaw, piano and reed organ; Louis Armstrong, Joe Smith, Ed Allen, Louis Metcalfe, cornet; Frank Newton, trumpet; Charlie Green, Jimmy Harrison, Joe Williams, Jack Teagarden, trombone; Garvin Bushell, alto saxophone; Chu Berry, Greely Walton, tenor saxophone; Robert Robbins, violin; Buddy Christian, Charlie Dixon, banjo; Eddie Lang, Bobby Johnson, guitar; Billy Taylor, bass; Cyrus St. Clair, tuba; The Bessemer Singers, vocals; Floyd Casey, drums.

Recorded 1923–1933

Bessie Smith's position in jazz history has been tenuous, because of the material she sang. Fair enough; her songs were blues, and even if her style wasn't blues from the country, it bore the mannerisms of blues singing more than it did what we consider, historically, to be those of jazz singing. But she represents the last point of this blurriness; after her came jazz singing.

You'd do well to make room for her, given the musicians who made appearances on her records and given her trajectory toward a jazz sense of dynamics, a jazz disposition. The list of instrumentalists on this collection, which extends from the beginning of her career to beyond the point of its slide into the Great Depression's commercial oblivion, represents an impressive portion of jazz's great figures in the twenties and early thirties.

All reports say that Smith, who had previously been a touring member of Ma Rainey's Rabbit Foot Minstrels, was nervous about making her first recordings. But five months after her initial sessions on Columbia, on "Jail-House Blues" she radiates confidence. She releases vowels with such force that it's sometimes hard to make out the sense of her long, stretched-out "the"s and "in"s and "here"s and "you"s. Her rhythm and rubbery intonation on the repeated first line—"thirty days in jail with my back turned to the wall"—are simply awesome.

From there, her style grew both bigger and meaner and, strangely, more decorous at times; the quality of her accompaniment, starting with the bare bones of Clarence Williams's piano, went through the roof. On "St. Louis Blues," from 1925—the period at which she became a million-selling artist—Smith is accompanied by Louis Armstrong on cornet and Fred Longshaw on reed organ, the kind of instrument you now hear on an old-fashioned carousel. It's a lovely textural mix of the wheezy and archaic with the clarion and modern. The song builds momentum over four choruses; Armstrong's obbligato inventions grow increasingly complex as the tune goes along, and he ends on a tangy F-sharp over Longshaw's dominant seventh chord, introducing a bit of major-minor drama at the last second. In "You've Been a Good Ole Wagon," cut later in the same session, he lays on more devices, wrapping a jagged discourse of wah-wah phrases around her vocal line.

Smith's voice grows rough and cutting and more hornlike in "I Ain't

Goin' to Play Second Fiddle," recorded a few months later. At the peak of her popularity, Smith grew into her persona, projecting bold assertions of independence. When she sang that she was "used to playing lead," her claim is commanding; you wouldn't want to mess with her.

Still, this was slight compared to her later songs. In "Gimme a Pigfoot and a Bottle of Beer," from 1933, she is impatient, reckless, competitive; she wants her demands satisfied without delay. "Give the piano player a drink because he's bringin' me down," she sings, and then: "He's got rhythm, YEAH!" The "yeah" is not cute or carefree; it's monstrous. (Choosing such small gestures to intensify beyond reasonable proportions is the mark of a great singer.) It's a kind of nihilistic, death-wish song, too; she revels in its extremity. "Gimme a reefer and a gang o' gin," she exhorts; "slay me, 'cause I'm in my sin."

Every time a female pop singer comes along who seems to be a sinner with a conscience—neither a Madonna nor a whore but an actual person with appetites, bluster, vulnerable emotions, and moral ambiguity—she is treated as if she invented a new state of mind. But this was Bessie Smith's complexity in the 1920s. She could adopt a cooler, more objective, cabaret flavor in "Backwater Blues," backed by James P. Johnson's Europeanized blues; and over the incongruously downcast, low-embers mood of "Need a Little Sugar in My Bowl," she lustily sang some of the most transparent metaphors in the history of nudge-wink songs.

The music improves as the collection moves along, culminating in her work with Buck and His Band, in which she finally sang against a truly sophisticated jazz combo. She absorbed some of Louis Armstrong's light-footed rhythm (listen to "Do Your Duty"); there is a similarly witty delicacy in the solos of Chu Berry and Frank Newton.

Finally, "Take Me for a Buggy Ride," one of her last great songs, hangs together on account of how closely she sticks to the melody's tonic note. In two stop-time verses, where all of the band comes in only to accent the first and third beats of each bar, she sticks almost exclusively, obsessively, to that one note. Bessie Smith was a master of creating tension, and here the tension comes from restraint.

4. FLETCHER HENDERSON:

A Study in Frustration: Thesaurus of Classic Jazz

(COLUMBIA/LEGACY 57596; 3 CDS)

Fletcher Henderson, piano, arranger; Don Redman, alto saxophone, clarinet, arranger; Louis Armstrong, Henry "Red" Allen, Russell Smith, Roy Eldridge, Dick Vance, Joe Thomas, Bobby Stark, Joe Smith, Emmett Berry, Elmer Chambers, Howard Scott, Tommy Ladnier, Leora Henderson, trumpet; Rex Stewart, cornet; J. C. Higginbotham, Dicky Wells, Sandy Williams, Teddy Nixon, Charlie Green, Benny Morton, Jimmy Harrison, Claude Jones, Ed Cuffee, Fernando Arbello, Al Wynn, John McConnell, trombone; Coleman Hawkins, Chu Berry, Ben Webster, Franz Jackson, Elmer Williams, tenor saxophone; Russell Procope, Carmelo Jejo, Scoops Carey, Buster Bailey, Eddie Barefield, Budd Johnson, clarinet and alto saxophone; Benny Carter, Harvey Boone, Hilton Jefferson, alto saxophone; Don Pasquall, alto and baritone saxophone; Edgar Sampson, alto saxophone and violin; Lonnie Brown, alto and C-melody saxophone; Jerry Blake, alto clarinet; Freddie White, Bernard Addison, Bob Lessey, Lawrence Lucie, guitar; Clarence Holiday, guitar and banjo; Charlie Dixon, banjo; Fats Waller, piano, organ; Horace Henderson, piano; Ralph Escudero, June Cole, Del Thomas, tuba; John Kirby, bass and tuba; Israel Crosby, bass; Walter Johnson, Sid Catlett, Kaiser Marshall, drums; Pete Suggs, drums and vibraphone.

Recorded 1923–1938

The Riverside History of Classic Jazz—with its booklet of interpretive history written by historians and critics—appeared five years earlier. But *A Study in Frustration*, initially issued in 1961 on four LPs, came very early for a critical-minded reissue of jazz, especially of a single artist.

A critical mind-set is a necessary precondition to approaching Fletcher Henderson. As the nominal bandleader, sometimes composer, sometimes arranger, usually pianist, Henderson created music that had high peaks and deep troughs; his hot streaks were short, and his oversights baffling.

Yet he is important for several reasons. One, he established the size of the big-band orchestra, making his instrumentation the standard. (He was the most popular black bandleader at the end of the 1920s, with his fan base growing constantly from his regular job at New York's Roseland Ballroom.) Two, look at the personnel list above, studded with the jackpot names of jazz history. The best players in the country were drawn to him. Three, the range of his work is a lesson in how far toward both art and commerce a bandleader could lean; in Henderson's case, the zigzagging becomes almost absurd, from treacly novelties, to a gleaming and influential mainstream big-band sound, to the stone avant-garde. At times it seems as if there was no consistent, guiding hand on the tiller. And four, his work includes important keys to understanding Louis Armstrong and Coleman Hawkins, Fats Waller and Roy Eldridge.

Don Redman, the arranger for all the material here up to late 1927—which is all of the first disc—set down several blueprint ideas about big-band arrangements. The interstitial sequences played by three clarinets, the spooky timbral feeling that later helped make Ellington's "Mood Indigo" so effective, were in place as early as 1924. And the separated section work was, too: brass posing the question, reeds giving the answer (or vice versa), both coming together for a summary statement.

Armstrong's airy syncopation, the annunciatory spirit of his playing, abounds on "Copenhagen," "Everybody Loves My Baby," "Sugarfoot Stomp," "T.N.T.," and others. And Coleman Hawkins—rhythmically pinched and far more invested in "legit" playing than he would be ten years later, yet still a jolting player—has his first great extended solo on "The Stampede," from 1926.

Some of the writing and arranging here is almost too tricky for its own good—whole-tone chord cycles, diminished chords, changing stop-time sections; for its studied sophistication, it's about four years ahead of Ellington. Nineteen twenty-seven's "Whiteman Stomp"—written by Fats Waller and sold to Henderson for ten dollars, then given to the Paul Whiteman orchestra (it is unknown whether Waller got another ten dollars for the second transaction)—is an examplary piece of writing and arranging. It's got so many sections that it almost seems through-composed; no wonder the Whiteman orchestra found it too difficult to play at first. But it is a full-blooded reading, with Waller playing the piano part more authoritatively than Henderson ever could. Hawkins's "Queer Notions," from 1933, harks back to that complex chord movement and restless, incident-stuffed arranging. But the Henderson band was also capable of something like the charging "Hop Off," a much more acceptable major-key dance tune—even though it changes strains several times, and even though the Hawkins solos, with their abrupt, slightly ugly, whipped-around arpeggios, sound like he's wrestling ostriches.

The drummer Walter Johnson replaced Kaiser Marshall in 1929, and things changed: the group began to breathe rhythmically, riding on something other than cleverness. (For this, "Wang Wang Blues," arranged by Benny Carter, was the turnaround moment.) Finally, by 1931 and "Singin' the Blues," the band's tuba player, John Kirby, traded his instrument for a bass and presto—not only a brilliant orchestra but a comfortable one, with a suddenly modern sense of swing.

Why did Henderson wait so late in the game to switch Kirby from tuba to bass? The tuba was starting to sound ancient by 1931, and yet it's amazing to realize that only nine years separate the last days of Kirby's tuba from Jimmy Blanton's first recordings with Duke Ellington, on which the bass sounds as if it could never be played better. (See ahead to Ellington, *The Blanton-Webster Band*, 1940–1942.) Why, in this sophisticated ensemble, should there be a place for Edgar Sampson's awful violin solo in "Sugar," or for the wretchedly saccharine tune itself? Why should Henderson have drafted Katherine Handy (the daughter of W. C. Handy, not that it makes her any more palatable) to sing "they just live on dancin' / they're never blue or forlorn / and it ain't no sin for them to guzzle down gin / now, that's just why darkies were born" ("Underneath the Harlem Moon," 1932)?

Sometimes there is no explaining the wine-dark sea of popular culture, and Henderson went adrift in it. He is said to have been a bad manager and never to have entirely recovered from a 1928 car accident. His orchestra lost much of its audience by the 1930s, though he pressed on, making his most direct orchestral swing in "Christopher Columbus" and "Stealin' Apples." In 1938, when this box set stops, Benny Goodman was known around the world as the "King of Swing," having derived his sound from the mid-thirties Henderson band; Henderson himself, without a band of his own, was put to work for Goodman in 1939 as a staff arranger. You can understand how racially charged this turn of events might have been, and how those who felt close to his music would never quite forget the sting.

5. LOUIS ARMSTRONG:

The Complete Hot Five and Hot Seven Recordings

(COLUMBIA LEGACY C4K 63257, 4 DISCS)

Louis Armstrong, Bill Wilson, trumpet; Kid Ory, John Thomas, Honore Dutrey, Roy Palmer, Fred Robinson, J. C. Higginbotham, Jack Teagarden, trombone; Johnny Dodds, Jimmie Noone, Jimmy Strong, Don Redman, clarinet; Barney Bigard, Happy Caldwell, tenor saxophone; Boyd Atkins, Joe Walker, Al Washington, Albert Nicholas, Charlie Holmes, Teddy Hill, reeds; Lil Armstrong, Hersal Thomas, Earl "Fatha" Hines, Luis Russell, Joe Sullivan, piano; Johnny St. Cyr, Bud Scott, Dave Wilborn, Eddie Condon, banjo; Rip Bassett, Mancy Carr, banjo and guitar; Lonnie Johnson, Eddie Lang, guitar; Peter Briggs, tuba; Pops Foster, bass; Warren "Baby" Dodds, Tubby Hall, Zutty Singleton, Paul Barbarin, Kaiser Marshall, drums; Joe "Butterbeans" Edwards and Susie Edwards, Hociel Thomas, Lillie Delk Christian, vocals.

Recorded 1925–1929

These days, young people within fifty miles of at least a third-string university town (and hence a used-record store) tend to find their way to jazz through rock music: groups like Medeski, Martin and Wood and Sonic Youth give them the keys to the kingdom, pointing them by homage, if not by scholarly liner-note directives, to jazz of the 1960s, which might, possibly, lead them on further to Louis Armstrong. (Young jazz musicians, of course, have teachers, who help them get there more directly.) But even at the tail end of the LP era, these Columbia records—among the best-known jazz in the world—were often the first jazz you'd hear. (Such, at least, was the case for me.)

They demand to be heard and reheard, enjoyed for their flash and their design and their incredible pulse of life. When you return to them later—having heard much else, with your capacity for surprise reduced—some of the tracks here still ask new questions.

They certainly don't settle passively into a clichéd conception of music from the late twenties. They represent the New Orleans sound, yes, but even by 1927 Armstrong was out front and center, a bold fact, playing entire phrases before or ahead of the beat, making a fool of time. An idea like "New Orleans" couldn't contain him. ("Weather Bird," his marvelous duet with Earl Hines—the only musician here who can properly respond to Armstrong's challenges and shines, at times, with equal brightness—is so full of both men's original aesthetics that it's not properly representative of anything outside themselves.)

Armstrong the trumpeter also found himself as Armstrong the singer during this period, originating a rhythmic vocal conception that flooded the world of jazz singing and the parallel world of pop singing, as it was later taught by Billie Holiday and Frank Sinatra. And immediately after Armstrong left Columbia, he began his career as a soloist in front of an orchestra, tackling American popular music in the largest possible context.

When Armstrong recorded this music—all in Chicago, save for the final three tracks—he had already been through several bands, all of which had scored hit singles thanks to his trumpet playing, including Clarence Williams's Blue Five, Fletcher Henderson's, and Bessie Smith's. OKeh records signed him in 1925, putting him in the studio with a group that never existed in the real world. Armstrong was an exception in all things, and these recordings are the exception to the rule that working bands make the best jazz.

The contrapuntal tangle of "Muskrat Ramble" is a two-and-a-half-minute force field of contained energy. Armstrong's improvisations (and those of Johnny Dodds on clarinet) in "Potato Head Blues" have no hesitation: they know exactly what they want to do, and are conceived as ends in themselves. (If Armstrong didn't invent the solo, he invented the importance of the solo and its function as a kind of musical heroism.) "Skid-Dat-De-Dat," with four-bar portions connected by short improvisations and then a scat-singing solo, is formally radical; its shocks are of the same sort that Ornette Coleman's early work provides. The magnificently touching "West End Blues" is a work of almost unparalleled power in jazz history—as influential upon trumpet players as it was upon singers.

This collection makes the Hot Fives and Sevens catalog—most of which has always been available separately—unified and manageable as a start-to-finish listening experience. As Columbia has reorganized it, the set is not without strangenesses. The reissue has been produced by Phil Schaap, and he presumes your familiarity with the programming buttons on the CD player. You are given full information, presented with all tracks and alternate takes in chronological order, and given a four-second pause track to program in between songs if you like. The tacit suggestion is that if you want to canonize any further, you go right ahead; as an example, "Cornet Chop Suey," released through the years in what's now thought to have been a slowed-down key of E-flat, is included both at its well-known speed and in proper F.

Schaap's drive to get things right has an interesting twist: it tends to respect the effect of the public imagination on culture. (Armstrong belongs to the public imagination; this set reflects that notion, issued as it was in 2000 to commemorate Armstrong's widely celebrated birthday, July 4, 1900, which wasn't really his birthday at all.) Schaap as producer isn't trying to rewrite history so much as give you the commonly accepted version as well as his own. Some of the tracks included here are not strictly recordings by the various Hot Fives or Hot Sevens but were released as such in the past. They've earned inclusion, if only by an error of history.

The sound here is bright and present, even more so than on the JSP reissues that were for a while the tolerable alternative to Columbia's muffled-sounding initial CD reissues of this material.

6. JELLY ROLL MORTON:

Birth of the Hot: The Classic Chicago "Red Hot Peppers" Sessions, 1926–27

(RCA BLUEBIRD 66641-2)

Jelly Roll Morton, piano, vocals; George Mitchell, cornet; Kid Ory, Gerald Reeves, trombones; Johnny St. Cyr, banjo and guitar; Bud Scott, guitar; Omer Simeon, Barney Bigard, Darnell Howard, clarinets; J. Wright Smith, Clarence Black, violins; John Lindsay, bass; Andrew Hilaire, Baby Dodds, drums; Quinn Wilson, tuba; Lew LaMar, vocal effects.

Recorded 1926–1927

By the time of his first great recordings, Jelly Roll Morton, the New Orleans–bred Creole pianist, was more than seasoned: he had been a pro for twenty years. He had begun in the whorehouses of New Orleans then went on the move, traveling around the South, the Midwest, to New York, to Los Angeles. He heard and absorbed ragtime, light opera, Cuban music, Tin Pan Alley tunes, hymns, spirituals, and the music of brass bands.

In music he had an orderly mind. New Orleans music before these sessions put a premium on improvised choruses of polyphony; there was aesthetic gold to be had there, but what you could call the improvisational fallacy quickly began to creep into recordings. (In the improvisational fallacy, all improvising is fresh, therefore improvisation is the key to making meaningful jazz. It's not true even half the time: unless you're a player with a great amount of ideas at your disposal, the improvising mind is more maddeningly repetitive than the composing mind.)

Morton assembled his Red Hot Peppers studio band, gave them written-out parts, and rehearsed them, for this was not to be a jam session. He set up a hyperactive pile of arranging devices: stop-time figures at the beginning of tunes, consistent dynamic and melodic variation between strains, and rhythmic change-ups, edging into Cuban territory, that got beyond the clichés of the New Orleans chugging two-beat. These were the first great jazz compositions.

He did what he could to make you listen. He used novelties, some of them as crude as Lew LaMar's laughing to the beat on "Hyena Stomp," some of them as ticklingly modern as the strange harmonies and key-shift breaks in "The Chant" (written by Mel Stitzel), some of them as romantic as the twin violins on "Someday Sweetheart." (That last is a track that even Morton obsessives tend to apologize for, averring that Morton was really a hard stomper, not a composer of gooey romance. But he was everything he put his hand to, and there was humor in all of it.) He was a boss soloist, as "Smoke House Blues," with one of the loveliest piano breaks in jazz, demonstrates. It begins in a New Orleans two-beat, glides over two bars of implied tango, winds up with some floridity, and leaves some sprinkled final notes hanging uneasily.

"Sidewalk Blues" is like a Public Enemy song of 1926: a seemingly anarchic statement that's actually immaculately controlled, with Morton using the record as a canvas for theatrical action. It starts with a whistle, a car horn, wild shouting, a Morton heckle. "Hey, get out of the way! What are you trying to do, knock a streetcar off the track? You're so dumb, you should be the president of the deaf-and-dumb society!" "I'm sorry, boss, but I got the Sidewalk Blues." A piano chord played eight times, setting the tempo. One note played tutti by the band, and the first line by the trombonist shoots out, setting up a stop-time figure. Then the cornet plays the melody, over the band chugging on the twos and fours. Controlled band polyphony. Second theme statement: clarinet over the twos and fours. A C section with a new line, carried by cornet. The goddamn car horn and more whistles. More polyphony. Brass out; reeds whining the countermelody while Morton bangs in the background. Some false endings. The car horn again, Morton shouts, "Let 'em roll!" and it's over. In three and a half minutes, you've looked at this band up, down, and sideways; you've heard different combinations of melodic instruments, different ways of exposing the beat.

The Red Hot Peppers sessions are the models that much serious jazz composition was henceforth based on; their constant shuffling of ideas and their suggestion of possibility influenced everyone from Armstrong to such maximum-form-in-minimum-time outfits as John Kirby's Orchestra and Artie Shaw's Gramercy Five. But anyone interested in the lore and literature of jazz should also get familiar with Morton's solo piano Library of Congress recordings from 1938, released on CD by Rounder. On them, Morton talks, sings, and plays, conscious of his place in history and the importance of the recorded document. All the musical examples are connected by fabulous self-serving lectures; he was too foxy to be the mere subject of a mere documentary recording.

7. BIX BEIDERBECKE:

Bix Beiderbecke, Volume 1: Singin' the Blues

(COLUMBIA 45450)

Bix Beiderbecke, cornet, piano; Bill Rank, Miff Mole, trombone; Jimmy Dorsey, clarinet, alto saxophone; Don Murray, clarinet, tenor and baritone saxophones; Frankie Trumbauer, C-melody saxophone; Stanley "Doc" Ryker, Bobby Davis, alto saxophone; Herman "Hymie" Farberman, Sylvester Ahola, trumpet; Adrian Rollini, bass saxophone; Paul Mertz, piano, arranger; Eddie Lang, guitar; Howdy Quicksell, John Cali, banjo; Irving "Itzy" Riskin, Frank Signorelli, piano; Joe Venuti, violin; Joe Tarto, tuba; Chauncey Morehouse, Vic Berton, drums; Seger Ellis, Irving Kaufman, vocals; Fud Livingston, Bill Challis, Don Murray, arrangers.

Recorded 1927

This CD reissue, one of a two-volume set released by Columbia, contains "Singin' the Blues," an easy-tempo number adorned with silky linear-melodic solos by Trumbauer and Beiderbecke. Along with Louis Armstrong, Trumbauer and Beiderbecke produced something very new: original solos—which is to say, solos that gave soloists a measure of freedom from the theme, allowing them to invent fresh lines instead.

Beiderbecke's solo was wonderful, but largely on the strength of Trumbauer's solo grew a large and important strain of jazz playing. Lester Young acknowledged his debt to Trumbauer several times—most famously in an interview with François Postif shortly before his death—and it's easy to see why: Trumbauer was the first saxophonist to caress a melody artfully and introspectively.

Young wasn't the only one who enthused about Trumbauer or "Singin' the Blues" long after. Johnny Hodges and Charlie Parker claimed Trumbauer as a primary influence. Benny Carter, the arranger, bandleader, and multi-instrumentalist, orchestrated Trumbauer's solo on "Singin' the Blues" for a full saxophone section, and Rex Stewart, the Ellington trumpeter, proved it by interpolating Beiderbecke's solo with the Fletcher Henderson band. All these men were black; these are significant early examples of black musicians claiming white (and rather definitively white, as opposed to white-and-trying-to-be-black) influences.

In fact, Trumbauer was actually part Indian. But that's the least of the issue's complexities. Jazz is primarily a black American music. Yet all jazz musicians, especially in the early days, were hungry to use anything at their disposal. Stewart, in October 1926, had played with the Fletcher Henderson band at the Roseland Ballroom, going up against Jean Goldkette's orchestra in a battle of the bands. Goldkette's group—a white band from Detroit—included Beiderbecke and Trumbauer. About the experience, Stewart later said with affection, "Those little tight-assed white boys creamed us." Black and white were not always in conflict in America at the time—and especially not in jazz. "Singin' the Blues" is a celebrated case of natural hybridization.

Trumbauer's up-tempo saxophone playing was not to have the same far-reaching influence. Fast and flashy, popping with slap-tongue effects, it now feels constricted, rather severely a thing of its time; this was the style of Coleman Hawkins when he was a star member of the Fletcher Henderson band, though he was already in the process of outgrowing it. The slow, luxurious Trumbauer from "Singin' the Blues," however, was a thing of permanence.

But we still have not dealt with Bix Beiderbecke. "Singin' the Blues"—and thirteen of the twenty selections on this CD—were recorded under Trumbauer's name. Why was Beiderbecke so much more important? Because the 1920s were an age for trumpets, not saxophones; because he was a multi-instrumental (piano as well as cornet) talent; because he could swing a bit, whereas Trumbauer's notes didn't have that rhythmic orientation; because Beiderbecke's early death before the end of the decade fixed his legend. And because—though it was never stated in any context of advertising—he was the first great white artist of jazz.

With Beiderbecke, there are more instances of pure, consistent beauty. His trumpet idol was, of course, Louis Armstrong; recordings included here, like "Ostrich Walk" and "Riverboat Shuffle," are modeled structurally after Armstrong's. But as soloists, the two men were different. As writer and trumpeter Richard Sudhalter put it: "Where Louis carries a solo to ever greater heights through serial invention—one phrase suggesting the next in content and fervor—Bix works diligently at the song's emotional core, prizing out ever-greater complexities." There is little funk in Bix's style (listen to his long solo in "I'm Coming Virginia" and imagine how differently, with how much more vigor, Armstrong would have phrased it), but there is a coherent lyricism.

There's another aspect to this music, too. When you think of jazz becoming known, at least on a small scale, as an intellectual's music—as opposed to a dancer's music—you first think of the 1940s, at the fault line between swing and bebop fans. So jazz history has taught us. But even in 1927 there were tremors of "serious," ahead-of-its-time music. You can hear it in the sporadically avant-gardist leaning of the Henderson band; you can also hear it in the intertwined careers of Beiderbecke and Trumbauer.

First, there was a new instrumental delicacy: "For No Reason at All in C," recorded by the trio of Trumbauer, Beiderbecke on piano, and Eddie Lang on guitar, sounds almost as if it could be an experimental, independent-label Lee Konitz record from the 1970s. Then there was Beiderbecke's strange, searching talent at piano composition, which he felt shy about committing to record; the solo piano "In a Mist," with overt harmonic references to Debussy and Ravel, suggests a foretaste of Mary Lou Williams's "Zodiac Suite" of 1946. Fud Livingston's "Humpty Dumpty," again recorded under Trumbauer's name, offered more European harmony and odd chord changes. These curious bits aren't the main reasons Beiderbecke and Trumbauer have made it through history. But they are reminders that jazz has harbored a strain of exotic Europeanism since the early days.

A note for further listening: a recent box-set release by Mosaic called *The Complete OKeh and Brunswick Bix Beiderbecke, Frank Trumbauer and Jack Teagarden Sessions (1924–36)* tells the Beiderbecke-Trumbauer story rather well and expands their overlapping narratives to include the trombonist and singer Jack Teagarden, suggesting that the highest pantheon of early white jazz should be a triumvirate, not a duo.

8. DUKE ELLINGTON:

The OKeh Ellington

(COLUMBIA/LEGACY 46177, 2 CDS)

Duke Ellington, piano; Bubber Miley, Louis Metcalf, Jabbo Smith, Arthur Whetsol, Freddie Jenkins, Cootie Williams, trumpets; Joe "Tricky Sam" Nanton, trombone; Juan Tizol, valve trombone; Rudy Jackson, Prince Robinson, clarinet, tenor saxophone; Johnny Hodges, clarinet, soprano and alto saxophones; Otto Hardwick, soprano, alto, and baritone saxophones; Harry Carney, clarinet, alto and baritone saxophones; Barney Bigard, clarinet, tenor saxophone; Lonnie Johnson, guitar; Fred Guy, banjo; Henry Edwards, tuba; Wellman Braud, string bass; Sonny Greer, drums; Adelaide Hall, Irving Mills, Baby Cox, Cootie Williams, Sid Garry, vocals.

Recorded 1927–1930

Duke Ellington and his orchestra were hired by the Cotton Club in Harlem in January 1928 and stayed for thirty-eight months, with intermittent breaks to perform shows on Broadway and elsewhere. But he and the band always came back to the club, which was their laboratory.

At the Cotton Club, black entertainers performed for white-only clients. The music was part of a stage show; the live tableaux were dreamlike caricatures of racial fear and loathing. The historian Marshall Stearns recalled one in which a black pilot falls out of the sky to find—to his delight!—a blond goddess, worshiped by dark savages. We can say that this is hardly a working context fit for a serious composer. But shaping a world-class band and becoming a great composer in a compromised situation was a typical feat for Ellington, who was an ingeniously fluid American—socially, musically, intellectually.

Ellington has often been described as a middle-class Washingtonian, though to be sure "middle-class black" in the early twentieth century didn't mean what it does now. His father was a butler for a well-to-do physician, and a great deal of the luxuries enjoyed by the Ellington family came by virtue of their position as servants of a rich white man. (But a *sense* of luxury, of tact, of self-importance was implicit; Ellington's father also worked for a time in the White House, instructing white guests on proper behavior.) Ellington was brought up with encouragement, even coddling, by his family; by his accounts, they saw him as nobility in the making, and if he wanted to be an aesthete that was all right with them. Pursuing music and art (painting, design, and sculpture) until college years, Ellington focused exclusively on music in 1919.

In 1923, with a band and emboldened by the desire to write songs for the new black-music record labels, he arrived in New York. Five years later, he was making some of the great new music of the century, and the first few years of it are collected here. Jazz seemed to him an open canvas of possibility, as it did until the end of his life in 1974.

Ellington rose to the challenge of the Cotton Club situation and created a dramatic music—serving, on one hand, the notion of exotic jungle Negroes and, on the other hand, his own purposes simply to write excitingly, with new colors and arrangements. So in "The Mooche," from the fall of 1928, when the band was sleek with practice and Ellington was writing for nightly shows, there was a ghostly line voiced by three clarinets in close, lemony harmony; there was a remarkable growling trumpet solo by Bubber Miley, one of the excellent musicians who never quite found his footing outside of the Ellington orchestra; and an expressive wordless vocal by Baby Cox. It was plenty dramatic, but take it away from a painted-jungle backdrop and it exists as three minutes of music as music: innovative, humorous, varied, well arranged.

As a more extreme example, to hear "Saturday Night Function," a dignified piece alternating blues and gospel-tinged strains, and to imagine it serving as light entertainment for happy-feet white tourists gone uptown for the evening, is to understand a bit about how self-possessed Ellington was. Though Miley's sandpaper growl typified the "jungle music" era of Ellington's work, it was far from the dominant flavor; Freddie Jenkins, another trumpeter in the band, plays two dreamy muted solos packed with Ellington's melodic content in "The Blues with a Feelin'," over solemn, bowed bass and a combined banjo–snare drum beat on the two and four.

The first nine tracks of *The OKeh Ellington* are roughly recorded; by "Take It Easy," the impressive studio sound begins. OKeh's engineers, as well as the natural discipline of Ellington's band (groups played live without microphones in those days), made it possible for the dynamism to be captured—not all of it, though, and that's the best argument for groups like the Lincoln Center Jazz Orchestra playing Ellington as repertory: you think you know this music, but you don't, not until you hear the physical effect of the cross-panning, the leaping of melody between terraced sections of the band, that Ellington intended.

The music on *The OKeh Ellington* isn't freewheeling. The soloists in the band were playing shaped music—solos with a structure that shored up the tune's main theme or that acted essentially as a second, variation melody. For timbral mixtures, especially, Ellington had a genius. In "Mood Indigo" he brought together trumpet, trombone, and clarinet; in other pieces he deftly stepped around convention, such as using the low bass clarinet in the middle of a chord voicing's range rather than simply having it state the chord's root note. Connoting the deepest kind of adult sensuality—as in "Mood Indigo" again—he could write breathtakingly tender melodies. Jazz was a masculine endeavor, and suddenly this was a new kind of masculinity. As Harold Bloom has argued on behalf of Shakespeare, so could you argue on behalf of Ellington: he introduced listeners and musicians to dispositions that they may not have known to exist within them, yet which have since become commonplace. He widened the palette of jazz enough that it could proceed naturally in the manner that it still does—as a fullfledged art music as well as a popular music.

9. LOUIS ARMSTRONG:

The Complete RCA Victor Recordings

(RCA/BMG 09026-68682-2, 4 CDS)

Louis Armstrong, trumpet, vocals; Louis Bacon, Louis Hunt, Billy Hicks, Charlie Gaines, Elmer Whitlock, Zilner Randolph, Charlie Shavers, Neal Hefti, Ludgwig Jordan, Ed Mullens, "Fats" Ford, Thomas Grider, Manny Klein, Zeke Zarchy, Frank Beach, William Scott, Louis Gray, Robert Butler, trumpet; Bobby Hackett, cornet; Charlie Green, Keg Johnson, Russell Moore, Adam Martin, Si Zentner, Ed Kusby, George Roberts, Norman Powe, Al Cobbs, Vic Dickerson, Alton Moore, Russell Moore, Nat Allen, James Whitney, Waddey Williams, Kid Ory, trombone; Jack Teagarden, trombone, vocals; Louis Jordan, Arthur Davey, Johnny Hodges, Don Hill, Amos Gordon, Arthur Dennis, alto saxophone; Ellsworth Blake, Don Byas, John Sparrow, Joe Garland, Elmer Williams, Lucky Thompson, tenor saxophone; Pete Clark, Scoville Browne, George Oldham, clarinet and alto saxophone; Jimmy Hamilton, Barney Bigard, Peanuts Hucko, clarinet; Albert "Budd" Johnson, clarinet, tenor saxophone, vocals; Ernie Caceres, clarinet, baritone saxophone; Edgar Sampson, alto saxophone, violin; Ernest Thompson, baritone saxophone; Don Kirkpatrick, Wesley Robinson, Teddy Wilson, Charlie Beal, Lil Hardin Armstrong, Billy Strayhorn, Duke Ellington, Ed Swanston, Leonard Feather, Earl Mason, Dick Carey, Johnny Guarneri, Gerald Wiggins, piano; John Trueheart, Remo Palmieri, Elmer Warner, Allan Reuss, Bud Scott, Al Casey, Al Hendrickson, guitar; Jimmie Rodgers, vocal, guitar; Mike McKendrick, banjo, dobro; Ed Hayes, tuba; Elmer James, tuba, bass; Bill Oldham, Chubby Jackson, Arvell Shaw, Al Hall, Red Callender, Bob Haggart, Joe Comfort, bass; Chick Webb, Benny Hill, Yank Porter, Sid Catlett, Harry Dial, Sonny Greer, Butch Ballard, Zutty Singleton, Ed McConney, Minor Hall, James Harris, George Wettling, Cozy Cole, Irv Cottler, drums; Mezz Mezzrow, bells; Velma Middleton, vocals.

Recorded 1930–1956

Immediately after his OKeh recordings with the Hot Fives and Hot Sevens, Louis Armstrong ceased to be a New Orleans jazzman. He didn't give up all of his traditional repertoire; he still peformed "St. James Infirmary," "When It's Sleepy Time Down South," "High Society," and other popular songs suggestive of his hometown. But he immediately graduated to trans-American pop material (chiefly Tin Pan Alley songs) and was the very opposite of a provincial or regional figure. In the choreographer Mark Morris's words (describing his own ideal audience), Armstrong appealed not to everybody but anybody. It wasn't that it was lowest-common-denominator art. It just affirmed basic joys, with a feeling of vitality and rhythm and defiance.

In the early 1930s, Armstrong's singing became as important an aspect of his art as his trumpet playing, and despite the strangeness of that singing, its overcooked quality, its lapses into the mawkish or perverse, it has aged well. For at the root it is highly improvised, volatile stuff—in fact, the most highly improvised, risky, expansive performing that existed in jazz during the early thirties.

And it is recognizable as such today, after a lot of other jazz that has been serious in intent but mawkish or perverse as well—including some of the free jazz of the 1960s and 1970s. It has been said (most eloquently in Gary Giddins's *Satchmo*) but bears repeating: Armstrong was a modern character, a mixture of a true artist and entertainer, of individualist and crowd pleaser. If you don't appreciate both sides you miss his essence.

It's a shame to recommend Armstrong as he was defined by one record label (he was recording for other labels in the 1930s, chief among them Columbia), considering the heights to which Armstrong ascended during that period. But the RCA collection is well restored and brings together works from a number of different contexts, from Armstrong and His Orchestra in 1932 ("That's My Home," the "When You're Smiling / St. James Infirmary / Dinah" medley, "Basin Street Blues"), to Armstrong with the early country-music icon Jimmie Rodgers ("Blue Yodel No. 9," which shows Rodgers's notion of the blues as a structure with variable section lengths), to the Esquire All-American 1946 Award Winners band, playing functional blues while the clock ticks, to the twenties throwback Armstrong and His All Stars with Jack Teagarden, recorded live ("Rockin' Chair") and in his workmanlike swing-orchestra session ("It Takes Time").

As for his singing, "That's My Home" verifies that excellence does not rule out looniness. The wordless vocal on "Dinah" is pure improvising, in a realm beyond the melody and changes of the song. In "I Gotta Right to Sing the Blues" and an updated version of "Basin Street Blues," Armstrong's voice mimics an instrument—it's not clear which—but he is not singing as anyone either sang or talked at the time. His singing is just another opportunity to exercise the experiments in legato and rhythmic displacement that captured his imagination as a trumpet player.

For his trumpet playing, there is his new version of "Basin Street Blues" again. Armstrong was brave in all kinds of ways: here, he repeats one rhythmic figure for six straight bars (early in the piece, after the trombone solo). He contrasts long tones against rapid phrasing, in the middle of the same chorus. He works up to the best of his high, operatic, annunciatory playing.

Armstrong's voice mellowed in the 1940s, losing some of its scabrous bite; much of his music took on a sentimental edge when a New Orleans revival began. Thus, the contrast of Armstrong playing quite confidently among the modernists in the 1946 Esquire band, then putting the other musicians to shame in the "Dixieland Seven" band of the same year. But even Armstrong in low-grade surroundings could yield excitement: "Mahogany Hall Stomp," with the Dixieland Seven, has an Armstrong solo, before the final ensemble chorus, that picks up the momentum of the song, magically gathering the attention of the musicians around him, in a similar way that Coleman Hawkins did on his "Sweet Lorraine" of 1944.

I would suggest that a mixed listening diet of universal masterpieces with rent-paying operations—such as this box set offers—is an accurate way to learn about jazz. However rigorously or loosely they may have been prepared for, these performances by Armstrong contain the excitement of casual discovery. At their best—which is without a doubt the early-thirties material—they suggest much of the future of jazz improvisation.

Billie Holiday

10. BILLIE HOLIDAY:

Lady Day: The Best of Billie Holiday

(SONY LEGACY C2K-85979, 2 CDS)

Billie Holiday, vocals; Roy Eldridge, Jonah Jones, Bunny Berigan, Gordon Griffin, Charlie Teagarden, Richard Clarke, Shirley Clay, Irving "Mouse" Randolph, Eddie Thomkins, Buck Clayton, Charlie Shavers, Hot Lips Page, Shad Collins, Emmett Berry, trumpet; Bobby Hackett, cornet; Jack Teagarden, Dicky Wells, Trummy Young, Tyree Glenn, trombone; Benny Goodman, Tom Mace, Rudy Powell, Artie Shaw, Irving Fazola, Vido Musso, Buster Bailey, Edmond Hall, Jimmy Powell, Jimmy Hamilton, clarinet; Harry Carney, clarinet, baritone saxophone; Edgar Sampson, Hymie Schertzer, clarinet, alto saxophone; Ernie Powell, Babe Russin, clarinet, tenor saxophone; Benny Carter, alto and tenor saxophones; Tab Smith, soprano and alto saxophones; Ben Webster, Chu Berry, Art Karle, Ted McRae, Lester Young, Joe Thomas, Babe Russin, Herschel Evans, Bud Freeman, Kermit Scott, Stanley Payne, Kenneth Hollon, Don Byas, Jimmy Hamilton, tenor saxophone; Johnny Hodges, Earle Warren, Jack Washington, Carl Frye, Joe Eldridge, Bill Bowen, Georgie Auld, Don Redman, Leslie Johnakins, Eddie Barefield, Lester Boone, Jimmy Powell, alto saxophone; Teddy Wilson, Buck Washington, Joe Bushkin, Clyde Hart, James Sherman, Claude Thornhill, Margaret Johnson, Sonny White, Kenny Kersey, Joe Sullivan, Eddie Heywood, Art Tatum, piano; John Truehart, Lawrence Lucie, Dave Barbour, Dick McDonough, Allan Reuss, Freddie Green, Carmen Mastren, Danny Barker, Jimmy McLin, Bernard Addison, Ulysses Livingston, Paul Chapman, guitar; John Kirby, Artie Bernstein, Grachan Moncur, Pete Peterson, Milt Hinton, Walter Page, John Williams, Wilson Myers, Ted Sturgis, Oscar Pettiford, bass; Cozy Cole, Gene Krupa, Jo Jones, Alphonse Steele, Eddie Dougherty, Hal West, J. C. Heard, Yank Porter, Kenny Clarke, Herbert Cowens, Sidney Catlett, drums.

Recorded 1933–1945

While still living out a terribly damaged girlhood—there was a musician father who disappeared early, becoming a good-bad role model; she followed her mother into prostitution at age twelve, singing as an extra treat for the johns—Billie Holiday got her chance to break into recording at eighteen. She recorded twice that year, with Benny Good-man's orchestra. And in the first number, "Your Mother's Son-in-Law," she wasted everyone's time with callow pretension, enunciating a hard "r" that wasn't hers in "banker" and all its rhyming syllables. Ethel Waters, who watched her, did not approve.

But she got another chance just before her twentieth birthday, and here her talent was easier to gauge. In "I Wished on the Moon"—the Teddy Wilson band, with Benny Goodman on clarinet, played the introduction beautifully—it was there in the second line: "for some-thing I . . . nevv-ver knew." The session would have been a beautiful, relaxed orientation for any singer; John Kirby on bass and Cozy Cole on drums stamped plump swing beats like deep cushions. But she quickly ignores what safety the situation offered, and her louche inde-pendence from show-business convention—rushing, holding back, implying an easy *sprechstimme* at medium register, pursing her lips at the vibrato word "do" (in "What a Little Moonlight Can Do") to change her tone—intimates real worldliness, and musicality: she had incorporated Louis Armstrong's rhythmic style, at a time when it was still mostly just the instrumentalists who were doing that.

By "This Year's Kisses" in 1937—her first recording session with Lester Young, whose tenor-saxophone solos gave her the comfort that her lyrics seemed to be asking for—she really had it. Her small, froggy voice became a means of confiding as well as projecting pure sound, like notes from a muted trumpet. She made music, and this is why so many of the trifling songs that these bands were importuned to play have had any consequence in jazz history.

Since the late 1950s, Holiday has been well served by the record industry, in small-dose reissues that promote the best of her work. A person can go through many years of listening to jazz without noticing that Holiday had to sing a lot of garbage in the first half of her career. If you investigate Columbia's entire ten-CD box set, you'll hear cute caramel apples such as "Eeenie Meenie Meiny Mo" and "Please Keep Me in Your Dreams"; you won't remember them.

Young transforms these songs, adds a pliability to them, an element of surprise, that even the best of them begin to need. Though there is a uniform excellence in the 1935 to 1939 material—much of it with Teddy Wilson's band, including (for some sessions) the great Kansas City rhythm section of Freddie Green, Walter Page, and Jo Jones—

there is a sameness, too. They're all concise and swinging, and where even the songwriting is slender the transformations are remarkable.

Holiday refashioned melodies according to her own style of phrasing. It wasn't anything as studied as a harmonic framework—the time was yet to come when even jazz singers would study the Schillinger system—but, using a handful of octave slides and swing-oriented accents, finding her way to the notes that provided the song's centers of gravity and then tagging them as often as possible, she could significantly change a song's melody.

What control there was in these bands: in "The Very Thought of You," to choose a high-quality example, the sound just oozes, with a richness suggesting an organization much larger than a sextet; the harmonized obbligatos, made cottony by Lester Young's clarinet sound, aerate the song. This, as it happens, comes from a preternaturally good session, of September 15, 1938. Holiday sounds somnolent and a touch slurry. But without evidence to prove otherwise one can only believe it was an affectation of craft. Whatever it was, her swing is better for it.

It was beginning in 1938, to judge from records, that Holiday could occasionally sound like a much older woman. There was a new, flattened-out, brazen edge in her voice, and she could sound like a tired mother who wanted her child to get his ass downstairs right now, or like an aging chippie who was too fucked-up to care, or like a doting grandmother. It was at this time that she began to record often under her own name. She was a brand. She needed as much distinction as she could get.

When she started working at Café Society in 1939, drawing a well-heeled, culturally sophisticated audience, she became a new kind of jazz singer—one with range, who could deal with roadhouse or supper club. (She would always be better at supper club; volume was not the fate of such an odd and narrow voice.) The records acquired a new, compressed intensity, with more piquancy: "Some Other Spring" is a delicate ballad with unusual harmonic movement, made perfect; "Swing, Brother, Swing" is a minor-key hothouse, where she's as percussive as a rapper, singing "Raring to go / and there ain't nobody gonna hold me down / say listen boy / hurry up and send me, let me go to town." And by 1940, she was making art of universal use and importance (exhibit A: "The Man I Love"), as well as more moody chanteuse material, such as "Gloomy Sunday," "Strange Fruit" (released on Commodore and therefore not on this box set), and "God Bless the Child."

She was changing the role of the jazz singer, finding a new cultural role to fulfill, and knowing how to become iconic.

11. BENNY GOODMAN:

The Complete RCA Victor Small Group Recordings

(RCA/BMG 09026-68764-2, 3 CDS)

Benny Goodman, clarinet; Teddy Wilson, Jess Stacy, piano; Lionel Hampton, vibraphone, drums, vocals; John Kirby, bass; Gene Krupa, Dave Tough, Buddy Schultz, drums; Helen Ward, Martha Tilton, vocals; Ziggy Elman, trumpet.

Recorded 1935–1939

In reassessing jazz recordings, one can overimagine the eagerness of the musicians and the special quality of the occasions. In many cases, they are small-denomination meal tickets, calling cards, or something owed a record company; their greatness often occurs in spite of the situation.

But Benny Goodman in the second half of the 1930s had a fairly unique situation. He had just been credited by a good deal of the national media with starting the swing craze; his West Coast arrival the previous year, with his nearly riot-causing gig at the Palomar Ballroom in Los Angeles and the youth culture it ignited, made him a star both in terms of record sales and in terms of popular myth. (The American media deeply respects the model of artistic change as defined by the tumult created by Stravinsky's *Rite of Spring* premiere; a photo-opportunity event trumps a quieter aesthetic shift.)

He was suddenly one of the best-known musicians, of any kind, in the world, representing an exciting new musical form that most people knew very little about. So when he set about putting together a small group, one can assume that there was a palpable excitement about it. Increasing that excitement, he created a band with the black musicians Teddy Wilson and Lionel Hampton, the first interracial band to play big theaters in America.

This is the first characteristic of the Goodman Trio, Quartet, and Quintet recordings, which start in 1935 (a six-take session just before the Palomar triumph), pick up in earnest in 1936, and continue with increasingly varied personnel into 1939, with John Kirby as bassist, giving the music a new bottom-level heft. They crackle with energy; the band has promises to fulfill.

But this small-group music was not the sound for which teenagers demolished gates and bum-rushed security guards. This was the more intricate "chamber-jazz" music that Goodman forced them to hear as a part of his concert program. The big band, that was something else, an occasionally exciting but forthrightly commercial unit that built its own aesthetic traps very quickly. And today, when the commercial big-band sound of the 1930s reminds the average person of elephants, the smaller-unit Goodman is what sounds more poignant and more like art.

This music was, first, about the nexus of Goodman and Teddy Wilson, an Art Tatum devotee who proved to be (unlike his hero) a consummate band pianist and also, that rarer thing, a consummate accompanist of singers. (His work on Billie Holiday's early Columbia recordings, as it sits in the memory, is almost inseparable from Holiday's voice.) Later, it was about a triangle: Goodman, Wilson, and vibraphonist Lionel Hampton. The drummer Gene Krupa, present in the groups until 1938, started out as a secondary presence. But Krupa's in-person charisma proved enough to start a cult of his own, which Goodman apparently resented and felt competitive with. Though Krupa is an enlivening drummer, he is an overbearing one; at times you want to tell his foot to ease up, not to mention his snare drum. Outside of some hookups with Wilson that propagate a rum-and-Coke sort of fun, he's not what propels this band into its special atmosphere.

Goodman's clarinet sound, driving and impeccably in tune, is riveting. In "China Boy," the first tune from the 1936 sessions, he nails the beat rapidly, right on top of it, while vibraphone, piano, and drums gather around his orientation to rhythm; his arpeggiated figures are followed hand in glove by Wilson. His ascent into the high register is palpable, like a time-elapsed film of a tree shooting out of the ground.

Wilson, for his part, grows out of the stride tradition into swing, with a technique that emphasizes both hands equally; the movement of the bass is nearly independent of his strong melodic drive. His ideas for embellishing other people's tunes (none of the material here is credited to Goodman, Wilson, or Krupa) were commanding and fruitful: his introduction for "All My Life," for example, might have given birth to the opening chord movement for Thelonious Monk's "Ask Me Now." He could play games with rhythm; in "Who?" he lags two beats behind for a portion of his solo, finding his way out into straight rhythm with Krupa in an easy pas de deux.

Wilson, later in his career, became a bit of a one-trick pony, not quite as frustrating as Art Tatum but similarly captive to his own mannerisms; he could never quite break out of the melodic-harmonic dimension he had built for himself and began to sound like a relic much too early. But here, playing a fresh, new music, he is authoritative. Hampton, for his part, doesn't have the flair for rhythmic invention of Wilson or Goodman, but the melody ideas are fresh in his solos. He was keeping up with Armstrong, as nearly everyone was trying to do, and his lines are willfully clean.

That's another quality of this music: its immaculate organization, even at its most creative. What kind of discipline did it take to get this ensemble to sound so crisp, so one-take perfect?

12. COUNT BASIE:

The Complete Decca Recordings

(DECCA/UNIVERSAL 3-611; 3 CDS)

Count Basie, piano; Buck Clayton, Joe Keyes, Carl Smith, Ed Lewis, Bobby Moore, Karl George, Harry Edison, Shad Collins, trumpet; George Hunt, Dan Minor, Benny Morton, Dicky Wells, trombone; Lester Young, Herschel Evans, Chu Berry, tenor saxophone and clarinet; Caughey Roberts, Earl Warren, alto saxophone; Jack Washington, alto and baritone saxophones; Eddie Durham, trombone and guitar; Freddie Green, Claude Williams, guitar; Walter Page, bass; Jo Jones, drums; Jimmy Rushing and Helen Humes, vocals.

Recorded 1937–1939

The Count Basie band derived from two crisscrossing tributaries of the southwest's nonstop musical activity in the 1930s: Walter Page's Blue

Devils band of Oklahoma City, and Bennie Moten's group of Kansas City. The horn players of the Basie band were to be its stars, but by 1937 it had the deepest rhythm section of the swing era.

There was Walter Page, "Big 'Un," the first great bass player in jazz, known for a deep, resonant sound and a walking rhythm; after he officially abandoned the tuba in 1932, his first all-bass record date with Moten, including "Toby" and "Lafayette," was a manifesto for the instrument. Jo Jones was the drummer; by the mid-thirties, he had found that stating the beat with the hi-hat instead of the bass drum gave the music a silky levitation and opened the possibilities for more arresting accents from other parts of the drums. Freddie Green, the guitarist, took very few solos in his life; he was the quintessential engine-room player, content with holding up the four-four beat and making an art out of a very modest role.

And there was Basie on piano, who had been through so much competition in his travels from New Jersey to the southwest that he discovered his own way of getting over: with silence, cunning, and timing. To become distinct in an atmosphere that heady, musicians had to be masters of rhetoric, and Basie found not only his touch but his manner of delivery; he came to own the pregnant pause, as well as the single closing note to wrap up a brass arrangement.

The band's front line included another kind of rhetoric in the juxtaposition of two tenor-saxophone players, Herschel Evans and Lester Young. Evans siphoned off the romance and the hard vibrato from Coleman Hawkins (some histories say he had his own style on the tenor saxophone before Hawkins, who is generally acknowledged to be the father of the instrument for jazz), while Young annexed the feathery poetry of Frank Trumbauer and the more relaxed rhythmic comportment of Louis Armstrong; both used the punctuation effect created by rough-and-ready honking. They stood at opposite ends of the bandstand, generating rumors of tension within the band, though before his early death in 1939 Evans ended up influencing Young.

These recordings—which begin just before the arrival of Freddie Green, and end just after the death of Herschel Evans—are the band's first, and they show what unity already existed. It had been hardened from the band's year-and-a-half, high-profile stint at the Reno Club in Kansas City, from which a radio broadcast could be heard as far north as Minnesota; that's what led Lester Young to come knocking for a job. Once the band hit New York, the group's sound increased its sheen through constant performances at Harlem's dance palaces, as well as through frequent practice sessions the band held in the basement of the Woodside Hotel.

To appease commercial tastes, the band tackled some hit songs and novelties on the Decca recordings: "My Heart Belongs to Daddy," "London Bridge Is Falling Down." But the group, even after it started gaining strength from single arrangers, was rooted in the cooperative "head" arrangement style of the Kansas City band, and it had a boisterous ring that has aged better than the all-over sheen of other popular swing bands, such as Jimmie Lunceford's.

Now, listening to the Basie band, we hear a version of the blues that was as confident and stylized an American product as a Cadillac—a version of the blues that, it turns out, has not been particularly durable. For the average person, the blues evokes a Robert Johnson figure, alone at the dust-swept crossroads, or the Albert King and Buddy Guy music, which accompanies the pay-per-view in sports bars. One tends not to think of this Kansas City model, with its bright bounce, with Jimmy Rushing's enormous, refined shout—the version of the blues that Ralph Ellison and Albert Murray typified as "antagonistic cooperation," a battle against the chaos of life that also affirms the right to live with style and grace.

Basie signed a standard contract with Decca, earning him a below-standard fee and no royalties; John Hammond helped move him to Columbia in 1939, making records that have better-known high points, including Lester Young's solos on "Lady Be Good" and "Taxi War Dance." (Look for them on Columbia's three volumes of early Basie.) But the Decca material achieves excellence more consistently; it is unparalleled for a glimpse of a band in the first flush of its prime, and the remastering is fine.

In many of these tracks, it's not the grand statements but the subtle details that contain the most power. For example: Basie's final, single bass-clef note after the ending brass shout in "The Glory of Love." The natural deconstruction at the ending of "John's Idea," where the brass riff gives way to Basie's rippling piano and then a long chord spread across the horns, dribbling off with Jo Jones's light patterns across the kit. The delicacy of "Time Out": Eddie Durham's scratchy wide-interval guitar improvisation, and Basie's one-chorus solo, with its bell tones, a double-octave arpeggio, tremelos, and a driving outro. Lester Young's subtle clarinet obbligato in the fade-out of "Texas Shuffle." Basie's iron single notes to kick off "Jumpin' at the Woodside." The vocal numbers, with Jimmy Rushing and Helen Humes, are first-rate, and a handful of tracks played by the rhythm-section quartet are sublime.

This is good-time music—not, on the surface of it, the IQ testing that lay just around the corner for jazz with early bebop. But the deeper you listen, the more there is.

13. DIZZY GILLESPIE:

The Complete RCA Victor Recordings

(RCA/BMG 66528-2, 2 CDS)

Dizzy Gillespie, trumpet, vocals; Bill Dillard, E. Wright, Lamar Wright, Jr., Benny Bailey, Shad Collins, Dave Burns, Elmon Wright, Benny Harris, Ted Kelly, Matthew McKay, Ray Orr, Willie Cook, Miles Davis, Fats Navarro, trumpet; Dicky Wells, Taswel Baird, William Shepherd, Andy Duryea, Kai Winding, J. J. Johnson, Sam Hurt, Jesse Tarrant, Charles Greenlea, trombone; Russell Procope, Howard Johnson, John Brown, Benny Carter, Ernie Henry, Charlie Parker, alto saxophone; Coleman Hawkins, Ben Webster, Chu Berry, Don Byas, James Moody, Yusef Lateef, "Big Nick" Nicholas, Joe Gayles, Budd Johnson, Robert Carroll, Charlie Ventura, tenor saxophone; Cecil Payne, Al Gibson, Ernie Caceres, baritone saxophone; Buddy DeFranco, clarinet; Sam Allen, Clyde Hart, Al Haig, John Lewis, James Forman, Lennie Tristano, piano; Lionel Hampton, Milt Jackson, vibraphone; John Smith, Charlie Christian, Bill DeArango, John Collins, Billy Bauer, guitar; Richard Fulbright, Milt Hinton, Ray Brown, Al McKibbon, Eddie Safranski, bass; Bill Beason, Cozy Cole, J. C. Heard, Joe Harris, Kenny Clarke, Teddy Stewart, Shelly Manne, drums; Chano Pozo, conga, bongo, vocals; Joe Harris, Vince Guerra, conga; Sabu Martinez, bongo; Johnny Hartman, vocals.

Recorded 1937–1949

Dizzy Gillespie

How overdone and drained of mystery Dizzy Gillespie's "A Night in Tunisia" is, as a piece of repertoire; it stands with "Autumn Leaves" and "Take the 'A' Train" as songs I'd rather not hear performed, if given the choice.

But what a pleasure it is to hear the Gillespie band's initial version in 1946. Gillespie had a past-into-future band; it included Don Byas, one of the great early-forties tenor players, as well as Milt Jackson on vibraphone and Ray Brown on bass. But Gillespie's solo on both takes is the high point, with fluent playing at the extremes of the horn, a sense of resolving logic, and incredible swing. It begins backed by silence after a slight pause, and it's an announcement, its full-fledged presence learned from the example of Armstrong. The same goes for his solo on "Anthropology"—it opens with a quotation from "We're in the Money," then blasts through self-sustaining rhythmic motifs, a flatted fifth, a tour of the high register. Gillespie was frightful, a man at the top of his game.

At the same time, he was recording hipsterisms like "Oop-Pop-A-Da," "Ool-Ya-Koo," and "Jump Did-Le Ba"—novelty tunes that, coincidentally, smuggled in some serious playing, providing the easy way into the bebop movement. It wasn't commercialism but a new kind of nonsense humor. In art, where there is nonsense, there is something at stake, something being purposefully obfuscated, a game being played.

This collection concentrates on the years 1946–1949; from the 1930s, there are only four cuts that Gillespie recorded as a sideman with Teddy Hill and with Lionel Hampton. It has a split focus: the early Afro-Cuban jazz, recorded with the *conguero* Chano Pozo, and the orchestral bebop of Gillespie's seventeen-piece bands. One of the bands here, in two different sessions—December 22 and 30, 1947—created four classics of big-band and Afro-Cuban jazz. He was straddling two worlds. (See Chano Pozo, *El Tambor de Cuba,* below, for elaboration on this theme.)

The most obvious examples of Gillespie's bravery are "Cubana Be" and "Cubana Bop," with their ensemble sections thornily arranged by George Russell. ("Cubana Be" is famous for the romping, dire minor mode that opens it, one of the early examples of modal jazz.) But many of these tracks—"Stay on It," for example, recorded with one of the big bands—aren't normal music of their time; they rewrite bebop in large type, with splashy cymbals, transferring a single horn's bebop licks to an orchestration for a whole trumpet section.

Gillespie seemed to hear music as a shrill, athletic blast, a hyena cackle. Introspection was not for him. He gravitated naturally toward the top of his horn; he was the leading show-business edge of what he and his peers considered a fine art. He put bebop's self-conscious musical transgressions—its flatted fifths, for instance—out front, using them as much as possible, until they became cute; this was a double-edged sword and led to the spectacle of the late Gillespie, who often went overboard in corny jokery, which the old-timers loved and the younger listeners could never quite condone.

Within Gillespie's shiny packages was brash, radical new music; what doesn't hold up well in it is a consequence, perhaps, of the same brashness.

Lester Young

14. LESTER YOUNG:

The "Kansas City" Sessions

(COMMODORE 402)

Lester Young, tenor saxophone and clarinet; Buck Clayton, Bill Coleman, trumpet; Eddie Durham, trombone and electric guitar; Dicky Wells, trombone; Joe Bushkin, piano; Freddie Green, guitar and vocals; Walter Page, John Simmons, bass; Jo Jones, drums.

Recorded 1938, 1944

In three different sessions while in New York and on leave from Count Basie, several members of the Basie orchestra—and a few others who were old friends from the spectrum of Kansas City jazz—recorded as The Kansas City Five or The Kansas City Six. They included some of the great soloists of the Basie band, including Lester Young, under whose name these recordings have often been reissued. But these are sessions where nobody tries athletically to outshine the others—at least not on the surface.

The mood is formed around Young, except for the four 1938 tracks at the end, on which he's not present. The music is muted but not wan, as in some of the sessions Young was to turn out in his final years. These recordings are half early Basie era, half post-Basie, and all previous to Young's army service—the chapter in his life that is usually put to blame for his subsequent depression and dissolution. Yet the difference between Young and any other saxophone player—especially Coleman Hawkins, the preeminent player of the day—is vast and made larger by these sessions. In his softness, Young takes a great stylistic stand.

"Pagin' the Devil," from the September 1938 session, takes its mood from Ellington's "Mood Indigo," with a creeping line of low-register clarinet and muted trumpet. Playing a metal clarinet, Young gives his best flowing-melody improvisations in this session, especially on "I Want a Little Girl"—slow, wounded, always diatonic, never very bluesy, and almost the obverse of the hard-edged technical brilliance displayed routinely by Benny Goodman and Artie Shaw.

Sorry to get paramusical, but when you talk of Young there are

issues of tone that force you to talk about human qualities, about ten-
derness and mellowness. It's too easy to hang this wreath at the door of
Frank Trumbauer and Tommy Dorsey, the two musicians whose tone
Young frequently said he admired and tried to emulate. Their music
making was more resolutely optimistic; they are the forerunners of
Young's famous "Lady Be Good" solo with Basie but not of this.

Young's remarkable playing has a sort of wise-zombie quality to it;
if an actor embodied it, he'd have Peter Lorre's enormous, haunted
eyes, hooded with hipster anomie. The art critic Arthur Danto once
wrote of Francis Bacon's screaming-pope paintings that they present a
philosophical impossibility: a picture with such high formal composition and high-religious symbolism depicting screaming just doesn't add
up. You cannot *say*, "I am screaming" while screaming. That gets at the
conundrum here: if a man were really this sad, how could he also be
this expressive?

Eddie Durham's guitar playing on "Way Down Yonder in New
Orleans," among other tracks, is beautiful, too, in its gnarled, spiraling
runs and leaps. People don't play guitar like this anymore, except perhaps for Marc Ribot, and when he does it the significance is the same:
this is a progressive version of a "country" (i.e., unsophisticated) style.

But back to Young. What he's playing here is the Chet Baker/bossa
nova/James Dean mood, the dyad of masculine terseness and feminine
tenderness, nearly twenty years before that posture became iconic.
Could it be that this temperament—call it beatnik, call it what you
want, but you know it well—began here?

15. LOUIS JORDAN:

Let the Good Times Roll: The Anthology 1938–1953

(DECCA/MCA 11907, 2 CDS)

*Louis Jordan, alto saxophone, clarinet, baritone saxophone, vocals; Court-
ney Williams, Freddie Webster, Kenneth Roane, Leonard Graham, Aaron
Izenhall, Emmett Perry, Bob Mitchell, Money Johnson, trumpet; Lem
Johnson, Stafford Simon, Freddie Simon, Josh Jackson, James Wright,*

Louis Jordan

Skinny Brown, Reuben Phillips, Maxwell Davis, tenor saxophone; Leon Comegys, Bob Burgess, Alfred Cobbs, trombone; Oliver Nelson, alto saxophone; Marty Flax, Pee-Wee Moore, baritone saxophone; Clarence Johnson, Arnold Thomas, William Austin, Wild Bill Davis, Bill Doggett, Jimmy Peterson, John Malachi, Chester Lane, piano; Carl Hogan, Ham Jackson, Bill Jennings, Bert Payne, electric guitar; Charlie Drayton, Henry Turner, Dallas Bartley, Jesse Simpkins, Al Morgan, Billy Hadnott, Bob Bushnell, Thurber Jay, bass; Walter Martin, Shadow Wilson, Slick Jones, Razz Mitchell, Eddie Byrd, Joe Morris, Charlie Rice, Johnny Kirkwood, drums.

Recorded 1938–1953

When touring with Chick Webb's swing orchestra in the 1930s—the period when Ella Fitzgerald sang with the band—Louis Jordan was the band's comedian and most dazzling stage presence; he made an impression on the young Dizzy Gillespie, who used similar clowning routines in his performances for his whole bandleading life. But what nobody expected was that the Webb band's third alto player would leave the big bands, start the most popular small group of the 1940s, and not so indirectly help invent rock and roll.

Jordan has survived mostly as a kitsch figure, except for the recent neoswing revivalists who base their music on his and the few jazz musicians who still openly admire his playing. (Sonny Rollins is one.) But he was one of the most important American musicians of the twentieth century, even if the major themes of his songs were fried food, women with screechy voices, and getting piss-drunk in roadhouses.

His genius was to take the private corners of black life—most of his routines seem taken from barbershops or bars, places where black people could congregate and trash-talk—and spin them into catchphrases, make them part of an American identity that everyone else (i.e., white people) could understand. He beat Chuck Berry to the punch at this by almost fifteen years. Taking songs from black and white writers, he popularized a kind of humor that black people had previously kept to themselves, and he did it without ever being accused of Uncle Tomming.

The history of "Open the Door, Richard" is an example. The song was based on a comedy routine by the entertainers Dusty Fletcher and

John Mason, who performed it in black theaters during the 1930s. It's about a hapless drinker who shares a room with another hapless drinker. The narrator finds himself without his house keys one night; as he bangs on the door to wake up the roommate, the sidelong glances of all the gossips in the town are set upon him. It's a little sketch in shame and cruelty, about a guy who's unable to transcend his inherent unclassiness, and about the condescending judgments that follow him around. Jack McVea, along with Fletcher, Mason, and Dan Howell, changed the words of the routine to soften the discomfort of the racial stereotyping, and set them to a rhythm-and-blues melody. McVea had the first hit with it, and Count Basie recorded it soon after, but Jordan's version, following within months, is the only one that has had any kind of life beyond 1947.

Jordan was a decent, spirited singer, though it was the whole original package of fun and games and social comedy that he was selling, not just a vocal style. (He was undoubtedly the model for Morris Day in the eighties funk group the Time.) But he was a pretty fine alto player, as you can hear from his poignant inroductions to "Rusty Dusty Blues" and "I'm Gonna Move to the Outskirts of Town," both from 1941.

In the mid-forties, Louis Jordan's Tympany Five acquired its killer sound, first with the jump-band speed of hits such as "Caldonia," then, in 1945, with the addition of electric guitarist Carl Hogan and pianist Wild Bill Davis. Tracks such as "Don't Worry 'bout That Mule," which put Aaron Izenhall's bebop trumpet and Josh Jackson's Jazz-at-the-Philharmonic style of tenor-saxophone playing to a new, driving rhythm, are the primary texts in how jazz is connected to rock and roll.

These songs were produced by Milt Gabler for Decca. In 1955, just after Jordan left Decca, Gabler produced Bill Haley and the Comets, a Western swing band. He persuaded Haley to adopt Louis Jordan's sound. "Rock Around the Clock" was the result. And check out Carl Hogan's double-stopped guitar opening from "Ain't That Just Like a Woman": it is the meat of "Johnny B. Goode."

16. CHANO POZO:

El Tambor de Cuba: Life and Music of the Legendary Cuban Conga Drummer

(TUMBAO TCD 305, 3 CDS)

Chano Pozo, conga, vocals; Miguelito Valdés, Antonio "Cheché" de la Cruz, Panchito Riset, Tito Rodríguez, Reinaldo Valdés "El Jabao," Orlando Guerra "Cascarita," Rubén Gonzalez, Oscar López, Tito Gomez, Joseito Núñez, Olga Guillot, Beny Moré, vocals. Orchestras: Orquesta Casino de la Playa, Orquesta Havana-Riverside, Xavier Cugat and His Waldorf Astoria Orchestra, Cuarteto Caney, Marcano y su Grupo, Machito and His Afro-Cubans, Orquesta Hermanos Palau, Julio Cueva y su Orquesta, Anselmo Sacasas y su Orquesta, Dizzy Gillespie and His Orchestra, Orquesta Hermanos Castro, Havana-Casino Orchestra, Orquesta Hotel Nacional, Chano Pozo y su Conjunto Azul, Miguelito Valdes y su Sexteto, Miguelito Valdes con la Orquesta de la Mil Diez, Chano Pozo y su Ritmo de Tambores, Chano Pozo y su Conjunto Con el Mago del Tres, Dizzy Gillespie and His Orchestra. Dizzy Gillespie, trumpet; James Moody, tenor saxophone; Milt Jackson, vibraphone; others.

Recorded 1939–1952

"On the night of Wednesday, May 7, 1947, the African Academy of Arts and Research presented the dancer Asadata Dafora in 'African Interlude,' a show of music and dance, which took place at the Hotel Diplomat in New York at 110 West 43rd Street. One of the most outstanding moments of the show was 'Bombastic Bebop,' a number which Dizzy presented with Charlie Parker, backed by a rhythm section formed by six percussionists: Billy Alvarez (bongos), Pepé Becké, Diego Iborra, Eladio González and Rafael Mora (conga drums), and Max Roach (drums)."

The above is taken from Jordi Pujol's narrative history accompanying the first Chano Pozo retrospective box set, issued in 2001. I include it because this performance looks like something that would today be funded by a foundation grant and organized by a well-informed, syncretism-minded, high-art concert or record producer. Possibly, it would include the saxophonist and bandleader Steve Coleman, who traveled to Cuba in the mid-nineties to record things just like this. It's a "world music" idea before that phrase had any meaning whatsoever.

It happened just as the Cuban *conguero* Chano Pozo was entering the New York City music scene, and his arrival hastened the strong feeling among jazz musicians that Cuban music was a natural relative of jazz.

It's too early to tell, but the archival research of *El Tambor de Cuba,* and the seriousness with which it has been issued, is bound to have consequences. It establishes the fact—in a way that has never been established before—that Chano Pozo wasn't just a muscular conga player from Cuba who joined Dizzy Gillespie's band in the late forties and drew excited crowd reactions, a footnote in most jazz histories. He was, in fact, a composer involved in many projects of Cuban music and Afro-Cuban jazz that were both "before their time"—a sort of meaningless phrase—and absolutely logical, inevitable, necessary. He was also an adherent of the African-derived Abákua religious faith, a fact that made him a natural conveyor of Old World culture in the New World.

There's a very Latin American obsession with connecting the past to the present and even to the imagined future; it's the logical mind-set of nations with Indian tribes in their interiors, industrial cities on their coasts, an African prehistory (in some cases), and computer technology connecting them quickly to the rest of the world. Brazilian singer-songwriters such as Caetano Veloso and Lucas Santtana, Mexican rock groups such as Café Tacuba, a pile of new Cuban hip-hoppers, and even the Puerto Rican heavy-metal band Puya are all doing it: putting the old up against the new. Religious music deriving from West Africa provides a convenient ingredient in these mixtures, because it's so rhythmically sensuous, so beautiful, and so complex. You can mix it with so much contemporary music of the New World—be it jazz, samba, or metal—and it not only works in sound but works in philosophy: immediately, with the introduction of Yoruban rhythms, these bands are playing their own cultural identities.

In Cuba, the first popularizations of Afro-Cuban religious music as "official culture" were in 1937. That was when a seventy-piece orchestra played the Afro-Cuban–influenced music of Gilberto Valdés—

a well-regarded scholar and composer in Cuba—in the Municipal Amphitheater of Cuba. Valdés's aim, aside from aesthetic ones, was surely to break down middle-class Cuban prejudice against a "cult" (that is, Negro) religion. With that in mind, listen to "Nagüe," on disc one of *El Tambor de Cuba,* recorded by Machito and His Afro-Cubans. Made in New York in 1942, with Mario Bauzá as arranger, it sets sophisticated, Ellingtonian big-band arrangements over a Yoruban chant and a Cuban rhythm matrix. Its composer is Chano Pozo; he was a full five years away from being a recognizable name to any non–Latin American.

We don't hear Pozo's conga playing on the first disc; it's only his compositions. (Pozo, according to legend, was too dark skinned to join the successsful Casino de la Playa orchestra, which nevertheless recorded his songs while he made a living as a bootblack.) On a handful of these recordings, the singer is Miguelito Valdés, a popular entertainer who in Cuba filled the role that later, in New York, was Gillespie's: he spread the word about Pozo's talent.

The second disc presents the Afro-Cuban music on which Pozo actually played, before and after moving to New York in 1947; it includes popular *son montunos* as well as a series called "Ritmo Afro-Cubano Nos. 1–4," recorded for the tiny label SMC; they are examples of Cuban religious music, recorded in documentary style.

Disc three arrives at Afro-Cuban jazz, Pozo's American glory period (which began with his appearance with the Gillespie band at Carnegie Hall on September 29, 1947), and the end of his story. Here are the recordings of Dizzy Gillespie's jazz orchestra with Pozo on conga, including the Gillespie–George Russell suite "Cubana Be"/"Cubana Bop," the immortal "Manteca," and the Latinization of the Gillespie piece "Woody 'n You," retitled "Algo Bueno." (These pieces are also included on Dizzy Gillespie's *The Complete RCA Victor Recordings,* above.) And this is where we hear the differences between Cuban and American swing, negotiated with hunger by musicians who probably had no idea whether what they were doing would end up being commercial music or art music. It also includes the less famous 1948 jazz sessions in which Pozo participated—with Milt Jackson's quintet and a wonderful James Moody session in which Pozo and Art Blakey battle each other for prominence in the mix.

Pozo died December 2, 1948, shot after a round of grievances started when he accused his drug dealer of selling him weak pot. The set ends with three musical tributes by Pérez Prado, Miguelito Valdés, and Beny Moré.

Much of this music is little known; several independent musicologists I know, Cuban-music specialists, had never heard many of these recordings before they surfaced here on the Spanish Tumbao label. For a history of the first wave of Afro-Cuban jazz, this is the place to look; Pozo was, more than a great player, a pivotal character.

17. DUKE ELLINGTON:

The Blanton-Webster Band

(RCA BLUEBIRD/BMG; 3 CDS)

Duke Ellington, piano; Wallace Jones, Cootie Williams, trumpet; Ray Nance, trumpet, violin, vocal; Rex Stewart, cornet; Joe "Tricky Sam" Nanton, Lawrence Brown, trombone; Juan Tizol, valve trombone; Barney Bigard, Chauncey Haughton, clarinet; Johnny Hodges, alto saxophone, soprano saxophone, clarinet; Harry Carney, baritone saxophone, clarinet, alto saxophone; Otto Hardwick, alto saxophone, bass saxophone; Ben Webster, tenor saxophone; Billy Strayhorn, piano; Fred Guy, guitar; Jimmy Blanton, Junior Raglin, bass; Sonny Greer, drums; Ivie Anderson, Herb Jeffries, vocals.

Recorded 1940–1942

By the late 1930s, Duke Ellington had made hit records, and had established himself as a popular and experimental composer. ("Creole Rhapsody," "Reminiscing in Tempo," and "Diminuendo and Crescendo in Blue" from 1931, 1935, and 1937 respectively had partially realized his urges to write longer, through-composed works.) He had taken control of his own business, having fired his longtime manager and publisher Irving Mills; on the domestic front, his troubled marriage was dissolved.

Duke Ellington

Having become something of a hero to black people, he now became widely admired among American whites as well; and a successful trip to Europe in 1939 proved that they loved him over there, too. He was suddenly in the clear to write his own ticket: the compass was set for an artistic future beyond what any other jazz bandleader could imagine.

With the advent of swing as a national spectator sport in the mid-thirties, Ellington's band had done well in battle-of-the-bands contests. (Even if Jimmie Lunceford brought a killing swing machine to dancers, Ellington had the better soloists, the more imagination, the more individuation of character.) Ellington invested in his musicians, so that they could become more than average swing players; they were allowed to show emotional palettes as well as technique and polish. "Duke was playing some weird stuff," remembered the Kansas City saxophonist Buster Smith, who used to see Ellington's band when it visited the Midwest in the early and mid-thirties. "He was a little over our heads in those days." And he was proud of his inscrutability: he admonished his musicians not to jam with other bands when they rolled into a new town.

Then a few acquisitions drove his art forward even more. He found the young composer and lyricist Billy Strayhorn in Pittsburgh; he found the young bass player Jimmy Blanton in Chicago; and he hired Ben Webster, an established tenor saxophonist in the southwestern scene of the early thirties, who had gone on to work with Fletcher Henderson and Cab Calloway before hooking up with Ellington.

Strayhorn became a friend, an amanuensis, and a beneficent competitor of sorts, reminding Duke of his own strength and possibility, helping to firm up his greatest arrangement effects. He also provided added stamina and resources of energy in a period when, as opposed to the other leading swing bandleaders with their hired staff arrangers, Ellington did almost all the work himself. Blanton filled out the bottom end. His rounded, resonant pizzicato notes at once kicked the band along in a new way and, for the first time, defined the bass as a melodic instrument. Ben Webster was simply one of the great musical character actors of jazz; the numbers featuring his gruff but shapely sound became instantly, and justly, famous.

Ellington hit a hot streak, regularly turning out benchmark classics at every recording session; *The Blanton-Webster Band* collects them all. Some were extensions of earlier breakthroughs. The dire, dramatic "Ko-Ko," combining thirty-two-bar song form, blues, and bass solos, served as an announcement that Blanton had arrived and extended the rhythms and timbres of his late-twenties "jungle band" period. "Dusk," with its subtle, muted effects, seemed a more progressive cousin of "Mood Indigo."

In general it was an unparalleled fertile stretch, and here are a few of its high points:

"Cotton Tail," built on the chords of George Gershwin's "I Got Rhythm," gave Webster his piece of history with a solo that has a plotted magnificence, rising to a terrifying apogee and then subsiding. In "Sepia Panorama," the segmented, hybrid nature of music from Fletcher Henderson's mature period grew organic and lovely; instead of tiny two- and four-bar pockets sounding like effortful contrivances, there was a compound structure of twelve-, sixteen-, and eight-bar sections with solos long enough to be savored. The piquant harmony in "Warm Valley"—its title a surrealist suggestion of sex—gave a close-dancing slow number intellectual heat. "Take the 'A' Train" became the band's introductory number to warm up dancers, and was a symbolic piece of American optimism in the early 1940s. "I Got It Bad (and That Ain't Good)," with its hill-and-dale interval of a ninth, became durable via Ivie Anderson's vocal. Following on the earlier success of "Caravan," Juan Tizol kept writing his witty, if not particularly profound semi-Cuban pieces, like "Conga Brava," "The Flaming Sword" (cowritten with Ellington), and "Moon over Cuba." Billy Strayhorn clocked in with four classics—"Take the 'A' Train," "Chelsea Bridge," "Raincheck," and "Johnny Come Lately."

From his earlier artistic successes (see *The OKeh Ellington*, above), Ellington had become canny at working with sound engineers and using the recording studio. "I Don't Know What Kind of Blues I Got" captures the woody, mentholated sound of the clarinet at soft volume better than anything until Jimmy Giuffre's recordings of the late 1950s. The mute-and-plunger brass soloists in the band—Nanton and Nance—developed their "talking" style until it sounded as if they were parting their lips directly to the microphone. And the Ellington band's control over dynamics—which became a do-or-die issue in the polished swing-band atmosphere of the time—became unparalleled in tunes such as "Cotton Tail" and "Harlem Air Shaft."

Who knows how much of the various musicians' solo material was composed by Ellington, or at least worked out in advance under his hand? Who knows, once Strayhorn entered the fold, how exactly they negotiated their collaborations? Or how Ellington got the best out of musicians who, once freed from him, never quite measured up in their own careers?

18. JOHN KIRBY AND HIS ORCHESTRA:

1941–1943

(CLASSICS 792)

John Kirby, bass; Charlie Shavers, trumpet; Buster Bailey, clarinet; Russell Procope, George Johnson, alto saxophone; Billy Kyle, Clyde Hart, piano; O'Neil Spencer, Specs Powell, Bill Beason, drums.

Recorded 1941–1943

The bebop and hard-bop traditions, in the long run, led to the trend of soloists going on at length. In the best hands, fifteen-minute tunes by four-piece bands can be just the right scale for revelatory heroism—look at John Coltrane. But at a lower level of achievement it's just kid stuff. A slightly earlier tradition, from the 1930s and 1940s, pointed toward the opposite ideal.

With the John Kirby orchestra, the goal was to present maximum form in minimum time. We are still in the 78 RPM era here, and of the twenty-one tracks on this disc, only two run a hair over three minutes long. The New Orleans standard "Royal Garden Blues" is a good example: it accommodates a strong introductory theme, tiny flurries of trumpet and clarinet as the rest of the band drops out, a second melodic strain, hocketing interludes (the device popular in prewar jazz of having a melody line pecked out note by note by different musicians), and even a trumpet solo. The music keeps changing size, contracting and expanding bar by bar; it's over in a minute and forty-three seconds.

Kirby was a strong-toned bass player and mostly a figurehead leader. (He didn't write tunes; the band's exceptional trumpeter, Charlie Shavers, shouldered most of the composing and arranging.) His band book offered witty jazz, even broad-brush corny at times; its swing was close cut. In the service of humor more than pretension, the band flirted with the classical canon, performing glosses on Beethoven ("Beethoven Riffs On") and Schubert ("Schubert's Serenade," included here); its self-consciously controlled dynamics were what jazz critics would start calling "chamber jazz" a little while later. Kirby was a light-skinned black man with strong, Orson Welles–like features, and his band was all black. It may have been calculatedly presentable music for a high-toned audience, but the records sold widely; this was popular music, full stop.

If you sense the mounting of an argument, I confess that I'm looking over my shoulder at the words of Gunther Schuller. In his book *The Swing Era,* so authoritative on so many things, Schuller makes an example of Kirby's music. He believes it was novelty music for squares and that its fluffball quality becomes most apparent when put next to Duke Ellington's music from the same period. Schuller writes: "It is difficult now, more than fifty years later, to imagine what prompted the Sextet's considerable popularity. Undoubtedly much of their repertory was created to wow the tourist customers who flocked to Fifty-second Street on their one visit to New York, to hear 'some o' that crazy new jazz.' Little did they know that the Kirby version was hardly jazz at all. But leaving labels aside, it wasn't very good or important music, by whatever name."

But jazz has long depended on wit, and sometimes (though they are not the best times) on corniness, and on technique and harmony taken from classical music. These were jazz musicians, this was intended as jazz, and therefore it becomes part of the history and tradition of the music; the Kirby jazz fits into a kind of muted-dynamics Café Society style, for lack of a better term, also practiced by Artie Shaw's Gramercy Five and the quartets of Jonah Jones and Bobby Hackett.

As Larry King likes to say on television, "perception is reality," and the perceptions of tourists are to be doubted at one's own peril. The ritual of musical performance is always two-sided: there are the performers, and there is the audience. Audiences are not always there to be transformed, socked in the gut, introduced to God. In the essay "Tradition and the Individual Talent," T. S. Eliot suggested that any aesthetic tradition becomes most meaningful in the work of those artists most alive to the present. Eliot's argument has been quoted to validate, and contextualize, the art of musicians who poke and challenge and grate against the ear. But it can also be applied in support of jazz musicians who are so shrewdly commercial minded (and I'm not sure that translates as "unchallenging") that they end up being excluded from the house of jazz.

No doubt, Shavers is the most exciting player on these records; the sense of time and pitch exhibited in his muted solos was impeccably accurate, and in his articulation of fast high notes he became influential on Clifford Brown and Dizzy Gillespie. But Billy Kyle, the band's pianist, also demands close attention. He derived from Earl Hines and Teddy Wilson, and he represents a line of tidy-sounding players (including Eddie Heywood, Nat Cole, and Johnny Guarneri) who shaped commercial jazz in the forties and whose bright rhythmic bounce was knocked out of favor with the advent of bebop and buried with the arrival of McCoy Tyner and Herbie Hancock.

It *is* a gimmick band. Listen to Buster Bailey's clarinet note held through twenty bars in "St. Louis Blues," while the background keeps changing as the song races to its close; the strength of the note falters only slightly toward the end. That note is a Houdini escape routine, something that you, the average Joe, cannot do. But there is great pleasure to be had in this music, and while its compression and organization can become stifling after an hour or so, its stimulations are relentless.

19. JAMES P. JOHNSON:

The Original James P. Johnson: 1942–1945, Piano Solos

(SMITHSONIAN FOLKWAYS 40812)

James P. Johnson, piano.

Recorded 1942–1945

James P. Johnson is generally credited as the patriarch of New York stride piano, a fiercely competitive, technique-obsessed scene of the 1920s that had about the same relationship to the rougher forms of honky-tonk piano playing as English horsemanship does to Western.

Jazz, in its infancy, was closely bound to prostitution, gambling, and theft. But many of the great early figures of the music weren't whorehouse wranglers; W. C. Handy, James Reese Europe, Johnson, and Willie "The Lion" Smith were studious, worldly, correct. Johnson was the earliest brilliant pianist-composer of jazz, and he got his work issued fast: 280 songs, nineteen extended concert works, and fifty-five piano rolls. His songs included "The Charleston"—one of the most famous songs of the early twentieth century—and "Carolina Shout," the finger-busting étude of choice for young stride pianists, including Duke Ellington. In New York, you had to be able to play it if you wanted to mingle among the "ticklers" in the cutting-sessions of black musical nightlife. Before isolating himself as a composer, Johnson was a major figure in that competitive scene.

Johnson and his crowd prided themselves on sophistication. "New York developed the orchestral piano," he said in an interview a few years before his death. "Full, round, big, widespread chords and tenths—a heavy bass moving against the right hand. The other boys from the South and West at that time played in smaller dimensions— like thirds played in unison. We wouldn't dare do that because the public was used to better playing."

Though Johnson and Willie "The Lion" Smith arrived in New York the same year, 1911, it was Johnson who corraled more interest and who went wider in his musical goals. If you're wondering who exactly were Wynton Marsalis's precedents—the Marsalis of recent years, the composer of sweeping, extended-form, jazz-history-in-miniature works—the story probably begins here. Johnson wrote the symphonic work "Yamekraw" in 1927, intending it as a combination of spirituals, jazz, and blues, weaving in what was considered "traditional Negro music" at the time—vernacular songs such as "Sam Jones Done Snagged His Britches" and "Georgia's Always on My Mind."

It is curious how the notion of the history-minded jazz symphony has drifted among different styles of musicians. Ellington, of course, knew all there was to know about Johnson when he wrote historically literate pieces such as "Black, Brown, and Beige" and his many suites and "tone parallels." From Ellington, the jazz-history-symphony idea branches out everywhere—to unclassifiable eclectics of the 1960s such as Jaki Byard (who recorded a section of "Yamekraw" with a trio) and Yusef Lateef (his "Afro-American Suite"), to avant-gardist works such as Julius Hemphill's "Long Tongues" and Hannibal Marvin Peterson's "African Portraits," to mainstream-jazz backward reckonings such as Jimmy Heath's "Afro-American Suite of Evolution," and finally to Marsalis. So you could correctly infer that James P. Johnson is important not only as a pianist but as a synthesizing conceptualist—much more important, actually, than he's given credit for.

"Yamekraw" had a pretty good life—it was performed in Carnegie Hall twice during Johnson's lifetime: once in 1928 as a concerto, with Fats Waller as soloist, and again as an orchestral piece in 1945, with Johnson at the piano. It is included on this CD as a single track in four sections, and sits among a curious selection of recordings, all made for the Asch label in the 1940s. Johnson was seldom seen then, writing concert music at his home in Queens, New York, and these are basically documentary recordings, not meant as commercial items.

Even if some of Johnson's early technique had left him behind (for technique, consult Johnson's late-twenties solo recordings, in one of their many reissues, and find "You've Got to Be Modernistic"), the Asch recordings are valuable for showing his range. Aside from his own compositions, the album includes George and Ira Gershwin's "Liza," the W. C. Handy song "Aunt Hagar's Blues," Scott Joplin's rag "Euphonic Sounds," and Jesse Pickett's "The Dream," possibly composed in 1890. "The Dream" has very Apollonian trills in the right hand and a tango-rhythm left hand playing changing-voiced bass chords; it swings hard even in its serenity, and the artiness of Johnson's approach can make him sound like a much more modern player—like Gonzalo Rubalcaba in 2000, say, playing boleros.

20. COLEMAN HAWKINS:

1943–1944

(CLASSICS 807)

Coleman Hawkins, tenor saxophone; Dizzy Gillespie, Victor Coulson, Ed Vandever, Cootie Williams, Roy Eldridge, trumpet; Leo Parker, Leonard Lowry, alto saxophone; Georgie Auld, Ben Webster, Don Byas, Ray Abrams, tenor saxophone; Budd Johnson, tenor and baritone saxophones; Edmond Hall, Andy Fitzgerald, clarinet; Clyde Hart, Bill Rowland, Art Tatum, Ellis Larkins, Eddie Heywood, piano; Hy White, Al Casey, Jimmy Shirley, guitar; Oscar Pettiford, Israel Crosby, bass; Max Roach, Specs Powell, Shelly Manne, drums.

Recorded 1943–1944

It is hard to find the essence of Coleman Hawkins, as it is with so many great soloists with long careers who made their greatest work before the LP era.

Coming to prominence as a member of McKinney's Cotton Pickers and later with Fletcher Henderson, Hawkins was a sideman—yet in Henderson's band he was the top player for more than a decade (1923–1934); the band's achievements would have been unthinkable without him. He created a role for the saxophone as a solo instrument, and everybody who later played the instrument flows from him; in a greater sense, he was a self-conscious artist, a serious entertainer, an experimenter with harmony. (His improvisations were based on chords more than melody.)

In 1934, he left the States for Europe. When he returned in 1939, he led a smallish big band and recorded "Body and Soul." The recording contains the first great solo that barely refers to a song's melody. (It is

Coleman Hawkins

available, among other career gems, on the RCA/Bluebird compilation *Coleman Hawkins: A Retrospective.*) He was already a gray eminence, and he was about to step into the waters of what was becoming, but was not yet known as, bebop. He dealt with it beautifully, finding his place, much as he dealt later on with Thelonious Monk and with Sonny Rollins; until his death in 1969, he was revered as an old master who remained curious about and unafraid of the new styles.

Hawkins had refined tastes. Those who visited with him noticed that he owned few jazz records; he preferred opera and the cello recordings of Pablo Casals. (He played cello as a young man, which helps to explain the richness and smoothness of his tenor-saxophone tone.) He would never be a run-of-the-mill jazz player, yet when he disbanded his big band in 1941, he got into the scrappy thick of it, recording for small labels, connecting with curious young players whom nobody had heard of—players like Max Roach, Ellis Larkins, Oscar Pettiford, Dizzy Gillespie.

Classics is a French label that releases complete available discographies of artists in chronological order; the period covered by this disc was a time in Hawkins's life when he was aesthetically hungry and wanting to record, as the ban on recording imposed by the American Federation of Musicians had just been lifted. (The AFM wanted a cut of every record's royalties, to make up for what it perceived as lost income from radio play; no commercial recordings were made for more than a year, thus blacking out the beginnings of bebop.) In the three-month span covered here, he recorded for Commodore, Signature, Brunswick, Keynote, and Apollo, in quartets, quintets, and big bands. Everything he did in this period—having moved on from the rather uptight, formal bearing of his playing with Henderson to a new, flowing style with longer phrases—is to be savored.

The album starts with "Mop Mop," a riff tune for swing dancers with a pothole on the fourth bar; it ends with a proto-bebop big-band date with young Gillespie and Roach. And at the middle of the arc are "Get Happy" and "The Man I Love," from a quartet date on Signature. A piano solo by Eddie Heywood on the former (a footnote at best in jazz—a leader of a sweet-music band, best known for writing the tune "Canadian Sunset"—but how he swings here) and Pettiford's bass solo on the latter are alive and pulsating; both musicians exhale loudly on each phrase, as if singing through their hands.

In "The Man I Love"—one of the single greatest performances in jazz—Hawkins carefully patrols his territory until he becomes incantational. You sense the space around him; you sense that he's filling up the area, creating a shape, a narrative. It's a heroic realm of improvisation closed off to all but the best—Armstrong, Hines, Parker, Rollins, a few others.

Hawkins enters with perfectly calculated indifference, splintering the rhythmic feel and introducing a touch of harmonic abstraction with some of his famous odd intervals, played as stylishly and genteely as possible. Then he begins a story and finds himself getting involved in the roll of it. At the bridge of the second chorus, there is the hint that he may lose his composure entirely; in its wake, he strikes his highest and loudest note. The last note of his solo ends the song. He has wound it up with withering perfection.

You must go on from here and hear Hawkins's "Body and Soul" and "Dinah," from 1939; you must also hear his lovely (and prescient) solo saxophone improvisation, "Picasso," from 1948, and his bizarre pairing with Sonny Rollins on the 1963 *Sonny Meets Hawk*. But the collaborative efforts of reissue labels to build a complete retrospective between separate recording companies, as has been done (at this writing) for Coltrane and a select few others, has yet to be done for Hawkins. *1943–1944* compresses much of his brilliance into a single disc.

21. DINAH WASHINGTON:

First Issue: The Dinah Washington Story
(The Original Recordings)

(MERCURY/UNIVERSAL 314-514-841-2)

Dinah Washington, vocals; Joe Morris, Frank Galbraith, Russell Royster, Bob Merrill, Cootie Williams, George Hudson, Clark Terry, Clifford Brown, Maynard Ferguson, Johnny Coles, Ray Copeland, Reunald Jones, Joe Newman, Ernie Royal, Doc Severinsen, Charlie Shavers, trumpet; Rudy Rutherford, clarinet; Arnett Cobb, Johnny Hicks, William Parker, Paul

Quinichette, Wardell Gray, Ben Webster, Paul Gonsalves, Eddie "Lockjaw" Davis, Eddie Chamblee, Benny Golson, Frank Wess, tenor saxophone; Tab Smith, Rupert Cole, Ernie Wilkins, Rick Henderson, Herb Geller, Julian "Cannonball" Adderley, Sahib Shihab, alto saxophone; Cecil Payne, Larry Belton, Charles Davis, baritone saxophone; Russell Procope, clarinet, alto saxophone; Mitch Miller, oboe, arrangements; Benny Powell, Gus Chappell, Jimmy Cleveland, Rod Levitt, Melba Liston, Julian Priester, Sonny Russo, Billy Byers, trombone; Jerome Richardson, flute, alto saxophone; Milt Buckner, Red Richards, Rudy Martin, Arnold Jarvis, Pattie Bown, Jack Wilson; Wynton Kelly, Beryl Booker, Sleepy Anderson, Junior Mance, Joe Zawinul, piano; Jackie Davis, organ; Mundell Lowe, Freddie Green, Barry Galbraith, guitar; Vernon King, Johnny Williams, Leonard Swain, Ray Brown, Keter Betts, Richard Evans, Paul West, Milt Hinton, bass; Lionel Hampton, Walter Johnson, Sylvester Payne, Teddy Stewart, Gus Johnson, Jimmy Cobb, Ed Thigpen, Max Roach, Charlie Persip, Shep Shephard, Panama Francis, drums; Candido Camero, bongo; Brook Benton, vocal.

Recorded 1943–1961

Dinah Washington grew up singing in the church, where forgiveness is a virtue, and she could be extremely forgiving of bad music. In twenty professional years, most of it with the Mercury label, she sang some absolutely awful material and some unimpeachably great material. Sometimes there is a difference in her intensity of approach between the two, sometimes not. "Embraceable You," from 1946, is delicious, refined, full of strategy, as is "Blue Skies," from 1954. But so is "Salty Papa Blues," from 1943, a short-order doggerel blues written by Leonard Feather, the record producer. ("T.V. Is the Thing This Year," from 1953, is a nadir, possibly included on a best-hits collection because it is the only sexual-innuendo song about manipulating a television set.)

In the mid-fifties, the soaring blues vowels of the early recordings gave way to skilled swing-song strategy; Washington's phrasing became more clipped and stylized. *After Hours with Miss D* and the live *Dinah Jams* were the peak albums during this period, and the Mercury anthology draws several key pieces from them: "Am I Blue?" and "Love For Sale" from the former, "I've Got You under My Skin" and "Lover,

Come Back to Me" from the latter. At this point, she still came from the black gospel style, but she was finally an American pop singer, plain and simple; to hear her rendition of "I Don't Hurt Anymore," a song also covered by the honky-tonk singer Ernest Tubb, is to be reminded that Dinah Washington and Patsy Cline had much in common.

Washington wasn't the greatest rhythmic singer of jazz; she was, however, one of the most emphatic, and she rightly saw herself as a student of Bessie Smith. Her voice was thin and piercing with a vigorous, narrow vibrato (picked up by Nina Simone), and she consistently returned to the same blues phrasing and microtonal shadings in relation to the tonic. She belted provocatively, with rather exact diction, and her early sessions—blues after blues, "Evil Gal Blues," "Salty Papa Blues," "Record Ban Blues"—become satisfying in their focus; at a limited range of formal singing, she achieves perfection.

But, lo, she was a jazz singer, too, and she could dim her blowtorch sufficiently to be understated. "Crazy He Calls Me"—recorded during a live-in-the-studio session including Clifford Brown and Max Roach that yielded *Dinah Jams*—shows that she could basically talk her way through a ballad. She did not give herself fully to a song, and that's one reason why in the end it didn't matter what she sang.

The success of "What a Diff'rence a Day Makes," from 1959, changed her into a pop icon, and she entered that in-between phase that female jazz singers both desire and are castigated for. She made pop records, very good ones, including *The Swingin' Miss D,* arranged by Quincy Jones, and "This Bitter Earth," which carried a hint of her gospel past. It is middle-of-the-road music, without question, and its kind of production—oohing choruses, an impasto of strings—represented an odd side trip for a jazz singer at her level. But her readings were always aggressive and stubborn, with her curious rests and still, always, that uncomfortably cutting voice.

There is something reassuring in the fact that Dinah Washington, and by extension any truly great jazz singer or artist, can make the middle of the road sound special, can explode any imposed critical standard of quality and taste.

22. CHARLIE PARKER:

The Complete Savoy and Dial Studio Recordings 1944–1948

(SAVOY/ATLANTIC 92911-2, 8 CDS)

Charlie Parker, alto and tenor saxophones; Dizzy Gillespie, Miles Davis, Howard McGhee, Shorty Rogers, Melvyn Broiles, trumpet; Jack McVea, Lucky Thompson, Wardell Gray, Flip Phillips, tenor saxophone; J. J. Johnson, trombone; Clyde Hart, Al Haig, Sadik Hakim, Dodo Marmorosa, Jimmy Bunn, Russ Freeman, Erroll Garner, Bud Powell, John Lewis, Duke Jordan, Teddy Wilson, piano; Red Norvo, vibraphone; Tiny Grimes, guitar, vocals; Slim Gaillard, piano, guitar, vocals; Remo Palmieri, Barney Kessel, guitar; Jimmy Butts, Slam Stewart, Curly Russell, Bam Brown, Robert Kesterton, Arnold Fishkin, Red Callender, Tommy Potter, Nelson Boyd, bass; Cozy Cole, Sid Catlett, Max Roach, Roy Porter, Harold "Doc" West, Zutty Singleton, Jimmy Pratt, Don Lamond, Specs Powell, J. C. Heard, drums; Earl Coleman, vocals.

Recorded 1944–1948

The story of Charlie Parker—more than being a story of an aesthetic rebel or a junkie—is a story of a virtuoso, and as in all stories of virtuosos the details can grow boring if seen too closely. Take after take of "Marmaduke"—there are eleven on the eighth disc in this box set—can wear you down; Parker's playing is like a stream of fresh water, but you come to hear the devices he used to get through the takes.

However, the beginnings of small-group bebop—one of the most enduring kinds of music in America and a natural consequence of the wartime rubber and gas shortages that shut down the era of the traveling big bands—are captured here, in slightly murky-sounding yet very exciting sessions. I have always preferred Parker's Savoy and Dial material to the recordings he made on Verve, because they bear a raw feeling, more suited to the music's status as an underground art form. It began as a music played after-hours; it was fast, aggressive, aesthetically shocking, and it didn't break out into national consciousness for years after it began.

Charlie Parker

The initial bebop sessions here—Dizzy Gillespie's Sextet and All-Star Quintet—don't have anything resembling bebop drumming on them, which negates them a little bit, drains them of energy. It isn't until the Charlie Parker's Reboppers date of November 1945—Parker's first as a leader—that this new music takes off, with Max Roach's perpetual high-frequency ride cymbal and his abrupt bass-drum bomb-dropping pulling the listener up short and throwing him off.

It is a dislocating music, and one of my favorite tracks in all of bebop is dislocated down to its essence: "Warming Up a Riff," a truncated excerpt of a jam on the chords of "Cherokee," with the tape turned on in medias res, as Parker comes toward the end of a chorus, spinning out a long thought in the high register.

Another track from the same session is "Ko-Ko," the masterpiece of bop: stealthy, fast, its introductory lines laid out unevenly across the bar, then going into a subversion of "Cherokee," with two Parker solo choruses. It is high-pitched, anxious music, and as succinct as any composition from Bach to Webern to the Beatles.

Bebop is possibly overrated as esoterica; there are ways to play it that don't shut down but actually encourage dancing. (People still dance to it in New Orleans bars.) I think the Los Angeles drummer Roy Porter, heard here in a brilliant session recorded in Hollywood in March 1946, grasped that as well as anyone; he gives the music a forthright bounce.

Mostly—there's no way to contradict it—this really is art music, a self-defining minority culture. Bebop lines, as composed by men such as Parker and Gillespie, had a new kind of beauty; they were fractured, high frequency (Parker gravitated toward phrases made from the middle-to-higher notes of a chord), stuffed with passing tones, and designed to be difficult to play and to count correctly. (In all their jutting jaggedness, the lines were still resolving and symmetrical.)

Parker, however, happened to be one of the great blues and ballad players, with a strong, bright, personal tone, as if making up for what emotional presence was lost in the hurly-burly of the fast-tempo material. And while his output on labels such as Savoy and Dial in the 1940s was made cheaply, without the benefit of strings, extensive rehearsals, or guest arrangers (quite the contrary: "Billie's Bounce," for one undying example, was written hours before it was recorded), there are some great slow- and medium-tempo performances here. They include "Embraceable You" and "My Old Flame," from Parker Quintet dates in 1947; "Parker's Mood," from 1948; and—one of the most argued-over records in all of jazz—"Lover Man," from a 1946 session in Hollywood at which Parker was so deep in heroin withdrawal that he sounded spastic, flopping through the changes.

Parker is best served by one or two discs at a time. In lieu of this set, I recommend Rhino's two-disc *Yardbird Suite: The Ultimate Charlie Parker Collection,* which combines performances originally released on Guild, Musicraft, Savoy, Dial, and Clef.

23. MARY LOU WILLIAMS:

Zodiac Suite

(SMITHSONIAN FOLKWAYS 40810)

Mary Lou Williams, piano; Al Lucas, bass; Jack Parker, drums.

Recorded 1945

Mary Lou Williams as a historical figure is hard to pin down, and if she never recorded a masterpiece album that caused the waves of a Miles, a Coltrane, or a Vaughan, she merits inclusion because she kept up with style after style, from stride piano to swing to bebop and even to funk. And also because of this single, lovely piece of music—remarkable for when it was made—which will have, if I can predict the future, a continuing life.

Having already been an arranger and pianist during ten years spent in Andy Kirk's big band—a band whose popularity was ultimately eclipsed by Basie's—Williams was a free agent in 1945, living in Harlem, and a mainstay of both branches of Barney Josephson's Café Society, uptown and downtown. Café Society audiences loved Williams's sophistication and her earthiness; this was just the ticket for a white-owned club, where political correctness was enforced to the point that

Mary Lou Williams

most bands were interracial and black customers, as a policy, were given priority seating. I don't mean this as an insult to Williams's music—just to point out that her mixture of vernacular blues and roots with playfully ambitious harmony and structure spoke to everyone; it was model music for a newly miscegenated scene.

The twelve parts of the suite, Williams's first long-form work (long-form works were the backbone of the rest of her composing life), were the twelve signs of the zodiac, but the piece was just as much a valentine to the musicians and jazz-scene habitués Williams knew. "Aries," for example, begins in a boogie-woogie romp with sparse bass accompaniment, then by 1:13 becomes ruminative, darkened by lingering dissonance, ending on the kind of carefully placed forte low notes that Erik Satie sprinkled his miniatures with. It was meant to sketch Ben Webster and Billie Holiday, who had the intense, changeable moods the sign is associated with.

In the spirit of Ellington, the piece pays tribute to loads of friends without actually approaching true tone painting of events. Ellington favored the phrase "tone parallels" for his evocative pieces, and so could Williams have described *Zodiac Suite*.

　　　　　　　　　　　　　　　　　　　　　　Mary Lou Williams

The pieces are short, airy, governed by cute compositional devices that are over almost as soon as they get started. But the main idea coming through here, in a beautifully coherent work—it's no mere jumble of tunes called a "suite"—is jazz as an expansive language, one that fits comfortably within early-twentieth-century classical composition. Williams loved putting the high-flown (unresolving chords, whole-tone scales, striking major-minor juxtapositions) and the earthbound side by side; listen to the arty European chords leading into the blues section of "Gemini."

If you're interested in music as an expression of gender, *Zodiac Suite* also can stand as a strong example of the feminine disposition in jazz. It's remarkably unmacho; her moments of pianistic prowess were embedded in sequential sparkling ideas rather than hanging out there as obvious shows of force. The short, zinging glissando in the piano solo following the bass solo during "Virgo"—almost a zitherlike sound— is a good example: her devices were compact and pinpointed, and she didn't approach the long, fast lines of a Tatum.

Zodiac Suite also serves as a prime example of what nurturing independent labels could do for musicians. It was recorded for Moses Asch, proprietor of Asch Records (and later Folkways), whose practice was generally to leave the room and put all his trust in the artist; he chose worthy subjects and was satisfied with a documentary recording if it came to that. (The sound quality is not good, even for its time.) But Williams, obsessed with form, made the work much more special.

24. CHARLES MINGUS:

Charles "Baron" Mingus, West Coast 1945–49

(UPTOWN UPCD 27-48)

Charles Mingus, bass, piano; N. R. "Nat" Bates, Karl George, John Plonsky, John Anderson, John Coppola, Vernon Carlson, Allen Smith, Andy Peele, Tommy Alexander, Buddy Childers, Hobart Dotson, Eddie Preston, trumpet; Henry Coker, Britt Woodman, Haig Eshow, Bob Lowry, Hawes

Coleman, Jimmy Knepper, Marty Smith, trombone; Maxwell Davis,
William Woodman, Lucky Thompson, Morrie Stewart, Alex Megyesy, Don
Smith, William Green, tenor saxophone; Willie Smith, Bud Hooven, alto
saxophone; Eric Dolphy, Bob Olney, alto saxophone, clarinet, flute; Buddy
Collette, Art Pepper, alto saxophone, clarinet; Dante Perfumo, flute; Jean
McGuire, cello; Gene Porter, Herb Caro, baritone saxophone; Robert
Mosley, Wilbert Barranco, Lady Will Carr, Jimmy Bunn, Richard Wyands,
Buzz Wheeler, Donn Trenner, Russ Freeman, piano; Buddy Harper, Louis
Speigner, guitar; Roy Porter, Lee Young, Chuck Thompson, Cal Tjader,
Warren Thompson, drums; Johnny Berger, percussion; Red Callender, bass;
Oradell Mitchell, Everett Pettis, Claude Trenier, Herb Gayle, Helen Carr,
vocals.

Recorded 1945–1949

The Los Angeles jazz scene of the 1940s remains fascinating for many reasons: because it was so well documented by its own musicians (in books by Art Pepper, Hampton Hawes, Horace Tapscott, and the oral history *Central Avenue Sounds*); because its hub, the Central Avenue scene, slowed to a police-assisted halt in the late 1940s, thus mowing down the careers of many good-to-great musicians; because its musicians sloshed between bebop and R&B with a great deal more fluidity than those in New York, where modern jazz, by the late forties, was powerful enough to generate a circle of players that one could join and stay with exclusively.

Not that West Coast jazz ended with the shutdown of the big Central Avenue clubs—not at all. But black West Coast jazz was dealt a serious blow. If there's a tremendous sense of what could have been surrounding musicians who made their first major statements in the fifties, such as Harold Land or Teddy Edwards (who had long careers but just didn't become iconic) or the mysterious Dupree Bolton (the first-rate trumpeter on Land's album *The Fox*), there's even more of one about black Los Angeles players from the forties, such as Wilbert Barranco, Jimmy Bunn, William "Brother" Woodman, and Maxwell Davis.

All of those musicians are heard on *West Coast 1945–49*, the first full reckoning of Mingus's earliest recordings. The twenty-four-track set begins modestly, with attempts at jukebox hits: "The Texas Hop" was recorded to be thrown on the bandwagon of a popular dance, and "Baby, Take a Chance with Me," sung by Everett Pettis (add his name to the list) in a manly Billy Eckstine croon, is typical balladry of the period. It's workmanlike in its sophistication; Mingus arranged a lovely recording date during this period for Dinah Washington, and the arrangements sound pretty much the same.

But then, beginning with "Weird Nightmare" and continuing through the next set of sides recorded under the name of "Baron" Mingus, the valve blows. Jazz musicians, then as now, listened broadly, but Mingus was one of the few musicians of the time who bulldogged the full extent of his modernism onto wax, combining Ellingtonian voicings, nineteenth-century symphonic writing, Scriabin, Charlie Parker, and R&B. (The notes in this reissue, written by coproducer Robert E. Sunenblick, mention that "most of these records were probably difficult to find even within days of their issue," since none of the small labels Mingus made them for, including Excelsior, Four Star, Dolphins of Hollywood, and Rex Hollywood, had distribution outside Los Angeles.)

As fussily European as the surroundings could be, Mingus's bass playing never loses its ferocious drive. This is a lesson we can take away from the record and apply to jazz in general: you don't necessarily have to subordinate swing, not for anything; if the intent is jazz, swing will fit in with pretty much anything. There's "Mingus Fingers," a no-nonsense tune recorded with a quartet, Mingus's first claim to Jimmy Blantonesque stature as a bass soloist. And in the following session there are some attempts at thick modernist orchestrations—the "Charles 'Baron' Mingus Presents His Symphonic Airs" sides—which get clotted up and clunky, almost insane with ungainly dissonance; they're failures by any measure except their incredible energy.

Mingus was involved in the integration of the Los Angeles musicians' union (black jazz players in Los Angeles were missing out on an awful lot of film work) and therefore got to know working musicians of all kinds; his kind of creative mind wouldn't have kept him ghettoized anyway. So here you have a black musician playing off of the totems of up-to-the-minute black art—Monk, Gillespie, Parker—even while he's knee-deep in what you might call white culture: modernized sweet dance-band arrangements including flute, cello, clarinet, and a white supper-club singer named Herb Gayle.

Remember that there was no vogue then for cross-cultural shufflings as such. If we heard Don Byron doing something similar now—and in many ways, Byron's destroy-all-stereotypes attitude about music making is Charles Mingus's gift—we'd understand it as a gesture that is expected of him. But for their time, these experiments are fascinatingly searching and earnest.

25. NAT "KING" COLE TRIO:

Live at the Circle Room

(CAPITOL 7243-5-21859-2-4)

Nat "King" Cole, piano, vocals; Oscar Moore, guitar; Johnny Miller, bass.

Recorded 1946

The great joke of "My Sugar Is So Refined," the new song Cole was plugging during this mid-forties Milwaukee nightclub engagement, is that his girlfriend has a different way of pronouncing everything—the only way she can pronounce her refinement is to put on airs and exhibit her differentness.

Cole was the most refined singer in jazz and one of its most refined pianists; by "refined" I refer to his control and his swing: he never appeared to make a mistake and exercised a controlling hand over his work as a whole that made it unified, smooth, and very rhythmic. There wasn't anything rarefied about him; he played perfectly in the American idiom. Everyone danced to him, black and white, young and old. Pianists are often the most original musicians in jazz. Like John Lewis, Ahmad Jamal, Jelly Roll Morton, and a few others, Cole was no outsider, yet in his slickness he was inimitable; as a person, let alone as a musician, he was light-years ahead of the average jazz musician of the day.

Cole was at his best in 1946, about to make the now-famous records with his trio that combined pop singing with real jazz improvisation. While an obvious choice for the best record from this period would be Capitol's *The Vocal Classics*—the studio-recorded hits of the mid-forties, essentially the music that Diana Krall's popular trio was based on, not to mention a band that influenced the likes of Ray Charles and Oscar Peterson—*Live at the Circle Room* can make for more penetrative listening.

Cole's hits are as ingrained in American consciousness as the images from *The Wizard of Oz* or the look of film noir cityscapes; hearing an average (but fabulous) live set by the trio from the period is the best way to break through the seal of familiarity. This recording—apparently the only available one of Cole in a nightclub—was done for radio but was a real concert, in the Circle Room of Milwaukee's Hotel LaSalle; so you get the announcer breaking in every once in a while, but you also get a dim fuzz of conversation, clinking glasses, cash registers. If you want to gauge how slick Cole was, check out the composure and precision of the trio together and then of Cole alone. (It's not a pristine recording, but here and there the sonic mist lifts over Cole's voice, and it's quite beautifully captured.)

His piano solo in "I Found a New Baby" is Cole at his most reminiscent of Earl Hines and Teddy Wilson, stretching out with effortless variations (though it doesn't "build" per se; coolness, not intensity, was his thing). It's punctuated by Oscar Moore's little string explosions, his zipping glissandos and sliding, popping two-note chords. (Listen to Moore, also, on "One O'clock Jump," from this album; far from plodding through a battened-down routine, he puts odd harmonies in his comping.) There's an awful lot to hang on to with this band.

26. BOB WILLS AND HIS TEXAS PLAYBOYS:

The Tiffany Transcriptions, Vol. 3: Basin Street Blues

(RHINO R2 71471)

Bob Wills, fiddle, vocals; Tommy Duncan, Dean McKinney, Evelyn McKinney, vocals; Joe Holley, fiddle; Louis Tierney, fiddle, saxophone; Millard Kelson, piano; Alex Brashear, trumpet; Noel Boggs, Herb Remington, steel guitar; Lester "Junior" Barnard, Eldon Shamblin, electric guitar; Tiny Moore, electric mandolin; Ocie Stockard, banjo; Billy Jack Wills, bass; Johnny Cuviello, Monty Mountjoy, drums.

Recorded 1946–1947

The greatest western swing was cowboy jazz; it came partially from the same sources as the other kinds of mid-twentieth-century jazz that need no qualifier.

Bob Wills himself, a short icon with meaty forearms, cowboy hat, cigar, and fiddle, was more a spur of talent, a Cab Calloway figure, a performance enhancer, than a singer or soloist. (There were usually additional fiddlers in the band.) He created a circle of players, and most of them were bona fide jazz freaks; many of them shared a generation and a locale with some of the great jazz instrumentalists of the day. They had naturally tuned into the Midwest and southwestern territory bands of the 1930s and to Ellington; the guitarists of western swing tended to love Eddie Lang and Charlie Christian (who was born the same year and grew up in the same town—Oklahoma City—as Eldon Shamblin, the great Bob Wills guitarist). Wills himself, with his exaggerated, bug-eyed grins and corn-pone falsetto *ah-hah!*s, was probably channeling the minstrel shows of his youth, which included a good deal of blues.

But among western swing bands, the Wills band was special. At its most lowdown and hottest, which is on these live-in-the-radio-studio recordings, it was a fighting unit. The rhythm-section accompanists absorbed swing feel to buoy the soloists, but the drummers' relentless one-TWO-one-TWO polka-tinged beat was more overbearing and aggressive than black swing. The whole sound had a fuzz-toned over-drive similar to what would later be the most aggressive rock and roll.

It's reading too much into it, but I've heard air checks of the Wills band from the fifties—dance-hall concerts broadcast over the radio—that sound like nothing so much as southern California punk, even when they're playing "In the Mood." There's a blasting energy, inten-sified by tripled electric instruments (guitar, steel guitar, mandolin) through overdriven amplifiers (favored at that moment by black gui-tarists spanning R&B and jazz, such as Tiny Grimes) and whatever felicities of radio compression that might have been involved in getting the sound onto record. That cumulative blast of sound and energy comes across not unlike Black Flag.

In any case, the Tiffany radio sessions of 1946 and 1947 caught the band during a hot period. The material on this volume of the *Tiffany Transcriptions* series—they are uniformly excellent—focuses on blues and jazz standards that had been made famous by Louis Armstrong, Bessie Smith, Jimmie Lunceford, and Duke Ellington, among others; though it's a selection imposed after the fact, the song choices reaffirm the band's natural connection to jazz.

27. THELONIOUS MONK:

Genius of Modern Music, Volume 1

(BLUE NOTE 7243-5-32138-2-4)

Thelonious Monk, piano; Idrees Sulieman, George Taitt, trumpet; Danny Quebec West, Sahib Shihab, alto saxophone; Billy Smith, tenor saxophone; Gene Ramey, Bob Paige, bass; Art Blakey, drums.

Recorded 1947

Some of jazz's best records are the liminal ones, when one musical sen-sibility coexists with another. They're useful not just for the historical frisson; the music itself tends to operate with a heightened consciousness.

Thelonious Monk's first recordings for Blue Note, made with a lot

Thelonious Monk

of musicians who never amounted to much and a drummer (Art Blakey) who did—are among these, although the era he was leading toward, out of his integrated stride, boogie, and bebop roots, was the era of himself. Monk was a liminal character: he combined the very old hymns and parlor songs and surely the Afro-Cuban music that had become a fascination in New York ballrooms as early as 1930.

His rhythmic and harmonic language in 1947 was not standard bebop language. His strategies—outside of the fast clip of the tunes, which he forswore ten years later to work almost exclusively with medium and ballad tempos—were not bebop strategies. (See *Charlie Parker: The Complete Savoy and Dial Studio Recordings 1944–1948,* above.) Bebop as an idea had existed since 1941, when the new music was practiced after-hours in Minton's and Monroe's, the Harlem clubs. But it hadn't been recorded as such until 1945. The word started showing up in the press; it had a name, but nobody knew exactly what it was or where it would lead.

These recordings, made with trio, quintet, and sextet, are small-group jazz that would forever sound new. Monk was already known among musicians; he had written "Epistrophy" and "'Round Midnight," both recorded by Cootie Williams. Listen to "Thelonious," with its contrary-motion horn harmonies in the head and then two stunning choruses of piano soloing. They weren't stunning for their smoothness: Monk was inventing a new kind of urbanity, one that challenged his audiences' assumptions by making them think he was just playing one unconscionable error after another.

Why would you hit a single note so obsessively, as he does in his second solo chorus of "Thelonious," if you weren't inept? In "Thelonious," a *Downbeat* critic wrote at the time, Monk sounds as if he were thinking about "the stock returns or the 7th at Pimlico—anything but his piano." It wasn't considered that he could be playing one key the way a *conguero* plays one drum or that he might have been embarking on the greatest gamesmanship jazz had ever seen.

One of Monk's healthiest bequests to jazz history is his penchant for letting the drums shine through: there are long moments in "Thelonious" and "Well, You Needn't" and "Off Minor" where all you hear is the steady thump of Gene Ramey's bass and Art Blakey's drums. At these moments, Monk is playing chicken: how long can I lay out?

There was more of this trick-bumbling sensibility in movie dancers than in jazz, and Monk's music is some of the most easily danced-to music in all of jazz—which is another way of saying it is some of the most immediately likable.

28. CHARLIE PARKER:

Charlie Parker with Strings: The Master Takes

(VERVE 314-523-984-2)

Charlie Parker, alto saxophone; Al Porcino, Doug Mettome, Ray Wetzel, Chris Griffin, Bernie Privin, trumpet; Will Bradley, Bill Harris, trombone; Bart Varsalona, bass trombone; Murray Williams, Toots Mondello, Sonny Salad, alto saxophone; Hank Ross, Pete Mondello, Flip Phillips, tenor saxophone; Stan Webb, Manny Albam, baritone saxophone; John LaPorta, clarinet; Mitch Miller, Eddie Brown, Tommy Mace, oboe; Joseph Singer, Vinnie Jacobs, French horn; Bronislaw Gimpel, Max Holander, Milt Lomask, Sam Caplan, Howard Kay, Harry Melnikoff, Sam Rand, Zelly Smirnoff, Ted Blume, Stank Karpenia, Sylvan Shulman, Jack Zayde, Gene Orloff, Manny Fiddler, Sid Harris, Harry Katzman, violin; Frank Brieff, Isador Zir, Dave Uchitel, Nat Nathanson, Fred Ruzilla, viola; Frank Miller, Maurice Brown, Joe Benaventi, cello; Myor Rosen, Verley Mills, Wallace McManus, harp; Art Ryerson, guitar; Stan Freeman, Bernie Leighton, Al Haig, Lou Stein, Tony Aless, piano; Ray Brown, Tommy Potter, Bob Haggart, Curly Russell, bass; Buddy Rich, Roy Haynes, Don Lamond, Shelly Manne, drums; Diego Iborra, percussion; Jimmy Carroll, Joe Lipman, Neal Hefti, arrangements, conducting.

Recorded 1947–1952

For anyone who has learned about Charlie Parker through his small-group recordings, in which bebop rhythm—both the rhythm section's and his own—is of enormous importance, the *Charlie Parker with Strings* sessions can seem like surprising frippery.

Bird is canonized by the virtues of speed and toughness—those sprayings of sixteenth notes, all that fragmented melody stuffed with passing tones as he and Dizzy Gillespie lunge toward a new rhythmic and harmonic vocabulary. The themes that have evolved from his biography suggest an outlaw status, cherished by Americans: the artist staying a step ahead of his public, confusing them, challenging them, angering them.

But when you talk about his ballad playing, you're talking about a different level of expertise, one that included speed but also a tenderer and possibly deeper beauty. And his sessions with strings are, almost without exception, lush ballads; though the dynamic Buddy Rich is the drummer for most of them, the recordings have nothing of the rhythmic vitality that was supplied in the small-group sessions by the first-wave bebop drummers.

Bird saw recording with strings as keeping an eye on the main chance, a way into popularity. Who really can say whether the arrangements of Jimmy Carroll and Joe Lipman satisfied him? The point was that Norman Granz was willing to organize it, Parker had the biggest seller of his short career with the 78 RPM single of the Carroll-arranged "Just Friends," and for several years the strings format allowed him to tour easily, because the music was written out and the star could improvise handily over a pickup band.

There's a variation of quality on this collection, made up of the three "Charlie Parker with Strings" EPs, five live tracks from a 1950 Carnegie Hall concert, and one uncollected piece, "Repetition," written and arranged by Neal Hefti. The CD is bookended by two fabulous pieces. Parker's opening salvo in "Just Friends," after the pizzicato strings introduction, is his improvising at its best—as light, here, as Lee Konitz's but with cracking speed, note stuffed but imaginative, its tonal center blurred by rapid, muscular reshuffling of patterns and lashing, wide-interval melodies. The song's second chorus, after Mitch Miller's oboe interlude, begins with an entirely new melodic thrust.

Hefti's "Repetition," at the back end of the disc, is an artful arrangement without the harps, oboes, and kitsch sweetness of the Carroll and Lipman sessions. In the middle, there are tracks in which Parker sounds less inspired; on David Raksin's theme song from the film *Laura*, for example, which served as the basis for one of Don Byas's greatest recordings (see *Savoy Jam Party* on the B-list at the end of this book), Parker's playing is predictable, barely getting away from the melody. It's a dreamy butterscotch fantasy, and he just seems bored.

But it's remarkable how sustaining so much of this music is and how geared to broad entertainment and Hollywood sensibilities it is, given that Parker was one of the preeminent artistic geniuses of the twentieth century, a figure sharing the same rarefied terrace as Eliot, Faulkner, Picasso, Welles, and Balanchine.

There's a judgmental sadness that accrues around this period of Parker's career in a lot of biographical and critical writing, a how-could-he tone. But what is jazz if not a complete confusion of popular and esoteric, highbrow and middlebrow and even lowbrow? Everybody who knew Parker remarks on his interest in an unusually wide range of things—not just unusual for a musician, unusual for anybody. He was also apparently attentive to all kinds of entertainments—comic acting and Hindemith and street musicians. I'm not at all convinced that he naively saw this recording as a ticket to classiness. I do suspect, though, that, aside from economic motivations, he enjoyed the idea of his music intersecting with what was actually a form of popular culture.

29. DJANGO REINHARDT:

Djangology 49

(BLUEBIRD/RCA ND90448)

Django Reinhardt, guitar; Stéphane Grappelli, violin; Gianni Safred, piano; Carlo Recori, bass; Aurelio de Carolis, drums.

Recorded 1949

Django Reinhardt enthusiasts are a peculiar subspecies: no excuses are offered for their fealty to a single artistic source. True Djangophilia— the standard of which is set by Sinti Gypsy guitar players such as Reinhardt himself—doesn't really mean building on Reinhardt's language. It means trying to sound as much like him as one can. Within the context of the jazz world, Djangophilia is an honorable pursuit; but to see it in action (and there are more and more contexts for this) is a bit like watching a bunch of talented actors stand around in fedoras and do Bogey for an hour.

This is because Reinhardt's music was rooted in Gallic joie de vivre; for its high craft, it's essentially chummy and lighthearted. The way the songs are played, sweet and fast, can sound like the only way to play them, and that's that. You don't want to be different from Django; you want to be Django, to share the same earthy humor and sweetness and light. It is a music of *copains,* and as it extended into the bebop era its soul was different from the American ethos of competition and survival. Reinhardt had a strong, loud sound—apparently whether or not he was playing a Maccaferri, with its oversized resonating chamber; his sound sliced through the air, and his strings rattled against the frets. It was a rough, gutsy music, possibly an overcompensation for his burned fretting hand, which left the third and fourth fingers disabled; in most pictures you see him using only his first two fingers, with sometimes his thumb reaching around the neck to grab a bass note.

Grappelli, on the other hand, manufactured an obsessively refined tension, especially in ballads, repeating short phrases in something like a patrician's elegant stammer, then tagging them with fast, wide-interval endings, concluding solos with whistling harmonics high up on the neck. They were very different (musically and personally), but their overwhelming technique and florid mannerisms yoked them together.

Recording and performing together in the Quintette of the Hot Club of France for thirteen years (1935–1948), Reinhardt and Grappelli were a team, one of the few great two-person batteries in jazz history, to be compared with Bird and Gillespie, Lester Young and Billie Holiday, or Louis Armstrong and Earl Hines. But they played together more than any of those others. Their fates were intertwined, as they hung on to a romantic kind of swing that was going out of style.

The sessions on *Djangology 49* are Reinhardt's and Grappelli's last ones together. They aren't universally regarded as their best; that honor usually goes to some sessions from September 1937 and available as a single disc as Classics 748. The Italian rhythm section in the 1949 sessions is often derided as not being up to the standards of the leaders. But I have never been able to hear the rhythm section much, so intent are Reinhardt and Grappelli at outflourishing each other; and if there is a wobbly feel to these sessions, with a piano player whose bop-like accompaniment gets tangled up in the soloists, it doesn't matter much. I find the earlier sessions too tight, too armored, too much of a good thing. Until 1939, too, the quintet was an all-strings group; the format is lovely in short doses.

Aside from its subplot of the Reinhardt/Grappelli reunion and farewell, *Djangology 49* is also interesting for a change in direction in both players' music. They were trying, in their own way, to accommodate the harmonic advances of bebop; there are flatted fifths all over "Honeysuckle Rose," and they make the decision to play "I Got Rhythm," the boppers' anthem.

Sometimes you have to give in to a bit of the sentimentality that surrounds jazz history; it is, after all, a series of great stories. If you're going to favor a flawed session over a perfect one, this is the session to favor. Reinhardt and Grappelli's relationship was rough by 1949; their careers were going in different directions, and each was increasingly following the call of the solo artist. They very well might have known they were saying good-bye to each other, and I believe I can hear the mutual fondness and the last challenge in their playing.

30. STAN KENTON:

New Concepts of Artistry in Rhythm

(CAPITOL 7-92865-2)

Stan Kenton, piano; Conte Candoli, Buddy Childers, Maynard Ferguson, Don Dennis, Ruben McFall, trumpet; Bob Fitzpatrick, Keith Moon, Frank Rosolino, Bill Russo, trombone; George Roberts, bass trombone; Lee Konitz, Vinnie Dean, alto saxophone; Richie Kamuca, Bill Holman, tenor saxophone; Bob Gioga, baritone saxophone; Sal Salvador, guitar; Don Bagley, bass; Stan Levey, drums; Derek Walton, conga; Kay Brown, vocals.

Recorded 1952

Stan Kenton

You don't have to be familiar with Stan Kenton's telegram to *Downbeat* in 1956, charging the magazine with reverse racism in its annual critics' polls—or even with his long-boned, Nordic appearance—to grasp the deep Caucasianness of this music.

When you hear a black comedian lampooning a white attitude—I'm thinking of Cedric the Entertainer in *The Kings of Comedy*, describing how black people are said to typically run from a scene of danger whereas white people walk toward it briskly and stiffly, saying, "Well, see here, I'm gonna get to the bottom of this!"—that voice and that attitude is something like Kenton's. And his swashbuckling walk into modernism—modernism! with many, many trombones!—did not admit of less is more. He wanted to get to the bottom of this modernism business, and his commitment to the mission gave much of his music a nearly hysterical drive.

I don't mean to imply that Kenton was racist, or that his aesthetic somehow gated out black people. He did hire black musicians for his bands over the years, including Jesse Price and Lucky Thompson. And he did have a following among black jazz fans; the historian Dan Morgenstern saw Kenton in 1949 at Carnegie Hall, and recalls that more than half the audience was black.

But Kenton left a trail to be interpreted as you like—as grandiose and monomaniacal, or simply as perspicacious, a rare example of an avant-garde composer elbowing his way into popular music.

This band was convened after Kenton had launched, and then abandoned, his forty-piece "Innovations in Modern Music" orchestra; Kenton's orchestral concept descended stylistically from that of Fletcher Henderson in the 1930s—lots of immaculately ordered brass arrangements—and included a number of excellent players, both those who confirm Kenton's heavy-handed manner of hearing music and those who refute it. There's the light-toned alto saxophonist Lee Konitz, who moves lissomely through juggernauts such as Gerry Mulligan's "Young Blood" and "Taboo" (an unusually bebop-adherent solo, in an ersatz Afro-Cuban setting) and makes Bill Russo's "Improvisation" a fascinating piece of shifting-theme music. There's Frank Rosolino, an easily recognized trombonist, a flawless technician in bop-tempo material, and a balladeer whose poignant high-register lyricism usually came grit-free. And there's Maynard Ferguson, the trumpeter who made his name on ear-shattering high notes. Kenton's bands were military both in their precision and in their genteel aggression, and Ferguson was the commando gunner.

New Concepts, half of which was written by Russo (who still leads an enlightening Kenton repertory band based in Chicago), presents a cross section of where Kenton was in the fifties. It begins with his overblown, shamelessly pedantic "Prologue (This Is an Orchestra!)," complete with Stan the Man's voice-overs about the role of each member. ("An asset to any group like this is the presence of versatility—a musician capable of creating all moods. At the moment: warm, melting, personal sounds. Conte Candoli.") Who is he talking to? The average clod, who wouldn't care? His faithful flock, who wouldn't need such prompting to understand the band members' individual styles? An abstract notion of posterity?

The album has thunderous tracks and quiet tracks, two examples of Kenton's Cuban obsession, an icy modernist vocal number ("Lonesome Train," with slow chug-chug beats). There's one bona fide orchestral classic (Russo's "Improvisation," densely contrapuntal, a successful amalgam of jazz and classical languages, built of two discrete themes) and the soloist vehicle "Invention for Guitar and Trumpet," which made the career of guitarist Sal Salvador. The album closes with a fair example of the work of Kenton's weirdest arranger, Bob Graettinger, who reupholsters "You Go to My Head" with escalating, cannonlike cycles of dissonant brass, while Rosolino warbles the melody as you know it in his velvety trombone tone.

No, Kenton's music doesn't sit comfortably amid the jazz tradition these days. It sounds like an artifact from a very hard-assed and rather pretentious planet. The second Basie big band really dominated the sound of American orchestral jazz; in the end, Americans will take jocularity, warmness, generosity, and shared cultural roots over Kenton's exercises in anxiety and holding the audience at bay. (A record like *New Concepts of Artistry in Rhythm*—or, even better, the cult favorite *City of Glass,* arranged by the way-out Graettinger—was fifties America's pop-culture form of Bertolt Brecht's *verfremdung* effect.) But did Kenton ever try hard. His passion remains impressive and, in a funny-sad way, beautiful.

31. GERRY MULLIGAN:

The Complete Pacific Jazz Recordings of the Gerry Mulligan Quartet with Chet Baker

(PACIFIC JAZZ/CAPITOL 7243-8-382632-2, 4 CDS)

Gerry Mulligan, baritone saxophone, piano; Chet Baker, trumpet; Jimmy Rowles, piano; Lee Konitz, alto saxophone; Red Mitchell, Bobby Whitlock, Carson Smith, Henry Grimes, Joe Mondragon, bass; Chico Hamilton, Larry Bunker, Dave Bailey, drums; Annie Ross, vocals.

Recorded 1952–1957

Few documents of an evolving style are easier to follow than this one, even if the prehistory is a bit vague.

Cool jazz did not necessarily evolve on the West Coast. There was the 1949 *Birth of the Cool* recording sessions, a brainstorm that rightly should be cocredited to Miles Davis, Gil Evans, Johnny Carisi, and Gerry Mulligan. (The nine-piece music, with French horn and other delicate sonorities, was the continuation of a conversation among all of the above, as well as others, at Gil Evans's Fifty-fifth Street apartment in New York; it was a rare, true collaborative effort between dogmatic personalities, and the way was smoothed by Evans's lovely temperament.) There was Dave Brubeck's octet music, recorded around the same time, if not before. (The dates are uncertain.) There was a precursor bandleader, Claude Thornhill, for whom both Evans and Mulligan had worked; his music was full of elegant, French-sounding harmony and slow tempos. And there was Lester Young, of course, who came up with his own serene, feline sound in the 1930s, inspired partly by Frank Trumbauer.

In any event, Mulligan carried the mood of *Birth of the Cool* with him when he moved to Los Angeles in the early 1950s. He made some recordings, quite restrained, with Red Mitchell and Chico Hamilton, on which he played dollops of piano; he made some more with Chet Baker, Jimmy Rowles, and Joe Mondragon, and Rowles's personality at the piano was so strong that the records sounded like products of coleadership. Then he was booked into a club called the Haig, which had had its piano removed for the previous attraction, the vibraphonist Red Norvo. Mulligan went along with the imposition, playing with a pianoless quartet. Suddenly, the music sounded different.

To make up for the chordal variety of a piano, Mulligan and Baker worked out contrapuntal sections, but all executed with fairly even, clean rhythm. Hamilton, who was interested in making a kind of jazz chamber music, was the perfect drummer; his small fills and bass-drum patterns worked into the counterpoint. "Bernie's Tune," the first song from the breakthrough pianoless recording session of 1952, nearly suggests (in the two-horn chorus after Baker's solo) a new kind of Dixieland—but its minor-key, organized, reflective sound seems utterly the opposite of good times on Bourbon Street. ("Utter Chaos #1," a thirty-two-second snippet made at the end of that session, sounds more traditional and suggests the kind of music they could have made if they had more commercial aims.)

They had barely started, and they were recording in cheap, fast circumstances, but they already had the plot, and it was relatively simple:

ditch the piano, play with chamber dynamics, and don't get wild. The subsequent Pacific Jazz recordings made Mulligan's name in California.

This music doesn't demand much of you; it is lazily reflective, very diatonic, mid-tempo, and its individual instruments don't make much of their textural qualities. (The music has a single, piquant, collective timbre from beginning to end.) It is pretty and compact, and it didn't hurt that it is the opposite of the perfervid, intimidating sound that black beboppers had already canonized and stylized back east.

Actually, the idea was simple enough for perfection to be achieved. "My Old Flame," from April 1953, brings the soloist-accompanist dance that Mulligan and Baker enact with each other—very much like the right- and left-hand actions in Bach's solo piano music—to a new level of severe pleasure.

The idea of the group was revived in 1957, with a different rhythm section. Mulligan and Baker here sound a good deal more secure; in Mulligan especially, there is a new openness to caress the slow-tempo songs, such as "Stardust" and "Festive Minor." (Charlie Parker and Bennie Harris's "Ornithology," on the other hand, the West Coast version of an East Coast anthem, sounds unnecessarily stodgy.)

Despite a brilliant idea, the shortcomings are obvious. There is enough open space to explore sound better, to bring out the beauty of the individual instruments, but it doesn't happen. Or at least it doesn't happen with the original lineup. Lee Konitz makes an appearance on disc four for twelve tracks, as a fifth wheel to the quartet in a live recording, and his playing is gorgeous—humid and drifting at times, sprightly at others, galloping through bop lines at others. He helps to humanize the music.

Those unwilling to buy the complete box set will appreciate a single-CD reduction of the same material, *The Best of the Gerry Mulligan Quartet with Chet Baker* (Pacfic Jazz/Capitol 7-95481-2).

Dave Brubeck

32. DAVE BRUBECK QUARTET:

Brubeck Time

(COLUMBIA/LEGACY CK 65724)

Dave Brubeck, piano; Paul Desmond, alto saxophone; Bob Bates, bass; Joe Dodge, drums.

Recorded 1954

Historically, it has been unbearably tempting for a jazz critic to be perverse when it comes to Dave Brubeck. Whether or not the fault can be placed at his feet, Brubeck represents everything old-world about today's aging jazz audience. Dave Brubeck wore chinos, the Gap ads do declare. So do most college men of the 1950s, in our family photo files. Many of them look amazingly like Dave Brubeck, in fact.

At the first moment when jazz became hot in the media and general consciousness, the mid-1950s, Brubeck's were the records that made the most sense to college kids. They're not intimidating; they're almost official representations of an underground cult, with a practicality, a professionalism about them. This was modern jazz, and the albums might as well have come packaged with diagrams. ("Stolid" was a word used widely to disparage Brubeck in print by the 1960s—and a word that Brubeck came to hate.)

I'm afraid that I shall live up to expectations and not select his most famous record by ten miles, 1959's *Take Five*. As confident and important as that record is, it's also too . . . stolid. For repeated listening, I like *Brubeck Time* from 1954.

From his start in the mid-forties, Brubeck did not represent mainstream jazz, which made his success all the more remarkable. He situated himself far from the dominant Bud Powell school of bebop rhythm and harmony; he relied much more on chords than on sizzling, hornlike right-hand lines.

It took a little while for him to capitalize on his greater visibility and distribution with Columbia, which signed him in 1954, and slowly jazz purists began to turn against him. (The 1957 album *Dave Digs Disney*, covering songs from Disney movies, didn't do his street credibility any favors.) But by the end of the decade, he had a commercial breakthrough. In 1958, the band traveled in the Middle East and India, and Brubeck grew intrigued by folk music that didn't stick to four-four time. The result was the 1959 album *Time Out*. With the hits "Take Five" (composed in five-four meter) and "Blue Rondo a la Turk" (in nine-eight), Brubeck found enormous financial success; those pieces, released on two sides of a 45 RPM single a year after the release of the full LP, sold more than one million copies.

But the earlier *Brubeck Time* isn't exactly obscure. It came out just after Brubeck made the cover of *Time* magazine; one imagines that it sold a few copies. (He had already dominated the college concert-committee scene and sold half a million with *Jazz at Oberlin* before Columbia approached him.) But in 1954, neither Brubeck nor his bosses had become wedded to the idea of the concept album, and he was still a chameleonic musician.

On *Brubeck Time,* he was several different piano players: a splashy, crowd-pleasing, chord-flashing Erroll Garner–like player (as heard on his solo in "Keepin' out of Mischief Now"); a dry, hard, percussive single-note player (the theme of "Brother, Can You Spare a Dime?" sounds like something from a Lennie Tristano album, and Paul Desmond sounds remarkably like Lee Konitz, Tristano's favorite foil); and a cool, shrewd, slightly oblique modernist like Dick Twardzik, with static harmonies and long, resounding, quiet chords.

Brubeck's slightly nerdy methods of rhythmic rearrangement are already in evidence here, in "Jeepers Creepers." The drummer and bassist, who were not to become part of his long-running quartet, are just there, keeping time; they swing adequately, and that's that. But Brubeck and Desmond are wonderful. "Pennies from Heaven" remains one of the best Brubeck quartet performances on record, from Desmond's patient thematic development and canny swing to Brubeck's quiet series of prewritten (I assume they are, anyway), cell-like solo ideas, built on one sturdy harmonic device after another, including a swinging bitonal blues section.

Cecil Taylor, of all people—whose music has always had a patina of inward-looking, anticommercial radicalism—has spoken admiringly of early Brubeck. One can imagine Taylor having focused on something like "Pennies from Heaven"; this confident, highly arranged solo, vaulting among distinct ideas, could have influenced Taylor when he recorded his own great solo on a ballad, "This Nearly Was Mine," in 1960.

This may seem like special pleading—as if, to merit inclusion in this book, it's not good enough for Brubeck to have been popular; he has to be radical, too. But that's not what I'm trying to express. It's truer to say that there is usually a radicalism of some sort in popular culture, and Brubeck probably understands that as well as Prince, Mick Jagger, or Madonna.

Sarah Vaughan

33. Sarah Vaughan:

Sarah Vaughan

(VERVE 314-543-305-2)

Sarah Vaughan, vocals; Clifford Brown, trumpet; Herbie Mann, flute; Paul Quinichette, tenor saxophone; Jimmy Jones, piano; Joe Benjamin, bass; Roy Haynes, drums; Ernie Wilkins, arranger, conductor.

Recorded 1954

Sarah Vaughan's voice was something to be amazed by, and, as so often happens with an abundance of talent, it was applied to questionable uses. Don't blame her too much: she was a woman singer coming into her stardom just as rock and roll hit, and the reconfigured needs of the record industry were at odds with the strengths of some of jazz's most brilliant artists. The breadth of her talent and interests—and the fact that she saw herself as a free agent who could sing whatever she wanted to sing—led her away from hard-core jazz, which in the abstract is good; the fact is, though, that she was an unparalleled jazz singer, and her hard-core jazz records are her best. This is one of them.

Some record sessions, it seems, are just blessed; on rare occasions, even middle-level musicians can sound like gods. The arrangements of the Count Basie saxophonist Ernie Wilkins, the microphone placement and engineering of the producer Bob Shad, the weather that day or how much sleep Vaughan had had—who knows what was most meaningful, what pulled the circle tight and made this the thing it is.

One among Wilkins's loveliest ideas was to have Vaughan harmonize wordlessly with some of the opening heads; the timbral blend of her voice with Herbie Mann's flute creates an eerie effect of voice and instrument in cosmic agreement that's seldom been duplicated in jazz. Mann's playing is weak in spots; the same can be said of that of the saxophonist Paul Quinichette, pianist Jimmy Jones, and bassist Joe Benjamin. But the weaknesses are soft-pedaled and mixed low: in "September Song," Vaughan sounds if she's an inch from your ear, while Jones is down at the other end of the block—and nearly undetectable in the overall elegant atmosphere.

Then there's Clifford Brown and Roy Haynes. Of Vaughan's generation, Brown was perhaps the one musician most analogous to Vaughan (the nonchalant mastery, the professionalism of the talent), playing assertive little masterpieces of trumpet improvisation. And Haynes swings with a gimlet eye, making bass-drum splats on the upbeats, militating against the glide of the band with drumming that suddenly pops and glides like the roll-and-dip limp of a hipster's walk.

Vaughan's diction, tone, and vocal range encompass a great deal of the possibilities for expression as a jazz singer; this album is something like an instruction manual. Some of what I like least about *Sarah Vaughan* are its schizy moments, when she rockets between hoity-toity ("Oi feel so sure, so positive" in "I'm Glad There Is You") and so blues-singer earthy, in certain low-register moments, that she approaches vulgarity. Vaughan is responsible for a lot of embarrassingly purple jazz singing since then. It's a commonplace that Vaughan had good "taste"—hey, she liked bossa nova—but based on the way she deployed her talents even on a straightforward record like this, I'm not sure how true that is.

There is something far more live and volatile than taste here and much deeper. Small emotional nuances keep revealing themselves. Brown's solo on "April in Paris" seems to render Vaughan slack, for once, with its beauty, to judge by her suddenly affectless reading of the title line; what follows is a little struggle to get herself back to full strength. Like Holiday, like Hawkins, like Young, this performance is a kind of acting, and on *Sarah Vaughan* elements of pure music and pure drama keep mixing together.

34. CLIFFORD BROWN AND MAX ROACH:

Clifford Brown and Max Roach

(VERVE 314-543-306-2)

Clifford Brown, trumpet; Max Roach, drums; George Morrow, bass; Harold Land, tenor saxophone; Richie Powell, piano.

Recorded 1954–1955

The Miles Davis quintet of the mid-fifties represented a version of post-bop that bridged art and popular taste; it was one of the greatest hard-core jazz small groups of the era. But it wasn't the only one.

The Clifford Brown–Max Roach quintet, active from early 1954 to June 1956, ending when both Brown and pianist Richie Powell died in a car crash, ran neck and neck with the Davis band, and the two groups had considerable stylistic overlap. Speculating about what would happen if so-and-so hadn't died is futile, but you can be almost certain of this: if Clifford Brown had lived, the profile of Miles Davis, which shot up by 1957, would have taken much longer to rise.

Perhaps the surer speculation is that the Brown-Roach band was just not meant to be.

Assembled in Los Angeles at the spurring of producer Gene Norman, the group gave Davis—just recovering from heroin addiction and recording in a different thrown-together assembly every month—something to compete against. Davis set up his band similarly. He hired an experienced drummer from a bebop background (his Philly Joe Jones to this band's Roach) and a tenor player, John Coltrane, who was an unknown toiler in jazz and R&B bands. Harold Land had just moved to Los Angeles from San Diego, where he had both worked in a jazz band and also, like Coltrane, toured with R&B bandleaders (in his case Jimmy and Joe Liggins). Within a year of Land's arrival, Brown heard him in a jam session at Eric Dolphy's home studio.

The band's sound is a long way from the alpha-dog attack of the first-wave bebop ten years before. It is more controlled and much less brittle; bebop, at first, gave off a high-pitched sound, with its heavy cymbal timekeeping and its trumpet high notes and its tempos; you can't play hard and fast very well in low registers. Roach, as coband-leader, was markedly less assertive with bass-drum accents and snare-and-tom polyrhythms than he had been up to that point; they're still there but newly polished.

The communication between Land, with a smoky, swing-era tenor sound, and Clifford Brown, so alert and bright toned, was wonderful: their traded improvisations on "The Blues Walk," growing shorter and shorter toward the end, dancing around each other to avoid a collision, brings excitement to formula. This was an articulate band with a rather weak link in Powell, who had his brother Bud's headlong fistfuls of chords without the streamlined execution. But both Brown and Roach were setting benchmarks—Roach for a highly improvisatory, melodic style of drum solos, and Brown for the clarity and speed of his playing.

Roach is discussed elsewhere in this book (see Duke Ellington's *Money Jungle,* below, for instance). But Brown's influence was strong and short. He picked up where Fats Navarro left off, in a swift, mature, amazingly musical style (by which I mean it retained the coherent quality of song) that was more dynamically controlled than Dizzy Gillespie's; he compressed his showmanship into a rigorous harmonic-rhythmic conception, and he didn't parade his high notes. His phrases on this album are rounded and easily swinging. Nor did he miss any notes, or so was the legend about him; unencumbered by addiction to alcohol or drugs, he gave it his all every night, polishing his technique so that all of his performances sparkled.

Many prefer the second incarnation of the quintet with Sonny Rollins, but this is one of the strongest studio-made albums up to that

time in the nascent LP era. It includes four of Brown's great performances in "Parisian Thoroughfare," "Jordu," "Daahoud," and "Joy
Spring"; and the last two are Brown's greatest compositions. The
"Jordu" solo, in particular, is masterly, crafted in discrete parts, never
at a loss for ideas about how to expand on the tune's chords or its
melody. Roach's solo in the same song, too, is a perfect example of his
development; it uses African-sounding repetition to an unnerving
degree, but there's a lid on his projection.

35. HORACE SILVER:

Horace Silver and the Jazz Messengers

(BLUE NOTE CDP 7 46140 2)

*Horace Silver, piano; Kenny Dorham, trumpet; Hank Mobley, tenor saxo-
phone; Doug Watkins, bass; Art Blakey, drums.*

Recorded 1954–1955

Lifted out of the jazz-bar scene of Hartford, Connecticut, by Stan Getz,
who happened to be passing through there in 1950, and recording in
New York for Blue Note by 1952, Silver had a career that progressed
efficiently for its first fifteen years. Discographers say he was able to
make albums in remarkably few takes; he had a forthright, can-do
approach that's apparent in his playing.

What Silver achieved, as the first major figure of the music called
hard bop, was the deeper connection of several of bebop's musical
ingredients with the cultural tradition of black America, winnowing
down bebop's curlicued melodies, skipping a few steps of its rhythmic
mazes, and creating a model for hipness that wasn't based on European
models of virtuosity or complexity. Blues and R&B vernaculars aren't
unnatural to modern jazz; they were already strong elements in bebop,
and today Charlie Parker's "Now's the Time" and "Billie's Bounce" are
still played by street-corner musicians. But Silver foregrounded these
elements. Essentially, he took what jazz had been since 1940 or so and

Horace Silver

made populist sense of it, smoothing out the disjunctions, the strivings for art music, and the comforts of the vernacular.

Not that he was a simple case, or a pianist whose style you could see right through. His bass-clef chords, supporting his barrelhouse right-hand improvisations, spit forth like gravel from under a squealing tire: small, nubby slivers of sound, more percussive and recondite than even Monk's and Powell's left-hand figures. (Listen to Silver's solo here on "Room 608.") As hard-blues as Silver's phrases are, he didn't have a barroom fixation; his music isn't stuck in one mood, and he wasn't creating only a self-consciously working-class art. That notion came a few years later, with tenor-and-organ music, which owed something to Silver; Jimmy Smith recorded Silver's "The Preacher" on his own first album in 1956.

Despite all Silver's blues language and his deep funk—and this was not a word much applied to music before Silver came along—he was a modernist. The frameworks of these tunes may sound overfamiliar, but there's a hungry imagination at work inside.

Above all, Silver had a structure and a plan in all his music. Broken up into eight-bar chunks, sometimes a blues segment alternates with a Latin segment; Silver also wrote two-bar tags that beautifully wrap up his themes. As quickly as anyone in jazz, he established not only his own pianistic style—to which he would stay true—but a foolproof style of small-group writing and arrangement. Usually created for trumpet, tenor saxophone, piano, drums, and bass, this was ideal road music; it played equally well anywhere in the United States and didn't exclude any listeners on aesthetic grounds.

For all that, Silver has been saddled with a critical reputation for creating boring music, a sort of straitjacket template for mainstream players. Well, he did create a template, that's for sure. But it was a beautiful one.

If you were Alfred Lion, the coproprietor of Blue Note, and a twenty-seven-year-old pianist handed in this recording to you, you would be a satisfied man. This musician understood variety: the strong uptempo beginning of "Room 608," the midnight tempo of "Creepin' In," the folk melody of "The Preacher" (it comes not from "I've Been Working on the Railroad," as is guessed in Ira Gitler's original liner notes for the album, but from the English dance-hall song "Show Me the Way to Go Home"; Silver wrote it as something to play for his final tune on a gig).

This marked the beginning of Art Blakey's Jazz Messengers, and Blakey's strong drumming helps establish the authority in this music. But it's Silver who built the landscape here, an incredibly influential one, holding sway through Blakey's long career and his different bands, through Mingus, through Cannonball Adderley, and certainly through Wynton Marsalis.

Chet Baker

36. CHET BAKER:

Chet in Paris: The Complete Barclay Recordings of Chet Baker, Volume 1

(EMARCY/POLYGRAM FRANCE)

Chet Baker, trumpet; Benny Vasseur, trombone; Jean Aldegon, alto saxophone; Dick Twardzik, Rene Urtreger, piano; Jimmy Bond, bass; Peter Littman, Nils-Bertil Dahlander, drums.

Recorded 1955

Here we enter two contiguous realms: that of Chet Baker and that of the famously weird pianist Dick Twardzik. Both are cult realms, and cults are generally sprung from empathy toward weaknesses rather than admiration of strengths. But jazz is a music that depends on cults, because since the advent of rock and roll jazz has been a choice, an optional mode of being that very few are born into. You aspire to see yourself as a person who loves jazz, and thus you are led toward all sorts of false idols, as well as real ones. There's no point in worrying about the truth of cults; their true value always becomes evident in time, by the process of history.

I retain qualified admiration for Twardzik and Baker, even if neither, on his own, was top–one hundred material. (Baker checked out of being a sentient, developing musician—in other words, one who gave a shit—barely after having gotten started, and he continued on the path of least resistance for thirty-five more years. Twardzik didn't live past twenty-seven.) This is certainly not the album it could have been with greater preparation. But it represents an unusual confluence of talent.

Baker's technical talent was slender and his sound unrelievedly wan; he was the possessor of a cultivated, second-generation Lester Young disposition—that is to say, Young's affectless melancholy, minus his rhythmic genius. (There was honk and grit in Young, not just willowy sensitivity.) But Baker did have a sound—one as plainspoken as his singing voice, with minimum vibrato and strangely even dynamics.

In the mid- and late 1950s, there was a poetic and historical logic to sounding this way. The young musicians at this time were operating in the boom period after a war; they didn't have much practical experience of the strangulated economy of the war years. And the famous postwar what-does-it-all-mean attitude had jazz correlatives, too. Charlie Parker had established a benchmark of virtuosity that, it was assumed, couldn't be bettered. In 1955, he was dead. Even before he died, what was there left to do? Make music that was even faster, that stuffed more passing tones among the sixteenth notes? Should jazz musicians stop pretending and actually become sewing machines? Baker—and West Coast jazz in general and Miles Davis and Dave Brubeck's early music—were early signs of this aesthetic shell shock.

Twardzik came from Boston and had been a student of Margaret Chaloff, who taught many musicians in the area during the 1940s and 1950s, including Jaki Byard, Chick Corea, Keith Jarrett, Herbie Hancock, and the concert producer George Wein, then a jazz pianist. Twardzik didn't swing hard; some of Bud Powell's ornamental trills were natural to his right hand, but he was a sluggish accompanist, and his solos (which always come after Baker's in these songs) were tremendously odd.

They began without ceremony, with an in medias res feeling, and then he would let go, allowing himself to sink away temporarily from the rhythm; after a while, he would work his way back by imposing his own scales and chord patterns on the music. He left gaping rests, rendered his left hand largely silent, kept repositioning himself and his relationship to the rhythm, and propelled himself into harmonic tangles and clashes, using the entire extent of the keyboard. The solos drawled—sometimes drained of passion, sometimes catching a great idea like a short wave. He thought with a rare compositional rigor, even if the results were rather abstract. And, indeed, Twardzik's own compositions—there aren't many of them, but those interested should hear "Albuquerque Social Swim" and "A Crutch for the Crab," available on a Capitol reissue of his own trio—echoed the tonal world of his improvisations.

That strange drifting feeling, as if tonality is all relative and the established rhetoric of exits and entrances is for squares, meant only one thing in the 1950s: heroin. Twardzik was a hopeless addict, and he doesn't spark happy memories among those who knew him. But this band featured him prominently and let him be himself, even on tunes that weren't his own.

Which brings us to the next point of recommendation for this album: the tunes (at least for the three quarters of the album featuring the quartet with Baker, Twardzik, Bond, and Littman) are by Bob Zieff, a Boston composer. They're strange, with melodies built of odd intervals, and are suffused with major-to-minor flux. There is a consistency on this album; all the tunes are slow to mid-tempo, and after Baker's sad but focused trumpet improvisations you get Twardzik's harmonic daydreams.

Especially after the success of Bruce Weber's documentary film *Let's Get Lost* (1988), Baker wasn't the minority figure he used to be; his vocal albums especially are talismanic among moody young adults who aren't into jazz per se. Twardzik—like the New Orleans drummer James Black or the Philadelphia pianist Hasaan Ibn Ali—remains fascinating to the inner core of jazz collectors. Like those others, he was a troubled soul, and there isn't much of his work available. (He died of a heroin overdose while in Paris, two weeks after the last of these recordings.) To look at it coldly, the biographical details enhance—if not define—the value.

37. ERROLL GARNER:

Concert by the Sea

(COLUMBIA LEGACY 40589)

Erroll Garner, piano; Eddie Calhoun, bass; Denzil Best, drums.

Recorded 1955

What was it that Erroll Garner had that Earl Hines didn't have, that Art Tatum didn't have, that Stanley Cowell didn't have? Obviously piano virtuosity isn't enough—all of the above possessed it (and Cowell still does). What was it that sold *Concert by the Sea* by the hundred thousand and made him one of the most commonly cited names in jazz in the 1950s? Was it some complicated aspect of timing? Was it his savvy repertoire, classy but fad conscious? Was he somehow an ideal performer for the infant years of the LP, which was at that moment being marketed excitedly to a new kind of consumer?

All of the above and also possibly a reputation, built by benign racism, as a sort of idiot savant. The facts of Garner's musical illiteracy were widely spread; it says something about American society at the time that this was such a significant part of his biography. He beamed as he thundered, his piano bench given more height by a phone book, the music world's tiny, brilliant Negro. He worked sequences of classical music into his music without knowing their provenance, thus tickling the sophistication of those who did. With his ear's obvious acuity, he was the perfect example of a "natural" talent. He loved rhapsodizing (the solo introduction to his "Autumn Leaves" here is a schmaltz classic) and perhaps he discriminated between the "tasteful" vernacular art practiced in nightclubs at the time and the semiclassical dreck on plastic—Mantovani, the 101 Strings—that was spinning in suburban rec rooms across the country.

The previous paragraph is the critic's cerebral, mean-spirited rationalization. The practical truth is that he was a more generous performer: he offered you a grand tour of sonic possibility and didn't play games with you. There were no chips on his shoulder. He would not be suggestive or play it cool. (Garner demonstrated the semantic difference between the terms "cool" and "quiet." When he is quiet, he is still not cool.)

He simply owned changes in dynamics, the more dramatic the better. He and Ahmad Jamal were the masters of that domain, but Jamal depended on silences whereas Garner abhorred them. Garner had preternatural stamina for swing and handled desperately slow and galloping tempos beautifully.

Concert by the Sea, the most authoritative document of his effulgent, gregarious art, offered an audience-friendly variation on the Bud Powell concept. Where Powell played single-note hornlike lines with the right hand and telegraphed bare-bones harmony with left-hand chords, Garner was slicker. He played melodies in rich chords with the right hand, almost as if he were strumming a guitar, while keeping a four-four beat evenly with an unchanging hand. But quite often, and with relish, he spanked notes in the bass clef with a loud, heavy thumb, making them ring above the dense chording. This was straight-up orchestral; there was no aesthetic of negation in it. You didn't have to fill in any blanks.

That right thumb was Garner's equivalent of the bebop bass-drum "bomb," the between-beat accent designed to catch you off guard. His music wasn't estranged from bebop. It was part of jazz, no matter if it was bought by many people who wouldn't know Charlie Parker from a pool cue.

38. HERBIE NICHOLS:

The Art of Herbie Nichols

(BLUE NOTE B2-99176)

Herbie Nichols, piano; Al McKibbon, Teddy Kotick, bass; Art Blakey, Max Roach, drums.

Recorded 1955–1956

Herbie Nichols, who died of leukemia in 1963, is one of jazz's more famous obscurities. Or, at least, he was, until recently. During his life, hardly anyone knew of his music. Until the mid-1980s, he was best known by a chapter devoted to him in A. B. Spellman's 1966 book *Four Lives in the Bebop Business,* as well as for having written "Lady Sings the Blues," which became one of Billie Holiday's signature songs.

Finally, a small Nichols revival started, in stages. In 1983, a band co-led by Roswell Rudd, Steve Lacy, and Misha Mengelberg made *Regeneration,* an album split between Nichols and Thelonious Monk tunes. In 1989, the ICP Orchestra, from Holland, with Mengelberg as pianist, released a similar album. In 1987, Mosaic issued *The Complete Herbie Nichols on Blue Note.* Geri Allen started playing "Shuffle Montgomery" on gigs. By 1991, pianist Frank Kimbrough and bassist Ben Allison were not only playing his tunes but hard at work on transcribing all of them, and they set up a kind of interpretive repertory band, the Herbie Nichols Project, to play them. The trombonist Roswell Rudd, who knew Nichols and worked with him in the early sixties, had been working only sporadically; right around that time he started getting more calls, to play Nichols's tunes and to explain the mysteries of his composition.

Nichols's melodies were short, jaunty, intense, and instantly likable. But many of them were so orchestral, indwelling, and embedded in harmony that they weren't very well suited to arrangements that included horn players, nor were they obvious choices for other musicians to cover. Phrases had odd lengths, and those odd lengths would repeat an unusual number of times. "It wasn't a jam, with Herbie," Rudd said, in a 1992 interview with *Cadence* magazine. "It was, like, you really had to know theory, and you really had to be well-schooled and really had to have accuracy and precision and a lot of training to play his stuff. . . . This is music of great detail. That's why it sounds so simple. If you examine this music up close, you realize that everything is very carefully placed. If you miss by a sixteenth note, or an eighth note, or a half tone, of if you're just a little off, forget it, man."

Nichols was a shy man, not an entertainer, and had no gift for self-promotion. Also, by Rudd's account, he never played his music in front of a live audience. While making his own art—an art that Alfred Lion and Francis Wolff of Blue Note Records invested in against all odds—he made his living playing in New York Dixieland combos, on gigs where musicians were learning tunes and arrangements on the spot. Nichols wrote that he composed "The Gig" as a portrait of a "happy, modern jam session," but it sounds much more like he's making fun of a subpar Dixieland gig: the melody line starts, then stops suddenly, gets played with hesitation, then gets replayed at an odd moment—a reference to musicians who don't quite know where to begin or end a theme. It's witty and composed with awesome control; with its little extensions, its uneven form, its introduction and coda, it's a wonder that it's so easily graspable. Even here, Nichols was never particularly oblique.

This album is a collation of the four sessions Nichols recorded for Blue Note; if you develop further interest, get the three-disc box set *The Complete Blue Note Recordings,* finally issued by Blue Note in 1997 after the Mosaic set had gone out of print.

There's a good deal of interaction between Nichols and his drummers in this music, but it's written interaction; what sounds like a solo will last for only a bar or so before feeding back into a recapitulation of one of a tune's themes. Among Blue Note records of the 1950s, Nichols's music is highly unusual for the little amount of soloing it has in it.

In that respect, it's a far cry from Thelonious Monk, though Nichols is often thought of as a kind of more marginal Monk. Why? Biographically, there are similarities: they were born two years apart, and both grew up in the San Juan Hill area of Manhattan; both participated in some of the bebop-spawning late-night sessions in Monroe's Uptown House in Harlem in the late 1930s (though Nichols was reportedly cowed by the atmosphere of competition); both went through stretches of being misunderstood and little heard. And once in a while Nichols will play close-harmony chords in a kind of Monk-like rhythm, splatting them down brusquely, as Monk did, but hardly with Monk's force, his percussive energy. The structure of Monk's tunes tends to be much more forthright and even, and Monk played with much greater economy; Nichols fills up space, if only with returns to theme.

It's perhaps that they were both mysterious, oddball black musicians playing with a black vernacular—Tin Pan Alley, Ellington, hymns, boogie-woogie—that they knew quite well but felt free to change. It was not a popular thing to do and something that they both did with style.

39. LENNIE TRISTANO:

Lennie Tristano/The New Tristano

(ATLANTIC/RHINO 71595)

Lennie Tristano, piano; Lee Konitz, alto saxophone; Peter Ind, Gene Ramey, bass; Jeff Morton, Art Taylor, drums.

Recorded 1955–1962

The pianist and composer Lennie Tristano left a legacy that seems to go radically against the grain of jazz in the bebop era: for the most part, his surviving music sacrifices dynamics and the ecstatic spilling over of swinging rhythm sections; on many of his records, drummers tick like metronomes, avoiding the emphasis of the second and fourth beats. (We've already gotten into loathsome cliché number one, according to the Tristano supporters, but note that I said "many of his records.") Anyway, this rhythmic difference is one of the prime reasons why he has been a footnote in the standard histories of bebop.

He was a tangential figure, a lover of Bud Powell and Art Tatum who also imagined ways to insert Bach into jazz before John Lewis of the Modern Jazz Quartet did, who created his own pedagogical and performative school of jazz, and who pioneered multitrack recording in jazz (not that there have been many to continue the trail).

Much of the official evidence—a spate of albums dating from the late 1940s to the early 1960s, when he turned to private teaching until his death in 1978—suggests that he wrote himself out of jazz's mid-century rhythmic revolution. But he wrote himself out of and into many things; he was an early example of a stiffly opinionated jazz musician, the artist as ideologue, which we've seen much more often since.

Part of Tristano's irritability may have been that he nursed the jazz man's oldest complaint: that other musicians borrowed elements of his style but didn't credit him enough. He nurtured a rebel pose; beginning in the 1950s, teaching was his primary channel of income, and it afforded him enough remove from the jazz market to lob widely quoted criticism into the jazz mainstream. George Shearing is the most famous example of the pianists who absorbed Tristano's locked-hands piano technique, but in 1950 Tristano told *Downbeat*: "If you give watered-down bop to the public, they'd rather hear that than the real thing. Has George Shearing helped jazz by making his bop a filling inside a sandwich of familiar melody? Obviously not, because there are fewer places where jazz can be played today than there were when George and his quintet started out."

To go back to the issue of rhythm, Tristano didn't have a grudge against it. He loved layering different meters, and his own piano playing, with its hammering legato, shows that he internalized the patterns of Charlie Parker and Fats Navarro. Also, he performed concerts with some of the most outgoing, challenging drummers in jazz, including Roy Haynes and Max Roach; unfortunately, little of that music got on tape. Tristano wasn't a player for hire, and didn't enter lightly into record contracts. He monitored his output carefully, as some of his pupils, including Liz Gorrill, Lenny Popkin, Connie Crothers, Warne Marsh, and Sal Mosca have monitored theirs. (In the 1970s, Tristano started his own label, Jazz Records, which still exists.) But *Lennie Tristano,* from 1955, began a sporadic association with Nesuhi Ertegun and Atlantic Records, followed up six years later by *The New Tristano,* a solo-piano album. The two records have been combined on this single reissue disc. I find Tristano's solo music more draggy and inward, overdominated by walking bass lines, whereas in the small-group album *Lennie Tristano* he was forced to become a social being; you can see how he related his musical theories to the real world.

Ertegun helped jazz musicians to make strong statements, and the album begins like a shot: the extended single-hand lines in "Line Up" are like striking cobras—sinewy, strong, uncoiling across bar lines to create a time-warping feeling, ending a thought rhythmically and harmonically later than you expect it to end. (Tristano called this device "bypassed resolution.") And from the beginning the sound of the record is arresting: the piano is high up in the mix, with a bit of echo giving it a live snap. A piano-trio piece that fades out after Tristano ends a not particularly winding-it-all-up phrase, "Line Up" is an essay on momentum: you feel that it's one chunk in an ongoing discourse that could have lasted for half an hour.

It's followed by "Requiem," apparently based on an original blues that Tristano played at Charlie Parker's funeral. Parker himself was a Tristano enthusiast, and "Requiem" returns the affection: it is a slow, lovingly played blues, the sort of thing you don't associate Tristano with. Again, it fades out, and does so abruptly; it's like the final good-bye of someone who loves the leaving party so much that he doesn't want to hang around waving. In "Turkish Mambo," Tristano superimposed three tracks of himself playing in different rhythms—in seven, five, and three—and the result is a bracing ice-water bath of counterpoint.

After the metallic aggression of the first four studio tracks—where the original LP switched over to side two—the record changes into a warmly recorded live quartet session, one of Tristano's most relaxed and swinging recordings, with Art Taylor (no metronome he) on drums. All of these are standards, with only one up-tempo number ("All the Things You Are"); none use his signature piano-and-saxophone arrangement on the themes. Lee Konitz, Tristano's frequent foil, has a transparent, willowy alto-saxophone sound; it's the opposite of Tristano's hard touch. What an album of contrasts—what aggression, what melancholy, what involvement and disinvolvement with the standard values of jazz performance. It's no wonder that Tristano has been a figure of fascination for some of the most important avant-gardists in jazz, including Anthony Braxton, Matthew Shipp, and Borah Bergman; on the other hand, his reach seems too wide to co-opt in one move.

40. ELLA FITZGERALD:

The Cole Porter Songbook

(VERVE 537257-2, 2 CDS)

Ella Fitzgerald, vocals; orchestra arranged and conducted by Buddy Bregman.

Recorded 1956

Another name deserves space in the credits above: Norman Granz. If it weren't for Granz and his obsessive, spare-no-expenses vision for the artists he produced and in some cases managed—including Fitzgerald, Oscar Peterson, and at certain points Basie, Ellington, and Tatum—these musicians might well not be part of mainstream American culture. These were people who, to the general public, came to transcend the particular social matrices of their race; in America, at the middle of the twentieth century, that was a considerable achievement.

After she had been in show business for more than twenty years, with a solid jazz fan base, Fitzgerald was taken by Granz out of the unimaginative situation that was her Decca contract in the mid-1950s and rerouted from the jazz circuit she seemed destined to play for the rest of her life. Having included her in his touring Jazz at the Philharmonic concerts during the 1940s—which put the after-hours jam-session ethic in concert halls and raised the stock of everyone who appeared in them—Granz had a vision that Fitzgerald would be singing the best of American song, presented as an artist who would fit perfectly between popular and high art.

So he made a series of albums with different orchestras and arrangers, the best in the business; as a key to the seriousness of the endeavor, Fitzgerald sang the opening verses of songs that jazz performers tended to leave out. Granz's album packages used the best designers, the best photographers, the best cardboard. They cost a dollar more than other albums, and they were seen as an affordable symbol of sophistication; they sold extraordinarily well.

It didn't necessarily take rare vision to imagine Fitzgerald as a mainstream singer. Lena Horne said it pretty well, with an unintentional hint of criticism, when she eulogized her at a Carnegie Hall concert shortly after Fitzgerald's death in 1996: the "First Lady of Song," she said, was like a "golden typewriter," by which she meant that Fitzgerald presented a song exactly as the composer intended it. But a typewriter isn't a bad metaphor for Fitzgerald, who made scads of professional, impeccable recordings from this point on that shivered with chilly uniformity.

Fitzgerald could give any material a good reading and never came across as remote, depressive, maudlin, or a minority taste. One mustn't underestimate how significant this is and the control over one's talent it takes to get to this point.

Cole Porter was the perfect songwriter with which to start the series, a composer who in 1956 already had fluid, all-access status in American society. Through the agency of sophisticated performers such as Coleman Hawkins, Don Byas, Billie Holiday, and Charlie Parker—all of whom performed Porter's songs before Fitzgerald made her album—jazz musicians who couldn't care less about the hyperurbane witticisms in his songs grabbed hold of them for their melodies. (America's various races shared a good amount of musical culture at that point, and it wasn't necessarily a case of people from one race needing to assume the attitudes of another; it was just a case of various performers from different backgrounds all trying to reach an aesthetic summit.) But Fitzgerald's album spread their appeal further and wider, making those who weren't musical-theater buffs understand, in many cases for the first time, that Cole Porter was a man with a formidable body of work.

Her better artistic successes in this five-year series lay elsewhere, most recognizably in *Ella Sings Gershwin*. But the Porter album was the icebreaker, proving that a jazz singer could put over musical-theater material as well and as classily as anyone.

Buddy Bregman's arrangements are sweet and amiable, running the gamut from maudlin mood pieces with violins ("Why Can't You Behave") to a charming, light Basie rhythm ("Ridin' High"); they have a predictability. The music isn't very swinging, the instrumental breaks are few and far between, and Fitzgerald's interpretations tend toward the conservative, without the genius scatting among wide intervals that made her reputation; there is just enough jazz here to remind you that she is a jazz singer.

But the album has a self-possession about it, and Fitzgerald's small voice has the necessary caution to sing the wit in the songs. (They're better when they're not belted.) Her delivery floats over nuances; when she sings in "You're the Top" about the best of the best—symphonies by Strauss, Shakespeare, an O'Neill drama—you might suspect that those names didn't really terrify her. It doesn't matter. The songs marched ahead optimistically, keeping your serotonin levels healthy; her coiled vibrato on well-selected vowels and the hoarse, scraping sound in Fitzgerald's lowest and highest notes, those just outside the range of her girlish voice, gave the album a signature.

It's consistent work, crafted for endurance. Beyond rhythmic prowess and perfect intonation, Fitzgerald's extramusical ace in the hole was something that one finds in only half of Porter's work: innocence. She left the sense of experience to other, darker-voiced singers, and she was able to make an album whose popularity dwarfed similar attempts at pop-crossover records by Dinah Washington and Sarah Vaughan.

41. MODERN JAZZ QUARTET:

Fontessa

(ATLANTIC JAZZ 1231-2)

John Lewis, piano; Milt Jackson, vibraharp; Percy Heath, bass; Connie Kay, drums.

Recorded 1956

The deaths of John Lewis and Milt Jackson—the pianist and vibra-phonist of the Modern Jazz Quartet—in less than a year's span during 2000 and 2001, erased two superior talents, to be obvious about it. But they also may have ignited an important historical revision. Which is this: talents of the Lewis and Jackson kind shouldn't be appreciated by means of a single epithet. Lewis was not a repressed, fussy pianist, and "understated" (the standout honorific of his *New York Times* obituary) isn't wrong but encompasses only about an eighth of him. Jackson, on the other hand, was not merely an instinctive blues player; his role wasn't to bring soul food to a fancy-dress dinner.

What you learn after spending enough time in jazz is that it's hope-less drawing straight divisions between the urbane/academic and the country/intuitive. All great American characters draw sustenance from both sides. What disabled the logic of even American intellectuals—presuming it was they who made the Modern Jazz Quartet popular in this country in the 1960s and 1970s—was, simply, the sight of four black men in tuxedos, playing with precision and without amplifica-tion. It led to easy and wrong assumptions and encouraged the past few generations of jazz hipsters to deposit them among soft or café-society bands.

The MJQ, counter to popular assumption, swung as deeply and originally as anyone named Horsecollar or Fats. I think that is what Stanley Crouch was getting at by his memorable suggestion, at Lewis's memorial service, that all four of them were actually a little bit "coun-try."

The MJQ was a jewel of dynamics and projection; like the old coun-try bands who had to play around a single radio microphone, the band learned to mix itself into a four-way equal ideal. Its bassist, Percy Heath, came from Philadelphia, which in the 1940s was the absolute nexus of urbane and country, a second-tier eastern-seaboard town filled with music theory–obsessed jazz hipsters. And in Connie Kay—who prior to his joining the MJQ in 1955 had played with Lester Young on a lot of rock-and-roll sessions for Atlantic Records but wasn't a well-known jazz drummer—it found its perfect fourth member.

Fontessa is the second album the MJQ made with Kay (the first being *Concorde*, five months earlier); it's where everything came together, and it's the first mixture of bebop and extended Lewis compositions that was to characterize much of the band's later work. The title track uses different kinds of jazz—a loose-swinging blues, an airy, shimmering ballad, a largely free, coloristic section anchored by cymbal improvisations—to stand for different members of the commedia dell'arte. Lewis, as long as we're busting his stereotypes, wasn't pedantic: he refers in his beautifully simple notes included with the original album simply to "older jazz," "less older jazz," and "still later jazz." He was being imaginative, not programmatic.

It was always surprising to hear Lewis talk about the first-wave Count Basie band of the 1930s and 1940s as an inspiration for the MJQ, for there was a certain outgoing fire in the Basie band, as opposed to a mutedness in the MJQ. But it's an example of how smart a listener Lewis was. When he heard Basie, he paid attention to economy and individuation between roles—which, of course, were the two elements that made that group so special.

42. ART TATUM:

The Tatum Group Masterpieces, Volume 8

(PABLO/FANTASY 2405-431-2)

Art Tatum, piano; Ben Webster, tenor saxophone; Red Callender, bass; Bill Douglass, drums.

Recorded 1956

Tatum, forty-six and in the last year of his life, and Webster, forty-seven with nearly two decades to go, met each other on their own terms. They were both grand old men, yesterday's heroes, but their careers had proceeded differently. Tatum continued along the line of virtuosity, since there was perhaps nowhere else for him to go. A blind man who felt most comfortable playing alone, virtuosity was Tatum's signature, the paint that cornered him, and he had been its standard-bearer since the late days of stride piano and into the bebop era. (Bud Powell adored him; Tatum's speed and prowess through difficult negotiations of harmony was one of the forerunning qualities of the whole movement.) Webster, once a self-possessed but quicksilver hotshot tenor player in the Ellington band, had winnowed down his playing to melody and tone, as simple as that.

Their meeting, an eleventh-hour small-band session produced by Norman Granz, proved as piquant as the later Ellington/Roach/Mingus *Money Jungle* session (see below) and the Sonny Rollins/Coleman Hawkins album *Sonny Meets Hawk*—effective records despite themselves, in that they weren't exactly meetings of like minds. But the fact is that Tatum and Webster came together harmoniously on songs that had strong melodies, not just on jamming workhorses.

There are no blues on this album; instead, it's the likes of "Gone with the Wind," "Night and Day," and "Have You Met Miss Jones?" (These are songs of brilliant structure, and if you want to understand how they work—and what chances they take—look at Alec Wilder's *American Popular Song,* one of the jewels of all writing about American music.) It's hard to find readings of these songs that are more persuasive, with Tatum shining lights on the harmonic movement from all angles as he dive-bombs around with long arpeggios, with Webster playing the lines in his dulcet huffing. This is boudoir music, but these are also careful demonstrations of some of this country's greatest cultural products.

It's hard to improve on the album's liner essay for a description of what happens. Its author, Benny Green (not the Benny Green who came to visibility in Betty Carter's group of the 1980s but the English jazz critic), transmits the significance of what's going on here, without recourse to verbal rondo or discographical data. "When Ben went into the studio to make music with Tatum," Green wrote, "he had in his possession the one musical quality which no amount of other people's brilliance can ever dilute: he had his tone, and I have always believed that it was because of his tone—and of course his professional wisdom in realizing it—that Ben made what was probably the most successful attempt of all time to match his personality against Tatum's."

The tempo seldom rises above a slow drag, except on "Night and Day," and Tatum's keyboard pyrotechnics are held back to their most decorous. I confess that this is fine by me. For anyone but pianists, Tatum can be a challenge to listen to. His solo recordings—and there are many great ones, from the astonishing early 1940s live recordings captured in amateur fidelity on *God Is in the House* (High Note), to the early 1950s salon recordings captured on *20th Century Piano Genius* (Verve), and the final reckoning preserved by Granz for *The Complete Pablo Solo Masterpieces* (Pablo/Fantasy)—capture the talent. But these recordings, like what survives of Lenny Bruce's routines or Frank Zappa's all-instrumental *Shut Up 'n Play Yer Guitar* series, can tire you quickly.

It is a good thing to know about Tatum, for he elevated piano technique through swing and tonal harmony to a place where it can scarcely be bettered. But even when he wasn't on his own, he might as well have been. The common stock of jazz musicians—which he hovered above, with few points of real contact—consisted of social animals, invested in a collective enterprise, and that dependence on others isn't a handicap. Tatum's talent for solo playing turned that rule on its head, but Tatum's talent applied only to Tatum. Despite his grounding in the stride style of James P. Johnson and Willie "The Lion" Smith, he will remain a kind of freak, an outsider.

43. MILES DAVIS:

Miles Ahead

(COLUMBIA LEGACY 65121)

Miles Davis, flügelhorn; Gil Evans, arranger, conductor; Ernie Royal, Bernie Glow, Louis Mucci, Taft Jordan, John Carisi, trumpet; Frank Rehak, Jimmy Cleveland, Joe Bennett, trombone; Tom Mitchell, bass trombone; Willie Ruff, Tony Miranda, Jim Buffington, French horn; Bill Barber, tuba; Lee Konitz, alto saxophone; Danny Bank, bass clarinet; Romeo Penque, Sid Cooper, Edwin Caine, flute, clarinet; Paul Chambers, bass; Arthur Taylor, drums.

Recorded 1957

The decline of the big band was belabored and cartoonish; it kept coming back long after it seemed to have drawn its last breath. World War II was what really did it in, since gas and rubber shortages prevented large groups from going on the road. But once the big band no longer played dance music, it morphed into some strange, decadent forms—Stan Kenton's small municipalities with five trombones, for instance, or intellectual ensembles like Boyd Raeburn's that magnified bebop's hustled rhythms and tricky harmonies.

One tradition that survived in altered form was that of the mood arranger, who went from scoring music for big bands to orchestrating tone poems for individual jazz artists. That role was honed to perfection by Gil Evans in his collaborations with Miles Davis between 1957 and 1968—deluxe, semiclassical, and exotic, hydroponic creatures of the recording studio.

Gil Evans got his start in the early 1930s arranging for a band in Stockton, California, that later made theme and incidental music for Bob Hope's radio show. He could have gone the way of Henry Mancini, a dance-band jazz pianist who realized that there would always be more money in Hollywood. But instead he walked the tightrope between commercial and art music. His keenest influence was another big-band leader, Claude Thornhill, who hired him to do extra arrangements. The music from that period was deliberately slow, moving like someone trying not to sweat on a boiling day. It had no vibrato and a lot of French horn, which was combined with clarinets or tubas in piquant, hothouse-flower voicings.

Davis, on the other hand, had been through small-group bebop in the forties and seemed to have found that music too intense and inward; as he wrote in his autobiography, he was struggling to find a way to make bop sound sweet. When he convened a nonet with Evans and Gerry Mulligan's help in 1948 and recorded the music that would later be released as *Birth of the Cool,* he was blending bebop with a reduced vision of Claude Thornhill's instrumentation. This new sound prefigured white, California cool jazz, but so had other things—Billy Strayhorn's arrangements for Duke Ellington through the forties, and Lester Young's diaphanous tenor-saxophone playing with Count Basie even earlier. Davis always insisted that cool jazz was as much (if not more) black as white music; likewise, he never had any problem with the notion that jazz was a form of pop.

The duality of high art and mass sensibility is at the heart of Miles

Davis and Gil Evans's work. *Miles Ahead*—to my mind, the most successful of those collaborations (the others are *Porgy and Bess* and *Sketches of Spain*)—is music of fantasy, of dreaming. The drums, usually so central to jazz, are generally rendered secondary by the intricately accented horn charts within the nineteen-piece ensemble sound. The orchestra gathers around the soloist, rather than the soloist trying to ride the waves of the orchestra, and every move is keyed to Davis's sighing sensibility. But the most impressive moments are Davis's tremulous theme readings, laid down as mere suggestions, like soft, wet clay.

What a weird assortment of music: notated jazz compositions by Johnny Carisi and Evans, a transcribed version of Ahmad Jamal's "New Rhumba," a Kurt Weill song, a Dave Brubeck song. But Evans as arranger (and let's not forget the producer Teo Macero for how beautiful this record *sounded*) made a coherence of them.

Evans's arrangements on *Miles Ahead* were plotted like wily preparations for a siege. In the first twelve measures of "The Meaning of the Blues," the contents of a rising counterpoint behind Davis's melody keep mutating: French horn and trumpet give way to oboe, which slides back into trumpets, and the progression into the fourth measure, with nothing but the treble of muted trumpets in unison, feels like an airplane taking off. (Its power as an organic whole is no accident: *Miles Ahead* was recorded in bits and pieces, and "The Meaning of the Blues" was the only full, unspliced ensemble performance on the album.) So much happens on these tracks, and Davis's trumpet voice sails over the tumult, unaffected, as cool as can be. It was the beginning of his sound as a cultural icon.

These were popular albums—*Sketches of Spain* especially—but they didn't transform jazz. (Strange as they were, how could they? It's more impressive that the records were made at all.) Few jazz composers followed Evans's lead, though fragments of his sound wash up here and there. His timbral combinations and unlikely harmonies surface in the work of Maria Schneider, a composer and bandleader who was Evans's assistant for three years before his death in 1988. But since it's mainly jazz educators and historians who grasp the significance of Evans, you hear his music most often being played by repertory bands.

44. BILLIE HOLIDAY:

Songs for Distingué Lovers

(VERVE 314-539-056-2)

Billie Holiday, vocals; Harry "Sweets" Edison, trumpet; Ben Webster, tenor saxophone; Jimmie Rowles, piano; Barney Kessel, guitar; Red Mitchell, bass; Larry Bunker, Alvin Stoller, drums.

Recorded 1957

The biography, which has become attached like a barnacle to the art, is unbearably sad: suffering, even more than dope and domineering, vicious men, was Holiday's mother addiction. Abbey Lincoln, one of the most self-conscious beneficiaries of Holiday's singing style, was to reinvent herself in the early 1960s as a reaction, in part, to the dead woman whom she understood to be a masochist.

There has long been the tendency, among those who are in a position to make money from performers, to push them out in public long past their sell-by date—or, to put it another way, to refuse to insist that such performers stop performing. But most jazz musicians don't have pensions. And the world of jazz performance is suffused with perverse nostalgia; a musician's pain can cause an audience member's pleasure.

One could guess that this has something to do with a perception of authenticity or the vestiges of racist cruelty perpetrated by condescending whites (does the idea of the "beautiful loser" exist at all in black culture?), but it really just comes down to money and force of habit. Jazz can accommodate age, and any musician who has to provide for herself and her dependents will push it as far as possible, will grind on until the end. Jazz musicians are musicians around the clock; they don't go home and leave their profession behind. Their entire lives are lived in those nightclubs and small theaters, with those bands and managers.

None of this rationalization prepares you for a glimpse of public frailty. Some years ago, I went to hear a saxophonist who was, when I was in grade school, of some importance. He had been sick and off the scene for quite a while; I didn't know how sick. His return was staged at a Manhattan music school, with semipro accompanists; the room was full of believers, a small but deep audience. From the first note, I knew there would be trouble. He had no breath, and he was playing a ballad. During a painfully slow solo, his top set of dentures shot out, coming down over the top of the mouthpiece, and for a gruesome moment they looked like costume-vampire teeth. My body got up and left the room before my mind could even process it. I couldn't be complicit in his demeaning of himself anymore.

To me, the cult of eleventh-hour Holiday makes sense only through the more ghoulish instincts of the jazz audience. Don't misunderstand: there is nothing ethically wrong in liking *Lady in Satin,* her final studio work. She made it; she released it; she was an artist, and she controlled her image. But if it's a religious experience, it's a bomb-blasted cathedral. It's depressing.

Songs for Distingué Lovers, recorded only thirteen months earlier, is a much more palatable experience. There is still resilience in Holiday's voice, even if the higher register is gone and if, when she drops down low, it sounds like a muffler scraping against the road. No matter: this is the newest stage of a pop hero. (Real pop heroes make bad health seem attractive.) Norman Granz, the album's producer, gave her an appropriate context: a sextet with Harry "Sweets" Edison, who was already a prince of understatement and concise melodic thinking, and Ben Webster, who had played with her as early as 1937 and had refined his own playing to heavy breath and melody.

So there was no pretension of the kind on the strings-drenched *Lady in Satin.* What Holiday could do well at the end (the same could be said for Edison, who toughed it out until 2000) was swing, weakly but authoritatively, and this session is predicated on the notion that swing is both the essence of life and no big deal. These aren't climactic performances; they're just twelve durable songs, about half of them staples of her repertoire. There is nostalgia here; the album includes "I Wished on the Moon," which Holiday recorded with Webster at the 1937 session, and Webster gets to take the solo that he couldn't twenty years earlier, when Roy Eldridge had surged to the lead position.

If Holiday's art, by 1957, was reduced to affectations of phrasing (the upticks of pitch that came at odd moments, the overused vibrato that sounded more than ever like a quiet trumpet's) and the remarkable swing that was encoded within her, it doesn't damage the record. *Songs for Distingué Lovers* succeeds as a mood record and creates the basis for Holiday as a wrecked but contented culture hero.

45. MACHITO:

Kenya

(ROULETTE/EMI 7243-5-22668-2-1)

Frank "Machito" Grillo, vocals, shakers; Julian "Cannonball" Adderley, alto saxophone; Joe Newman, trumpet; Mario Bauza, musical director; Eddie Bert, Bart Varsalona, Santo Russo, trombone; Paul Cohen, Doc Cheatham, Paquito Davilla, Joe Livramento, Francis Williams, trumpet; Ray Santos, Jr., Jose Madera, tenor saxophone; Leslie Johnakins, baritone saxophone; Rene Hernandez, piano; Roberto Rodriguez, bass; Jose Mangual, bongos; Uba Nieto, timbales; Carlos "Patato" Valdez, conga.

Recorded 1957

Afro-Cuban jazz is only one part of the music originating in Cuba, with its rhythmic roots in West African drumming, that has influenced all of jazz. *Kenya* is a perfect and textbook example of Afro-Cuban jazz. But it seems a slight not to open up this book to further reaches of Cuban and Puerto Rican music—including the country *son* of Sabu's *Palo Congo,* the early salsa of Willie Colon's *Lo Mato,* Tito Puente's Yoruban-influenced *Top Percussion* and *Cuban Carnival,* the elegant big-band jazz of Chico O'Farrill's *Cuban Blues,* and the recently released field recordings of Lydia Cabrera on Smithsonian/Folkways, *Havana c. 1957* and *Matanzas c. 1957,* which capture elders of the Yoruban religion singing and playing in a style that comes directly from Africa. Get them all; the only reason they're not in here is that they're too hard to find, distinguished by single tracks rather than by an album's worth of them, or a few steps too far away from jazz.

Recorded seventeen years into Machito's career and at the height of the mambo craze in New York, *Kenya* is a slick, roaring record, informed by Basie's "New Testament" 1950s band as much as by the young Latin dancers at the Palladium; the Machito band was specially enlarged by jazz soloists including Cannonball Adderley, Joe Newman, and Doc Cheatham.

The record merits space here for a few reasons. One is the high quality of back-to-back improvisations in different idioms; on the fast rumba "Wild Jungle," Cheatham and the Machito-band trumpeter Joe Livramento alternate solos, and some lovely cognitive dissonance takes place in the shift between the jazz soloists and their Cuban background. Cuban swing, to put it in basic terms, is squarer, sharper; the swing of American jazz undulates. So the honey-dripping solos of Adderley and Newman over the *bata* rhythm in "Congo Mulence" attains cultural fusion.

Another reason this album is special is its evenhanded featuring of the Machito band's best arrangers. Mario Bauza, who arranges a few pieces here with Rene Hernandez, is rightly considered the pioneering architect of the band's sound; Machito himself was the charismatic, handsome leader. But on nine of the twelve tracks here, the arranger is A. K. Salim, a little-known figure (he made some recordings in the late fifties and early sixties for Savoy and Prestige before dropping off the map), and they're masterpieces, full of composure even as they grow towering structures off of telescoping brass chords. (He also had the benefit of Newman and Adderley on his tracks, whereas Bauza did not.)

Kenya, dedicated to the independence movement in what would soon be a brand-new African republic, was a special project during a time when the music of Machito's band threatened to become generic. The made-to-order mambo music of the late fifties by the best Latin bands is by and large wonderful but a bit watered-down; its immediate purpose, which is to reach the most dancers possible, threatened its long-term relevance. *Kenya,* however, is the real thing and one of the most widely studied documents of Afro-Cuban jazz; the Lincoln Center Jazz Orchestra has worked "Congo Mulence" into its repertory, and tracks such as "Conversation" and "Tururato" are exemplary pieces of jazz-Latin fusion.

A note of warning: there are some postproduction edits here, presumably made by Ralph Seijo, the album's original producer, that are embarrassingly rough as the band empties out of an ensemble passage and into a conga solo; also, in the CD version, there are some over-modulated passages that crest into fuzz in the speakers.

One further note for thrill seekers: *Kenya* may be more canonical, but you have to hear Machito's late forties–early fifties live recordings, particularly *Carambola*, recorded live at New York's Birdland in 1951. This band—with completely different personnel (though Bauza is there) and playing a tighter, more clipped style in earlier days—may be the tightest one I have ever heard. It constantly flicks between Cuban and American idioms, as in the ballad "Esto Es Felicidad," when the singer Graciela slips in a verse of "I Love You for Sentimental Reasons," and as in the lovely solos by Zoot Sims and Brew Moore adorning different versions of "Tanga," the great Afro-Cuban jazz anthem. It's a document, too: these recordings were made for Symphony Sid's radio show on WMCA, and his hucksterish, jiving interchanges with Machito are amazing. But for muffled sound quality and an unfortunate live mix—it's hard to hear Rene Hernandez's piano throughout—*Carambola* (released by the Spanish label Tumbao) would easily qualify as one of the hundred records to own, from all music of all time.

46. THELONIOUS MONK:

Thelonious Monk with John Coltrane

(RIVERSIDE/FANTASY 039-2)

Thelonious Monk, piano; John Coltrane, Coleman Hawkins, tenor saxophone; Ray Copeland, trumpet; Gigi Gryce, alto saxophone; Wilbur Ware, bass; Shadow Wilson, Art Blakey, drums.

Recorded 1957

In 1957, John Coltrane joined Thelonious Monk's band for a nearly six-month gig at the Five Spot club in New York. It was the point at which Coltrane turned around—from a talented, if muddled, improviser with bad personal habits to the focused, directed, well-formed musician that he was until his death ten years later.

The Five Spot gig—like Ornette Coleman's long stay at the same club in 1959—became a marker in jazz history not only for the music that was made but for the range of people who came to hear it. At the Five Spot there was a good representation of New York's high-powered intellectual community—writers, musicians, dancers, artists. As the pianist Ethan Iverson has said, that gig served the same function among intellectuals in New York that Mark Morris dance performances do now. (Iverson wasn't there, but as a jazz pianist in New York he lives with the myth of the Five Spot gig. And as the music director of the Mark Morris company, he knows what it is like to encounter an intellectually hungry audience in an artist's hometown.) There was palpable excitement coming from the stage, and it indicated what level jazz had climbed to as an art form. People looked to this gig to keep current about jazz and also to run into one another.

The one studio document of the band from the time inevitably falls short of its performance myth. There are only three tracks of the quartet as such; two more are a septet with three saxophones and trumpet; and one is a piano solo. But it is a strong, delightful record. Those three tracks are evidence of a strong, practical jazz quartet, captured in documentary style—not at the club, but the nearest approximation. It's a glimpse at the apex of Coltrane's early period.

Before this album, during the first of Coltrane's two tenures with Miles Davis's 1950s quintet, Coltrane could never quite organize his strengths enough to come to a good resting place. He had trouble ending solos. Here he is still noticeably long-winded; compare his breathlessly extended phrases to the concision of his work on Davis's *Kind of Blue* two years later. But he is quite incredible; the curious, flurrying phrases and rhythms are original, not the garbled versions of Dexter Gordon and Coleman Hawkins that his earlier work suggested.

Working with Monk did several things for Coltrane. It presented him with a difficult body of work, with complex melodies and unusual chord changes; it made him think in different directions. It encouraged his rhythmic growth, because if musicians played the rhythms a shade wrong with Monk, they sounded terrible. Monk insisted that improvisers in his band keep returning to the melodies; it forced Coltrane to recognize the wealth in the melody that was before him, which served him well as a ballad player later on. And, to serve Coltrane's ends,

Monk had a canny sense about when he should accompany with some punched chords (thus sharpening Coltrane's rhythm) and when to lay out entirely and let the saxophonist's towering structures lean against bass and drums alone. (In "Nutty," Monk comps for the first half chorus of Coltrane's solo and then lets go; there is a great difference in Coltrane's playing—as if he is first dutifully going by the rules, coloring in around Monk's hard, rhythmically organizing accents, then later set free to create a mural by running chords up and down.)

Monk's work on the record is a look ahead to how he would sound in the 1960s, when Charlie Rouse would be his saxophone partner. He functions as a band pianist, a role that the Genius of Modern Music is less famous for. Nevertheless, at that craft he was one of the best.

47. ART PEPPER:

Art Pepper Meets the Rhythm Section

(CONTEMPORARY/FANTASY OJCCD-338-2)

Art Pepper, alto saxophone; Red Garland, piano; Paul Chambers, bass; Philly Joe Jones, drums.

Recorded 1957

On the cover, Pepper's got on a killing dot-dash–pattern wool jacket and a windowpane pink shirt open to the third button; he's leaning against a tree, his alto saxophone's neck resting against his shoulder. It's cool: pastoral composure with a Dean Martin haircut, Los Angeles, 1957.

But the details of the session that produced *Art Pepper Meets the Rhythm Section* resemble those of a Hubert Selby nightmare. In his memoir, *Straight Life,* Pepper wrote that he hadn't touched his saxophone in the previous six months. How does this happen to a jazz musician who is, at the time, actually popular? A Stan Kenton sideman in the early fifties, he'd started to make his own records in 1952 and became one of the famous faces of West Coast jazz. But by the mid-fifties he was also famous for being an addict; he had even given a soul-baring but optimistic interview to *Downbeat* in late 1956 about how he was on the way to cleaning up. He wasn't, really. By his own account, around that time he spent most of his days nodding out, blood running down his arms.

In a sort of scared-straight A&R move, his wife, Diane, urged Lester Koenig of Contemporary Records to book Pepper for a recording date with Miles Davis's rhythm section—the backbone of the most popular small jazz group in the country. Part of Diane's strategy was not to tell Pepper about the session until the day it was happening. Pepper wrote that when he took his horn out of its case, the instrument was so disused that the cork had stuck to the mouthpiece, and when he adjusted the mouthpiece the cork ripped off. There was no time to get a new one; he had to play on a faulty instrument, and he entered the studio never having met Red Garland, Paul Chambers, and Philly Joe Jones, never having thought about what they might play together.

Pepper is a self-serving narrator; the point of the story is that only a genius can make a good record in such circumstances. But even if you ignore the details about the layoff, the cork, and the heroin daze, it's amazing that such a remarkably forthright record got made with such little preparation.

If you're interested in the great unmasterpiece, workmanlike toss-offs of jazz—if you feel like you have to enter a soundproof chamber before you can properly deal with carefully considered concept records like *Kind of Blue* or *A Love Supreme* or *Take Five*—this is a good place to start.

Informality worked for Pepper. His saxophone sound combined opposites: a light sound and floating rhythm (Pepper was a Lester Young fan from early on and came under the spell of Coltrane only a few years after this recording) with a jigger of grit and honk added.

The rhythm section is tough but delicate, full of imaginative ways to break up a tune (never underrate Philly Joe Jones), and against their hard East Coast swing he produces a wonderful contrast. "Waltz Me Blues" is an almost abstract melody; credited to Pepper and Chambers, there's a good chance that the line wasn't worked out much at all before the tape rolled. Pepper's improvising is clean and lovely, especially in his contrapuntal solo over Red Garland's parallel-hands octaves.

The record is interesting for repertoire, too: it includes "Jazz Me Blues," a song from 1921 recorded by Bix Beiderbecke, which at the time was pretty much exclusively the property of Bobby Hackett and other Dixieland nostalgists, unhip by modern jazz standards. And there's evidence that Dizzy Gillespie was on his mind, with both "Tin Tin Deo," a staple of Gillespie's Latin jazz bands, as well as Gillespie's own "Birks' Works."

It is an honest record; if you believe the story of its making, you'd have to conclude that Pepper, unprepared and unarmored, was forced to pull the music out of himself, since tepid run-throughs and stock licks weren't going to work in such exalted company.

48. SONNY ROLLINS:

Way Out West

(RIVERSIDE/FANTASY 357)

Sonny Rollins, tenor saxophone; Ray Brown, bass; Shelly Manne, drums.

Recorded 1957

By the late 1950s, there was a debate about who was the better tenor player, Sonny Rollins or John Coltrane. That there were only two "top tenors" wasn't a sign of how few tenor saxophonists there were; it was a sign of how incredibly well Rollins and Coltrane played and thought. They had power, promise, conception, daring, youth.

Certainly in 1957, and perhaps even in 1959, Coltrane seemed the more constrained of the two; his manner of playing games with harmony in his improvisations was seen by some as a potential death ride. Martin Williams, in the great and short-lived publication *The Jazz Review,* likened him to a rat in a maze. Such a pronouncement would never have been made about Sonny Rollins, who had a playful, linear style, much more in the storytelling manner of a Coleman Hawkins than someone who was trying to give you great gobs of chordal material in a moving piece of music. He had a big, marvelous tone and drive, and, as gruff and modern as he could sound, at the bottom of all his experiments was a traditional eighth-note swing, in which notes are accented loud/soft/loud/soft. He had a logic, an on-the-fly form in his improvisations, which Coltrane didn't come close to until his solos on Miles Davis's *Kind of Blue* in 1959. And Rollins's sound—the sheer physical nature of it, its size and flexibility—was new; it didn't provide a clue to what kind of jazz he felt closest to but established him as an individual. "Sound itself supersedes ideas in general," he has said.

He also made some of the most significant early saxophone trio albums—a daring concept, since jazz was still very tied to the notion of a piano lending guidance and support to the music's chord-by-chord motion. *Way Out West* was the first saxophone-trio album, with its amusing cover image of Rollins as a grinning cowboy in a desert scene. It was a visual pun: Rollins had been playing in California on his first extended trip from New York with the Clifford Brown–Max Roach group, so he was literally way out west. But in the album's heady feeling of Rollins out front without a chordal instrument, there's also a kind of gold-rush aspect, a pioneering, pickax-swinging feeling of discovery.

Rollins was funny: that was the most striking extramusical attribute that separated him from Coltrane. In the ballad "Solitude," included here, he plays with a japing quality; he stays hovering above the sadness of the tune. And in "I'm an Old Cowhand," he drags behind the beat, moving like a wary, lumbering cowboy—like John Wayne, in fact, who has also been an influence on Wayne Shorter.

"Come, Gone" is an offhanded sketchbook piece, a piece for blowing across changes until an improvised density is reached. He uses everything at his disposal: a Coleman Hawkins chordal approach, a raunchy, gutbucket-blues sound, repeating phrases like a Jazz at the Philharmonic soloist, silences and smeared phrases, some Parker rhythms. It's a grab bag and an endurance test, the kind of piece that Rollins excels in, then and now.

49. COUNT BASIE:

The Complete Atomic Basie

(CAPITOL 7243-8-28635-2-6)

Count Basie, piano; Wendell Culley, Snooky Young, Thad Jones, Joe New-
man, trumpet; Henry Coker, Al Grey, Benny Powell, trombone; Marshall
Royal, Frank Wess, Eddie "Lockjaw" Davis, Frank Foster, Charles Fowlkes,
reeds; Freddie Green, guitar; Eddie Jones, bass; Sonny Payne, drums; Joe
Williams, vocals; Neal Hefti, Jimmy Mundy, arrangements.

Recorded 1957–1958

The Count Basie "New Testament" bands—those that recorded after 1952, when he reconvened a big band after the collapse of the first great one (a brief small-group period came between)—had the best of both worlds. They were rhythm-section bands, in which you could hear the locomotive science of piano, guitar, bass, and drums powering the unit; the columns of brass sound kept giving way to the powerful core rhythm. But these bands also employed skilled, full-time arrangers to fashion slick, memorable humor and variation out of the relatively simple chord progressions that made up their repertoire.

Where Ellington enlarged his sensibility until he became all things to all people, Basie tended to localize, relying on a good deal more mother wit as a person, as a bandleader, as a musician. Ellington and Billy Strayhorn wrote arrangements that spread out, like the city design of Paris; Basie favored arrangements that bunched together and shot up, like skyscrapers. Ellington had universalist tendencies, and Basie was resolutely American.

Both men suffered from underrecognition of their piano abilities, but perhaps Basie even more: it wasn't just that he didn't spotlight himself a great deal, he played fewer notes. What notes they were, though: teasing, laying back, like a viper choosing its moment.

The Atomic Basie, a reissue made largely from an original album called $E=MC^2$, displays Basie at his most recondite. "The Kid from Red Bank" (Basie came from Red Bank, New Jersey) is a portrait of the artist in show business: stride-piano blues choruses colliding with Las

Count Basie

Vegas brass-section knockout punches. Basie's dallying right hand on the piano leaves acres of clear-cut space, making you feel as if you're alone in the woods, noticing the steam from your breath. Then the horns come in, and suddenly you're in Times Square, dazzled by light and sound. In the glacially slow blues "After Supper," Basie keeps perversely quiet in his solo. (The solo nearly begs the question, Why did you come to work if you don't want to play?) The sound is revealed in tiny dots; in some places, there's silence for almost a whole bar and no sustain pedal until the final quarter-note slide into the gnashing maw of the full band.

This is the band that included Eddie "Lockjaw" Davis, a rough-toned, Ben Webster–ish tenor saxophonist, and the trumpeter Thad Jones and saxophonist/flutist Frank Wess, who both had modernist tendencies. The concept of $E=MC^2$ was entirely arranged by Neal Hefti, who went on to write memorable film and television music (for *Batman,* among other things). It was a band that prided itself on precision and was often derided for not having strong enough soloists, but the unity of the ensemble sound was the key.

An album like *The Complete Atomic Basie,* with its mix of raging up-tempo pieces and ultraslow pieces such as "Li'l Darlin," remains good proof of why the Basie New Testament band became the most influential large group in jazz history, with a sound traceable into the Thad Jones–Mel Lewis band of the 1960s and 1970s (which became the Village Vanguard's Monday-night Vanguard Jazz Orchestra) and all the best high-school and college bands in America. It wasn't just because of logistical reality (Basie's hired arrangers went on to work for many other units and spread the sound around). It was more that Basie's own unpretentious sensibility (lack of pretension is a mark of Hefti's style as well), with its continually refigured blues, its generous humor, and its playing-for-the-cheap-seats projection, became a perfect curriculum for developing players; it teaches them how to function in a big band.

50. SUN RA AND HIS ARKESTRA:

Jazz in Silhouette

(EVIDENCE ECD 22012-2)

"Le Sun Ra," piano, celeste; Pat Patrick, baritone saxophone and flute; Marshall Allen, James Spaulding, alto saxophone, flute; Hobart Dotson, trumpet; William Cochran, drums; John Gilmore, tenor saxophone; Ronnie Boykins, bass; Charles Davis, baritone saxophone; Julian Priester, trombone.

Recorded 1958

"IMAGES AND FORECASTS OF TOMORROW / DISGUISED AS JAZZ," reads a poem included on the original record sleeve of *Jazz in Silhouette,* released on Ra's own label, Saturn. Just so: to judge by his own pronouncements, Sun Ra wanted to make music about outer space and time travel, about the magic of ancient Egypt; he was using jazz, his field of expertise, merely as a vessel. It was the corollary of his claim that he was originally from Saturn—he just was deposited here and given to an earth family.

This is the Sun Ra problem in a nutshell: if you like the music, do you have to sign on with all the cosmic stuff that was its context? Can you be a skeptical person and love Sun Ra? If you love Sun Ra, do you have to love all of it? Where does the extramusical stop and the intramusical start?

Behind the obscurantism, Sun Ra obviously wanted to entertain: that's what the spangly red caps were for, the rare African instruments, the parading through clubs at the beginning and end of a set. He respected an audience's need for grounding in the reality of a known cultural context. It's just that his output over his life—more than 120 albums in thirty-six years, with an Arkestra held together with limited resources for that whole period of time—was so vast that at certain points he had to follow his whimsy. If you caught him on a night when he was playing otherworldly stuff in no known musical language, you might catch him on the next night playing Fletcher Henderson charts. It didn't matter to him whether you liked him that night or not; the evidence of his breadth was out there for you to judge.

What's valuable about *Jazz in Silhouette* is that it can silence the severest Sun Ra skeptics with its red-hot swing and bop-tradition playing, its solid horn-section charts, its steady rhythm; and yet it also smuggles in a respectable chunk of the no-known-language. Sun Ra of the 1980s wasn't the same; by the time I got to the band, I liked it mostly as a diversion. In 1958, the band had monster players in Patrick, Allen, Dotson, and especially Gilmore, who had gotten the speed and controlled improvisational intricacy of Paul Gonsalves under his fingers. (Allen had done the same with Charlie Parker.) They were adepts at the mainstream language of jazz; they and Sun Ra weren't faking anything.

But they did like to pull the rug up from underneath jazz's majority sound, and there are nice moments of disjunction here. "Blues at Midnight" is a big-band bebop piece, the kind of thing that had been very impressive for the previous ten years, but spiked with dissonant voicings from Ra; after some rapid, superhip solos by the horn players, Ra ends the round of improvisations with a solo at the end on celeste— that's right, celeste, the instrument from the "Dance of the Sugar Plum Fairy" in Tchaikovsky's *Nutcracker Suite*.

I like Ra's humor, but I never found his self-conscious radical tendencies so fascinating. If you look hard enough, you find bits of madness everywhere in lots of popular music—in Raymond Scott of the thirties, or that oddly provocative year of 1947, which offered Duke Ellington's atonal miniature "The Clothed Woman," June Christy's little-known atonal duet with Stan Kenton, "This Is My Theme," the Coleman Hawkins solo-saxophone improvisation "Picasso," with its multiple tonal centers, and the famous free-improvisation recordings of the Lennie Tristano sextet. (A couple of years ago, clarinetist Joe Maneri revealed that he was playing free improvisation in 1946; without disputing its truth, I hear a desperate ring to the claim.) It seems like a futile race. That Scott or Kenton or Tristano didn't choose to play transgressive music every day of their lives is no sign of weakness. You look at one supposed breakaway moment after another, and they begin to look the same; you wonder if there is an intrinsic value in a transgressive act, or at least a value that can be judged on the same plane as musical values. The point is whether the act works as music, with shape and resonance and beauty.

By that logic, the track "Ancient Aethopia" remains impressive— for 1958 or any year. The trumpeter here, Hobart Dotson—little recognized in jazz history outside of this session, Ra's later *Sound Sun Pleasure,* and a mid-sixties Charles Mingus recording—plays an improvisation in a chordless context, with no other instruments except a thumping rumba rhythm; it has logic, form, and great beauty.

51. AHMAD JAMAL TRIO:

Cross Country Tour: 1958–1961

(CHESS/UNIVERSAL 18132, 2 CDS)

Ahmad Jamal, piano; Israel Crosby, bass; Vernel Fournier, drums.

Recorded 1958–1961

To this day, there's an amount of bandleader control in Ahmad Jamal's performances that you seldom see in any jazz trio. After the completion of each short, self-contained notion, his left hand shoots up, to indicate a change in tempo; or he uses a loud, declarative figure to introduce a new vamping or melody pattern. Every so often, he abruptly stands, leaning with his back to the keyboard—he has to turn around to face his sidemen—and scrutinizes his charges, arms folded.

The blueprint for this kind of performance was in place in the late 1950s, when Jamal recorded his astonishing live albums at the Pershing Hotel in Chicago, which are included here. This set packages together *At the Pershing* volumes one and two, as well as *Portfolio of Ahmad, Ahmad Jamal's Alhambra,* bits of *All of Me,* and *Ahmad Jamal at the Blackhawk.* All of them are live recordings; Jamal simply felt less constrained outside the recording studio.

They are his earliest available recordings, though he had been gaining speed professionally since 1951; his trio concept began then, first starting as a piano-guitar-bass lineup, like Nat "King" Cole's. In 1957, drummer Vernel Fournier entered the group, replacing the guitarist Ray Crawford, and everything changed. A year later, they had one of the freshest, cleanest sounds in all of jazz, an orchestral idea of the jazz small group, in which all players move as a unified organism—as opposed to the model of the harmony-obsessed pianist leading an inter-active band, which gained ground around that time with the arrival of Bill Evans and Herbie Hancock. About *At the Pershing,* Jamal pulls no punches these days: "It's a perfect record," he is quoted as saying in the new liner notes.

And it is. Jamal, like Ellington, is drawn to the extreme ranges of the piano, and in this period he tinkled melodies with the right hand alone or chimed small parallel harmonies with the left; Israel Crosby's walking bass connected with Vernel Fournier's brushed drums. Jamal was also known back then for his soft/loud shifts, and as Nirvana found out soon after they released *Nevermind,* a major dynamic tran-sition between verse and chorus can drive audiences wild. This was one of the reasons that Jamal seemed too obvious to jazz critics back then; the words "effete," "entertainer," and—sacrilege—"cocktail pianist" were tossed around.

But Miles Davis loved him for the way he was able to mine profun-dity from the most sparkling mainstream entertainment and for his use of space. Davis became his champion, and his quintet arrangements from 1955–1957 (compare his "Woody'n You" and "Billy Boy" to Jamal's) were outright homages. "Listen how he slips into the other key," Davis told writer Nat Hentoff in the mid-fifties, after hearing that Hentoff, too, thought of Jamal as lite jazz. "You can hardly tell it's happening. He doesn't throw his technique around like Oscar Peter-son. Things flow into and out of each other."

Indeed, there's a lot to be learned in appreciating Jamal on his own terms. When he first became known—the first volume of *At the Persh-ing* catapulted him from no-name to headlining status and stayed on the *Billboard* charts for more than two years—it was a golden moment for jazz, though one that worked to his disadvantage. The first Persh-ing record appeared right after Ornette Coleman's first LP, a year after John Coltrane improbably turned into a first-class improviser with the Miles Davis Quintet in 1957, and a couple of years after Lennie Tris-tano's bebopper-baiting cerebrations had been appreciably recorded and absorbed. These other figures were quickly interpreted as rebels, opposers, overturners; a superficial listen to Jamal leaves you with the opposite impression, as if he actually wants to entertain you.

When Martin Williams disparagingly wrote that "Jamal's real

instrument is not the piano at all, but his audience," it signaled a paradigm shift in jazz, when gentility and finesse were suddenly signs of artistic fraud (and of Uncle Tomming as well, though less so; jazz critics had already been confounded by Louis Armstrong's wide stage smiles and had come to appreciate him as a sort of professionalized genius).

To a certain extent, a jazz that's generous and forthcoming and that tries to exist as a form of popular music is still regarded suspiciously. These records still have something major to teach us, to pry us away from the underdog/oppressed/oppositional mind-set of jazz appreciation.

Jamal himself, in fact, may have finally proved himself to be a crank and iconoclast; his precise rhythm section sounds so sweet that you have to ask yourself whether you're allowed to enjoy swing this precise. Fournier, an underappreciated drummer, is superb on this material, following the dictates of the arrangements exactly—his bass-drum foot sometimes seems electronically wired to Jamal's left hand—and interjecting lovely superswinging fills. He left the group right after these recordings, so his Jamal-trio legacy is all here to be savored. (Fournier was from New Orleans, and New Orleans rhythm is encoded in that right foot; I doubt it's a coincidence that two other drummers who later played with Jamal for long stretches, Herlin Riley and Idris Muhammad, are also from New Orleans.) Jamal's practice of sifting among melodic ideas within extended vamps was picked up not only by Miles Davis at the time but by later pianists, including Keith Jarrett and Jacky Terrasson; it's a modern structural idea couched within pearly, perfect music.

Of course, this music can sometimes be too sweet and too micromanaged. I've had the experience, after watching Jamal play for an hour, of being ready to pay a surcharge for a decent groove uninterrupted by Jamal's control-freak tendency. But if you're looking for an argument that pleasurable, mainstream art can assume radical status at the same time, Jamal is your guide.

52. MILES DAVIS:

Kind of Blue

(COLUMBIA LEGACY 64935)

Miles Davis, trumpet; Julian "Cannonball" Adderley, alto saxophone; John Coltrane, tenor saxophone; Bill Evans, Wynton Kelly, piano; Paul Chambers, bass; Jimmy Cobb, drums.

Recorded 1959

"So you're doing a book on the hundred best jazz records? OK, let me guess. *Kind of Blue* . . . uh . . . what else?"

In 1959, jazz provided thunderclap after thunderclap, records and performances of great consequences. Jazz was going in many different directions at once, and, theoretically, some of them seemed at odds.

John Coltrane's *Giant Steps* pushed harmonic intricacy to its limit theretofore; to play it, you had to navigate chord after chord. On the other hand, Miles Davis's *Kind of Blue* did away with chords almost entirely, freeing the improviser in new ways. He wasn't tied to a sequence of chords; all he had to ground him at any given time was a single mode or scale. But if one turns to metaphors of freedom and constriction, as one is so often tempted to do in writing about jazz—largely because the history of jazz is so intricately entwined with the history of racism in America—one can misunderstand *Kind of Blue*. For all the implicit freedoms in the modal form that Davis popularized here, the record really gets by on structure. That it is largely improvised structure—some of the most convincing solos in the history of jazz are here—only makes it more impressive.

The interplay between Davis and Coltrane—they had been playing together, on and off, for four years—had reached a special point. Coltrane had absorbed Davis's sense of improvisational structure; his solos on "So What" present a new Coltrane, one that collects his energies into narrative instead of spraying speed and technique and influences, which he had been doing, to an extent, until 1957. And Coltrane, at that moment, had reached critical mass in terms of influencing his colleagues.

Both of them were deeply emotional players—both, in fact, projecting a similar kind of elegant, romantic sorrow. Bill Evans, too, had this; Cannonball Adderley seemed not to have it at his core, but even he was becoming technically influenced by Coltrane. All this created a cumulative force; *Kind of Blue* is an intensely emotional record, for all its serenity. It's a democratic emotion; compared to Coltrane's own records, which can be forbidding, *Kind of Blue* represents an emotional spectrum that's more available to the average person. You can attribute that to the cheery presence of Adderley or to the lightness of Evans's touch or to the agreeable nature of the blues (see "Freddie Freeloader" and "All Blues"), but you can't say for sure.

The piano role in the band is one of the most interesting aspects of *Kind of Blue*. Bill Evans, of course, had already created his own style, soft and harmony rich; it's the style that dominates "Blue in Green," the only track without Adderley, and a real change in mood from the rest of the album. (All compositions are credited to Davis, and there has been controversy over how much of the music was cocomposed with Evans. I find it hard to believe that Evans didn't have a hand in writing "Blue in Green.") But one track, "Freddie Freeloader," features the pianist Wynton Kelly instead, and how different he is from Evans. He swings; he's funky; his chords are lean.

Hear it, if you're one of the few who haven't. This is the only jazz album that sells five thousand copies a week, every week. Try to get beyond its landmark status. Listen to it as foreground music; listen to the solos, not just the full picture, as instantly attractive as that may be. (A curious book written a few years ago by the artists Komar and Melamid, called *Painting by Numbers,* determined through polling that blue landscapes were the paintings most people wanted to look at. *Kind of Blue,* with its openness, harmonic stasis, and muted dynamics, is jazz's definitive blue landscape.)

The 1956 Davis quintet—which made a series of offhanded, almost documentary recordings for Prestige—was an archetype; you could copy it for a living. But you couldn't do *Kind of Blue* for a living, or at least for not very long. Modal jazz turned out to be a flavor, not a whole cuisine. As is the case with most bestselling jazz records, melody—and I mean improvised melody, because there isn't much composed melody here—is the strongest link in *Kind of Blue,* rhythm the weakest. In the spirit of Davis, who hated platitudes and received opinions, try to listen for its shortcomings, too.

53. CHARLES MINGUS:

Blues and Roots

(ATLANTIC/RHINO 75205)

Charles Mingus, bass; Willie Dennis, Jimmy Knepper, trombone; John Handy, Jackie McLean, alto saxophone; Booker Ervin, tenor saxophone; Pepper Adams, baritone saxophone; Horace Parlan, Mal Waldron, piano; Dannie Richmond, drums.

Recorded 1959

Charles Mingus is one of the greatest American composers, and one of the two or three best in jazz. He was passionately interested in the long-form jazz composition and eagerly took up the challenge of combining jazz and classical music offered by the third-stream movement. He kept a sharp eye on his contemporaries; he was outrageously competitive and strenuously individual, never allowing his musicians to be hijacked by the styles of Charlie Parker and Bud Powell. He knew as well as any academic or historian what the root elements of jazz are, and he knew better how to reshuffle and transform them in order to make an art that provoked and pleased.

Given all that, why include here an album that collects six blues-form pieces? Not because *Blues and Roots,* from February 1959, is the "primitive" Mingus, I assure you. (Mingus, like Ornette Coleman, suffers a bit from a rockist appreciation of him that cherishes the primal.) It's because it shows how Mingus was an incredible spontaneous organizer of musicians—a skill that being a "good bandleader" doesn't always encompass.

In the 1950s, Mingus's idea of a "Jazz Workshop" (it eventually became the proper name of his band for concerts and recordings) had

Charles Mingus

developed to the point where he wanted to encourage a good deal of spontaneity; he was interested in risk. This wasn't just an aesthetic imperative; Mingus was as career-minded as any bandleader, and he wanted his music to sound different. He found a willing conspirator in Nesuhi Ertegun, who produced his Atlantic studio sessions between 1956 and 1961. The performances are ragged at the edges but are sublimely energized; it's a high-water mark pursued still by groups in the free-music sphere, like William Parker's In Order to Survive and Peter Brotzmann's Die Like a Dog.

The music for *Blues and Roots* wasn't handed out before the recording date. Mingus explained lines, riffs, and arrangements on the spot to his nine-piece group, a kind of little big band. The whole thing had a character of motion, of restlessness about it; Tom Dowd, Atlantic's engineer, wrote that recording Mingus's bass tended to be difficult because Mingus couldn't stop walking around with his instrument during sessions. At that point, Mingus knew better than anyone in jazz how to turn a mess into a virtue and still retain something of the mess. And any mess with Mingus and Dannie Richmond at its heart is going to be acceptable: they had as perfect a communication as any bassist and drummer in jazz.

Mingus's background was as an Ellington acolyte and as an earnest student of classical music; Buddy Collette was one of his friends and mentors, and there are few more disciplined musicians than Buddy Collette. But by the late 1950s, Mingus began striving to make himself transparent, to show the audience how he ticked. He found a way to make his jazz full of himself—a sticky issue, since jazz often derives so much strength from the subordination of individual talent to tradition.

For all the self-confidence and earthy bravado associated with Mingus, his autobiography (*Beneath the Underdog*) and his interviews show a man crackling with insecurities, crying out that he doesn't belong: with bebop, with white people, with black people, with his image as perceived by the press, with himself. The best of his music (even the third-stream piece "Revelations" from the LP *Modern Jazz Concert* [1957], collected on the reissue CD *The Birth of the Third Stream*) glows with gospel and blues, the deeper traditions of black American culture. But it's also an outsider's music, with harsh juxtapositions and a degree of anxiety and skepticism about those traditions.

Throughout *Blues and Roots*, the metaphor of self-revelation is made literal: Mingus shows you the layers of the music. Individual voices enter one by one into counterpoint, piling atop one another. Tempos seem to get faster, then slower. The bandleader shouts commands. These pieces work like instructional records, dissolving the mystery of music.

54. ORNETTE COLEMAN:

The Shape of Jazz to Come

(ATLANTIC 8122 72398-2)

Ornette Coleman, alto saxophone; Don Cherry, pocket trumpet; Charlie Haden, bass; Billy Higgins, drums.

Recorded 1959–1960

The first twenty seconds of "Focus on Sanity" tell you all you need to know: a drum roll, a squiggling, rushing figure obviously conceived on saxophone but arranged for saxophone, trumpet, bass, and drums, then a free-ranging, blues-scale solo on the bass, then a lowdown ching-a-ching bass-and-drums groove. It's the sharp-smelling anxiety of the missile-crisis age fusing into the imperturbable soil of American rhythm.

No, it's really the first five minutes, hearing the twinning and then differentiation, through individual solos, of Coleman and Don Cherry, two players who forged one of the most special connections in all of jazz.

No, actually, it's the entire album, which still has such freshness: it spills all over your idea of what jazz is but makes inherent sense, cohering with the like-mindedness of a suite.

Coleman crashed into the jazz audience in 1959, coming from Los Angeles with some durable melodies and a free, almost untutored way of improvising, with references made to chord changes whenever he felt like it. His two albums on Contemporary, recorded in California in 1958 and early 1959, were promising; the two years he spent under

Ornette Coleman (center)

contract with Atlantic Records, resulting in seven albums, changed jazz totally. He seemed to hear music in a light, high register, and his music came out like speech—not oratory, just conversation. It's amazingly unself-conscious, and it has the normal cracks of normal voices; it's not that it sounded as if it rebelled against the idea of "proper" saxophone tone—rather, it felt unhostile to and uninterested in the idea.

If any of this sounds phony—I admit that the "music like speech" idea is shopworn, having been the central tenet of Coleman appreciation since 1959—the music never does. The fact is, when Coleman and Cherry are playing a similar idea simultaneously in clashing keys, it does clash; then they bring it together, and it doesn't. So does that give more value to the clashing part?

With Coleman, it sounded fine either way. Every great musician sells confidence, along with whatever particular discipline and skill they bring to the table; Coleman's form of confidence was the natural-man sort. He was the kind of guy who questioned everything, but in the sweetest, most naive way. If it was an act of some sort, don't protest: it worked for him and for jazz. A charmer and a master of the aphorism,

Coleman once explained the hang-up about tonality in western music this way: food tastes the same whether you eat it with a fork or with your hands, so music should sound the same whether you have an assigned tonal center or not. There was shifting tonality in Coleman's music, even atonality, but in this early record—Coleman's first great statement—tonality is *referred* to constantly. It gave the listener a grounding, a foothold.

Technique can be a tricky issue in jazz. Lester Young—as Benny Goodman once remarked—played clarinet a lot better than a lot of clarinetists who played better than him. Coltrane played a touch sharp, as do Jackie McLean and Greg Osby. You can't hold someone to standards of tone, intonation, and attack if those standards don't assure great music. There are still relatively sane people who can't stand the sound of Ornette Coleman because he doesn't play in tune, and if that's the way your hearing is wired, fine. But I think the question of Ornette's technique or lack thereof isn't just an intellectual issue. That slurred half-step rise that he often turned to as an expressive device on *The Shape of Jazz to Come*—sharp as all hell, but modest in its projection—is beautiful. This is where technique breaks down; one step further and you're into mysticism.

The rhythm sections were crucial. With Billy Higgins on drums and Charlie Haden on bass, the band here achieved a dancing, simmering rhythm—fast, exact, hot stuff. Haden, whose early background was in country music, liked playing double stops; harmonic openness was the key to his sound, and if he wanted to bounce on the tonic for minutes at a time, he knew how to make that into rhythmic momentum, not just a harmonic holding position for the soloist.

For all the "feeling" that has been associated with Coleman's playing—and you ought to be skeptical when this word comes up too much around any brilliant black artist—he played no traditional ballad-style music on *The Shape of Jazz to Come*. ("Just for You," recorded at the same six-hour session but left off the album, comes closest; "Lonely Woman," the album's famous ballad, has free rhythm and a subtext of near agony—a flamenco mood of surging and subsiding.) But there was scant evidence—there if you wanted to listen for it, not there if you didn't care to—of Coleman and Cherry as beboppers or swing enthusiasts. It didn't sound like anything else, except something rustic—blues, it was supposed; Coleman was from Texas, after all.

The big question about Coleman, when he first got the ear of musicians and critics, was when he would get to where he seemed to be going. Why didn't he bring his chordal-movement imagination to bear on his improvisations? It was as if he and his band spelled out these beautiful, haunting compositions in the theme, then junked them in the improvisation section out of boredom or disability. In *The Jazz Review,* famous jazz musicians were often drafted to make sense of Coleman in record reviews. They all strike a similar tone: *hurry up and develop; get it together.* Art Farmer: "I'd like to hear him play a solo constituted around the chords of the tune and then I'd like to hear him play another melody on those same chords." (In other words, prove that he knows what he's doing, prove that those written themes weren't accidents.) Quincy Jones: "A teenager talks with not too much authority because he's not really sure what he's talking about. When Coleman does get authority, he'll be able to say more and say it more deeply with less. . . . His present occasional incoherence is probably the price he's paid for seeking originality, but he hasn't found anything really original yet."

What they couldn't have known was that Coleman had already found what he was looking for.

55. MILES DAVIS WITH JOHN COLTRANE AND SONNY STITT:

In Stockholm 1960 Complete

(DRAGON DRCD 228, 4 CDS)

Miles Davis, trumpet; John Coltrane, tenor saxophone; Sonny Stitt, alto and tenor saxophones; Wynton Kelly, piano; Paul Chambers, bass; Jimmy Cobb, drums.

Recorded 1960

This is a favorite record of musicians: it is the breaking point, the moment where Coltrane pulled ahead and left the jazz of the 1950s behind.

It didn't happen in a private environment, with a band all in his corner and signed on for the new sound; it didn't happen in small clubs and form an outsider coterie around itself. It happened in Miles Davis's band, the most visible and mainstream jazz band of the period, onstage, with Davis's blessing. There's a rare feeling in it of Davis letting go, releasing control. It was March 1960, and Coltrane had already given notice that he would leave the band at the end of the tour. Davis, who valued Coltrane dearly, might have been flummoxed, if not completely distracted, about who to hire that would properly replace him.

Coltrane didn't want to be on tour. He wanted to move on. "All he had with him were his horn, an airlines bag, and a toilet kit," Jimmy Cobb said of Coltrane. "He sat next to me on the bus, looking like he was ready to split at any time. He spent most of the time looking out the window and playing oriental-sounding scales on soprano." Coltrane may have mentally checked out, but he decided to play what he was hearing, rather than killing time on the bandstand. It's one of the most disconnected moments in the music's history.

The format of the Stockholm concerts are familiar, road tested; the band plays the theme, Davis begins his solo in short order, Coltrane comes second, Kelly comes third. The material was set, even rote: pieces from *Kind of Blue,* recorded a year and three weeks previously; a few standards that had become second nature to Davis, like "On Green Dolphin Street" and "Autumn Leaves." Coltrane's solos are longer than Davis's, and they build until he's in a trance, connecting ideas like crazy. Perhaps the microphones couldn't pick up the audience reaction, but on the recordings Coltrane's effusions meet an eerie silence. If a musician were to do this today in a New York jazz club, the patrons would be ecstatic, losing their minds. In Stockholm, there's no applause; it's tempting to conclude that these people hadn't the slightest idea what to think.

Davis's solos on the record are tight, concise, with dramatic use of space in rapid lines. Coltrane's are anything but concise. They begin with low moans and grow into wild, gnashing electrical storms. They turn what were once harmonic convolutions into a sensuous new way of phrase smearing; they sound, absolutely, like a new way of speaking an established language. (Not long before this, according to saxophonist Wayne Shorter, Coltrane had mentioned—apparently in earnest— that he was curious to learn how to speak English backward.)

It's possible that Davis used so much of the *Kind of Blue* music on this tour—which is all written simply, in modes, where the soloist plays on one preset scale until he's ready to move to the next—*because* Coltrane was playing such chromatic, dissonant improvisations. That is to say, as long as the tune was modal, it would be possible for Wynton Kelly to accompany him and not sound clashing or lost.

But there's no way to mask what's going on. The great Miles Davis rhythm section, with Wynton Kelly on piano, Paul Chambers on bass, and Jimmy Cobb on drums, sounds antiquated by comparison. Kelly happens to play a solo following Coltrane on "All Blues" that by normal standards could be rated as top-shelf; but it's made considerably less important by its context. For most of the record, his clean, crisp funkiness as accompaniment—he was known as the greatest accompanist in modern jazz—seems so inapposite to Coltrane's onslaught that at certain points Kelly simply stops, letting Coltrane roll. It wasn't a generational matter of young outstripping old: Coltrane was thirty-three, Kelly twenty-eight. It just sounds like one.

Coltrane is in this for himself. He's making references to his own albums, his own music, his own emergent career: on "So What," he swipes some of the melody of "Fifth House," from the album *Coltrane Jazz,* recorded a few months earlier; he also takes the notion of split tones (playing two saxophone tones at once), which he had worked into a short, neat étude on *Coltrane Jazz* called "Harmonique," and constructs a solo in "All Blues" where he works split tones into surging blues figures, repeating them for two whole minutes.

When Davis returned to Stockholm in October 1960, Sonny Stitt was his saxophone player. Davis loved experiment, but he also loved the mainstream of jazz language, and that's what Stitt brought: bebop, refined, lyrical, classical. The open-harmony *Kind of Blue* material is largely gone, because Wynton Kelly knew exactly how to work with a musician like this; they were on the same page. It's still music of a high order ("All Blues" on the third disc, especially), but there's no way to know what kind of aesthetic crisis Davis was going through. It was to be four years before he developed a new group language with the second Miles Davis quintet, and that was an eternity in the context of the quick stylistic advances he'd made all through the 1950s.

56. ERIC DOLPHY:

Eric Dolphy at the Five Spot

(PRESTIGE/FANTASY OJCCD 133)

Eric Dolphy, alto saxophone, bass clarinet, flute; Booker Little, trumpet; Mal Waldron, piano; Richard Davis, bass; Ed Blackwell, drums.

Recorded 1961

Eric Dolphy was beloved among the Los Angeles players of the late 1950s. Charles Mingus, Buddy Collette, Chico Hamilton, Gerald Wilson—they all adored him, all hired him; it was clear early on that he would get on the map. Like Coltrane, he had a mania for practicing and for developing a new language. He apprenticed in bebop, but when he grew to full maturity—before he arrived in New York (check out a disc called *Chico Hamilton Quintet,* on Fresh Sound, and hear his ripping solo on "Frou Frou")—he was an original.

Dolphy rearranged the priorities of his instruments—alto saxophone, bass clarinet, and flute. He often thought like a percussionist; you can hear his sound as purely rhythmic quantities by tapping out his rhythms on a snare drum. He liked speed and did keep referring back to any song's given tonality, but they were short, comforting touchdowns amid blizzards of notes, especially high-register chirps and quick glissandos. He favored strings of sixteenth notes, occasionally double-timed for a quarter measure, leaping between registers within a single line. His licks weren't sweet or tied to the blues; his idées fixes were some of the most asymmetrical moments of his playing. But they were dancing, quick-action figures, bold and exciting and, finally, not particularly influential. (The contemporary alto saxophonists Oliver Lake, Michael Marcus, and Justin Robinson have all incorporated parts of Dolphy's sound, but it's hard to think of others.)

Dolphy's own style, like Art Tatum's, was a kind of brilliant gizmo that worked for only one person. But he was a willing sideman who even made a middle-of-the-road Latin album while under contract with Prestige records; he wanted to blend his ideas with the existing mainstream of jazz, and he's heard to good effect on other leaders' albums, such as Oliver Nelson's *The Blues and the Abstract Truth,* Charles Mingus's series of records for Candid, and John Coltrane's *Africa/Brass.* (I hesitate to add Coltrane's *Live at the Village Vanguard* because the material from that recording that Dolphy *isn't* on holds up, to my mind, better.) In his prime—from 1961 to his death in 1964 of undiagnosed diabetes—he served three roles: as a journeyman, as an exoticist, and as a true-blue member of the hard-core jazz underground, a nightclub player.

Out to Lunch, Dolphy's one album for Blue Note, is beautifully recorded, with wonderful playing and composing; the only mark against it is chilliness. But *Eric Dolphy at the Five Spot* presents him at his most relaxed. Here he sounds like part of a larger aesthetic history, not a marginal figure.

His band is the reason why. Booker Little, the trumpeter, had terrific energy, joining bebop harmony to wilder intervallic leaps; Richard Davis, the bassist, played with a deep, rich tone; Mal Waldron was at his insistent, monochromatic, stubborn best; and Ed Blackwell, the great New Orleans drummer who drew upon Max Roach's bebop patterns and West African drumming, wielded such strong rhythmic presence that he didn't need to add colors or flashy solos.

This was the only public appearance of a quintet that could have become very basic to modern jazz and didn't; Little died of uremia less than three months later. This group played hard and risked mistakes all the time, welcoming the possibility of clashes. (A Booker Little quotation of the time, from an interview in *Metronome* magazine: "The more dissonance, the bigger the sound. . . . I can't think in terms of wrong notes—in fact I don't hear any notes as being wrong.") Recorded at the end of a week's (possibly two, though historians aren't sure) engagement at the club, it's the most practiced group on any of Dolphy's recordings.

In "The Prophet," one of Dolphy's greatest contributions to jazz composition, Dolphy delivers a great solo—a rough, discursive essay. Whereas elsewhere within the concert his flashes come off as discrete brainstorms, like a series of vaguely related theses, here he links the parts into logically connected plateaus, using an intonation so hard as he races down these potential blind alleys that at times his alto sounds like an electronic oscillator.

For all his self-conscious differentness, Dolphy was a serious musician and one who showed signs of great growth in a short period. As with Bix Beiderbecke, Booker Little, and Clifford Brown, it's painful to think of what Dolphy could have achieved had his life been a little longer.

57. BILL EVANS TRIO:

Sunday at the Village Vanguard

(RIVERSIDE/FANTASY OJCCD-140-2)

Bill Evans, piano; Scott LaFaro, bass; Paul Motian, drums.

Recorded in 1961

There's a single-minded, amiable rapture suffusing most of Bill Evans's music that just doesn't do it for me in the long run. It's not my mood; it's not one of the things that satisfies my thrill seeking.

I'm not alone in this. But I feel compelled to say it—possibly because Evans was so original and so influential that it seems like one should like him if one likes jazz. Evans was one of the pianists who started the entire process of really dismantling song material, making it sub-servient to the force of improvisation; this is genuine trio music, much of it made from the stuff that is inside the players rather than the stuff inside the compositions.

I have a block against his dreamy left-hand chord voicings, artfully positioned in relation to his right-hand lines but never quite forthright enough. They tend toward the higher notes of a chord, and the usual lack of a root suits Evans's style of shifting harmony; to me, the music doesn't feel planted enough on the ground.

But the potency of this record on a higher, more conceptual level is hard to ignore. Evans's notion for a new sort of jazz trio, formulated in the late fifties, was to have the musicians interacting more, a kind of natural, well-rehearsed trialogue that would meld the instruments' roles together and yet wouldn't become dense or tangled. It had

Bill Evans

become high time for that sort of change, and it subverted small-group jazz, which had become dependent on the notion of a star soloist with sidemen in support roles. The idea was well in place by the time of *Sunday at the Village Vanguard*, drawn from the several sets that the Vanguard used to present on Sunday afternoons.

Listening to this record, I pay attention not only to Evans, but to the bassist, Scott LaFaro, and the drummer, Paul Motian. LaFaro's sound is liquid; in the few years before his death (this album was recorded ten days before LaFaro was killed in a car accident) he had been developing a new kind of bass playing that was like a less aggressive Mingus or a more abstract Jimmy Blanton, a singing, soloistic style. And Motian, who has changed much since 1961—he's grown ever more fascinating, a tabula-rasa drummer whose every beat comes in a different package than the last—certainly took much in the conceptual realm from this music with him. His trio since the early 1980s with Bill Frisell and Joe Lovano has been a high-water mark in three-way improvisation over a piece of music's prenegotiated markers; it gets as far away from the guts of a tune as is possible without simply leaving it for dead. And in pursuing this strategy, Motian has been one of Evans's beneficiaries.

Evans's keyboard sound here is chiming, a music-box twinkle at its thinnest and a creamy legato at its most impressive. He takes you through the matrix of a tune and his embellishments on that matrix with an easeful, welcoming gait; he's never rushing, being imperious or convoluted. His brand of obscurantism is to dive into the chords of French impressionism and ancient modes, but he never shoves anything too oblique at you.

In fact, he's never shoving anything at you, particularly. Critic Martin Williams, writing at the time of this album, wondered why it was that to enjoy Evans he had to concentrate particularly hard—considering that this was not unlikable music by any stretch of the imagination. Well, I can relate to that. He called Evans an "introspect" and worried about the effect of his introspection: could it ever really communicate? The answer, obviously, is yes, and it has spoken deeply to pianists such as Bruce Barth and Fred Hersch, among hundreds of others. *Sunday at the Village Vanguard* communicates, strongly, but on subtle levels; it's an album you can spend a great deal of time with and still not feel sure you've heard properly.

58. JIMMY GIUFFRE 3,

1961

(ECM 849644-2, 2 CDS)

Jimmy Giuffre, clarinet; Paul Bley, piano; Steve Swallow, bass.

Recorded 1961

Younger jazz listeners these days can feel frustration that we don't have more obsessions and epiphanal discoveries in *our* generation; it's a drag to live on old criteria carried over from the sixties, that explosive age when the whole country, it seemed, was tuned in to jazz. So in singling out Jimmy Giuffre's best CD I felt divided among several options, then went with what I felt to be the conscience of my generation.

Jimmy Giuffre (far right)

Giuffre, the clarinetist and saxophonist, played in big bands of the late forties and fifties with Buddy Rich and Woody Herman, then joined the West Coast scene with Shelly Manne and Shorty Rogers. In the late 1950s, he located his own sound. Influenced, he has said, by Debussy's "Sonata for Flute, Viola, and Harp," he put together several drummerless trios, exploring different textures than those that jazz audiences were accustomed to, and creating a jazz that had syncopation, improvisation, interaction, and a folk quality as well.

His clarinet tone helped a great deal in the presentation of the music; it was woody and clean and often stayed in the low register. Thinking about himself not just as a jazzman but an American composer *tout court*—as did Nina Simone, Gary Burton, Cassandra Wilson, and Bill Frisell after him—he found a way to incorporate the major-triad feel of the blues, gospel hymns, and pre–Tin Pan Alley popular American music into a cool, smooth, tempered setting. (His short involvement with Spade Cooley's western swing band may have had a deeper effect on him than most jazz listeners realize.)

In 1956, he recorded an original and extremely accessible album for Atlantic, *The Jimmy Giuffre Trio,* with the guitarist Jim Hall and bassist Ralph Peña; one of its tracks, "The Train and the River," made it into the beginning of the famous documentary film about the 1957 Newport Jazz Festival, *Jazz on a Summer's Day*. By the time the song was filmed, the band had switched Peña for trombonist Bob Brookmeyer; now it had neither drums nor bass and was achieving some of the most gorgeous jazz (though with its high quotient of written arrangements, with its lack of blues qua blues, was it really jazz? Must we really care?) ever heard. That band was captured on some Atlantic releases available these days only on Mosaic's large, expensive box set, *The Complete Capitol & Atlantic Recordings of Jimmy Giuffre*; the Newport performance is available on an excellent, if not definitive, single disc from the Spanish label Fresh Sound, *Hollywood & Newport, 1957–1958*.

In 1961, Giuffre changed the band again to include pianist Paul Bley and bassist Steve Swallow, came under the influence of the more tonally abstract, miniaturist jazz chamber music being written by Paul Bley's wife, Carla, and recorded two albums for Verve, *Fusion* and *Thesis*. The band made one more album together, this time for Columbia, under the direction of Teo Macero, who doubtless encouraged their radical tendencies, putting out *Free Fall*—a far-out album for its time, freely improvised and utterly committed to forging a new language, even if it wasn't pretty, even if it took Giuffre out of his penchant for gentle textures and consonance. In a move surely not motivated by commerce, *Free Fall* was reissued well by Columbia in the late nineties; the authors of the *Penguin Guide to Jazz on CD* have given it their highest rating.

But it was *Fusion* and *Thesis*—repackaged by ECM in 1992 as the double disc *1961*—that really spoke to those who had been paying attention to "downtown music," as it was known in New York in the early nineties, and all its equivalents elsewhere. Few knew this Giuffre music; it came as a surprise, sounding so new, so contemporary. The old records mirrored what was being explored in our own time. There was new instrumentation; new rapprochements between classical music and improvised music; new ways to swing without lining out the beat; and, not least, the clarinet, which was just then becoming interesting again via Don Byron, Andy Statman, Chris Speed, Joe Maneri, and other musicians poking around on the margins of jazz. Surely this was why ECM put it out, cleverly securing licensing rights away from Verve, who would surely have put it out again by the late nineties, when its CD-reissue program gathered steam.

"Jesus Maria," by Carla Bley, is the solemn-toned ballad of the recordings, and one of the only pieces in Giuffre's repertoire from this period to be covered by another musician. (Mark Turner recorded a version on *Ballad Session*.) Both "Carla" and "Me Too," on disc two, are in blues form—at least Swallow's bass follows a blues progression. In fact, disc two as a whole—the complete original *Thesis* LP—is more sprightly, more capable of speed, humor, and catchy tunes than its predecessor. Funny that it all predated Giuffre's completely free music, rather than coming on the other side of it, because *1961* has the tenderness of a music using a new language, not the aggression of a music that tries to break apart an old language.

59. JEANNE LEE AND RAN BLAKE:

The Newest Sound Around

(RCA/BMG FRANCE, 74321748052)

Jeanne Lee, vocals; Ran Blake, piano; George Duvivier, bass.

Recorded 1961

In 1961, singer Jeanne Lee and pianist Ran Blake, classmates at Bard College who had just graduated, entered the Amateur Night at the Apollo contest and won. A couple of the right people heard them, and in short order they were able to make an album for RCA. "If there's going to be an enduring 'new wave' in jazz styling," read the chipper album-cover copy, "this voice, this piano may well be the beginning."

Jeanne Lee went on to have a career split between a sort of avant-garde jazz singing—of her contemporaries, she sounds most like Abbey Lincoln, with underlying traces of earlier singers—and multimedia art, working with Fluxus artists, poets, and dancers. She died in 2000, having traveled a long way from this initial statement. Ran Blake, on the other hand, still inhabits the peculiar place this album constructs: a dream world of film noir, gospel music, early-twentieth-century French-impressionist composers, and jazz.

The program for the record comprises standards such as "Summertime" and "Lover Man," film-score songs such as "Laura," a Monk piece, some Billie Holiday–identified tunes, a folk song, and some Blake originals. A few tracks—specifically, the ones with George Duvivier added on bass—actually swing, and Lee knew how to give her voice the insouciant fillips and curves that Sarah Vaughan used to such great effect. Most of the music is connected to jazz by a slender thread yet retains a strong Americanism throughout all its chill oddness.

A great number of jazz musicians are athletes of a sort. They've accepted the challenges of the music as the challenges of an instrument or of a particular group sound. Along the way, they meet all sorts of people who push them in interesting directions: someone will play them a samba record or introduce them to martial arts or take them to the opera or a Santeria ceremony. Many of them are enlivened by the new ideas they see and go so far as to wonder whether they can build it into their art. But multicultural multimedia jazz works have short lives and little funding, and there's (still) only a small tradition for their success even on aesthetic grounds. If the musicians are sidemen, their band bosses don't particularly want them to change direction. If they're bandleaders with a small constituency, their record labels and their audiences don't particularly want them to change direction. The music may be played on a very high level, but nothing much changes, and the opportunity to deal with music as art—not just as jazz—has been lost.

Lee and Blake, with the wisdom that only comes from naïveté, went in the opposite direction. When they made the record they had nothing to lose, and they created a music that intuits the connections between jazz itself and the idea of jazz. They're looking through the window in awe of and with humility at jazz; they're bringing in whatever other experience they have, singing popular tunes or folk tunes. This album could never have been made by musicians who played jazz for a living; it's too sheltered, too interior, too romanticized. Blake, for one, had outsider status in his bones from having being the only white attendant at black churches in Massachusetts during his adolescence. (You can imagine him soaking up Pentecostal services but not being allowed, exactly, to get involved; that sad sense of passion for, but barred entry from, black music is the backbone of his sound.)

In "Church on Russell Street," Blake improvises off a handful of chords; it's slow, dolorous, dissonant, and exactly what he does in performances today. Jeanne Lee's forthright voice does connote a hint of the paradigm shift that was happening in jazz: it's a proud black woman's voice, a bit nasal, a bit deep, very serious. It's naive, too, in the extent that Lee was clearly bowled over by Abbey Lincoln: *Straight Ahead* came out less than a year before *The Newest Sound Around*, and its title track appears on the Lee/Blake album. But this is from a young, tender artist's world, in which the beauty of the traditional "He's Got the Whole World in His Hands" is taken at face value, rather than slotted into the style of a practiced professional.

Sun Ra? Hardened by years of hard band work in Chicago before he ever wore a funny hat. Mingus? A professional. The free-jazz radicals of the late 1960s? They went where the work was and kept their eye on the main chance. There are not many outsider-art works in jazz; *The Newest Sound Around* is one of the best and the few.

60. ABBEY LINCOLN:

Straight Ahead

(CANDID 79015)

Abbey Lincoln, vocals; Max Roach, drums; Coleman Hawkins, tenor saxophone; Eric Dolphy, reeds; Mal Waldron, piano; Booker Little, trumpet; Julian Priester, trombone; Art Davis, bass; Walter Benton, tenor saxophone; Roger Sanders, Robert Whitley, congas.

Recorded 1961

This album was at the heart of one of the great paradigm shifts in jazz and born in a context of self-conscious political radicalism.

Lincoln, a supper-club singer and movie actress who became disgusted by doing what she didn't want to do to suit the desires of white managers, became involved in civil rights, changed the style of her singing, and took up with the drummer Max Roach. In recording *We Insist! Freedom Now Suite* with Roach in 1960, Lincoln made her first step toward establishing herself as a jazz singer who had something substantially different to offer.

Nearly the same crew as on *We Insist!* was assembled by critic and then–record producer Nat Hentoff, with arrangements by Booker Little and Mal Waldron; Coleman Hawkins, the great elder of jazz, came in with ebb-tide, bluer-than-blue solos on several tracks. Lincoln's new mood was honesty. She meant to speak for the fed-up feeling of black women and of black people in general; it seems clear that she was also conscious of the West African griot tradition, in which a singer carries on traditions by telling local stories in song. This is the beginning, too, of Lincoln's new identity as a singer of poems, with lyrics by Paul Laurence Dunbar, Langston Hughes, and herself. Looked at in long view, Lincoln is almost a poet first; the common-meter prosody of Dunbar's "When Malindy Sings" has served as a basis for lots of her songs.

In 1961, she was riding a wave of encouragement; as Hentoff's admiring liner notes point out, she was president of an organization called the Cultural Association for Women of African Heritage and was associating with African nationalists. Talking to Hentoff, she used the language of recovery, of facing down her demons. "I'm not holding back anymore," she said. "It's a hell of a good feeling to come out into the light."

The music is laden with honesty: occasionally radiant, occasionally bedraggled, struggling, pushing, rage filled. The horn arrangements are tart, rich with the dissonance that Dolphy and Little were exploring on their own albums; Lincoln was almost oversinging—did she *need* to project so loudly over medium-soft accompaniment? Yes, she did, and toward the end of "African Lady" she growled, less in the manner of Eartha Kitt than of Ima Ripyourheadoff. She was possessed with righteousness and confidence.

But the white jazz intelligentsia never wants to be considered demonizers. Ira Gitler, reviewing the album in *Downbeat,* accused Lincoln of being a "professional Negro," warning her against further involvement with retributive black politics, as opposed to the quieter, more harmonious kind. He wanted to know what was so enslaving about the jazz scene. Doesn't the cream rise to the top? Isn't this an aesthetic game, not a political one?

Lincoln and Roach were furious at the review and suggested a roundtable conversation, to be printed in *Downbeat*. The transcription of that conversation remains a primary document of the change that occurred in American popular culture at that moment: many black musicians were not going to be entertainers anymore, and they had problems with the white power structure controlling their music and their lives that they were ready to reveal. The musicians were ready to get comfortable with their own anger, ready to start that difficult process of educating the educated, showing perfectly well-intentioned white people why there was something fundamentally wrong in their thinking.

Black nationalism and political radicalism in general didn't end up being particularly nurturing for jazz as music. It led, perhaps indirectly, to the establishing of a grassroots, independent-label record business. But politics receded in jazz, even in Lincoln's own music. What remains, however, is the value of Lincoln's self-awareness (historically, culturally, sexually, business-wise) as a tool of art, as opposed to a tool of demagoguery.

61. "BABY FACE" WILLETTE:

Face to Face

(BLUE NOTE 59382-2-1)

"Baby Face" Willette, organ; Fred Jackson, tenor saxophone; Grant Green, guitar; Ben Dixon, drums.

Recorded 1961

Organ jazz, as pioneered by Wild Bill Davis and Bill Doggett in the 1940s, popularized by Jimmy Smith in the 1950s, and extended into the present by players such as Joey DeFrancesco and John Medeski, is

---

essentially tavern stuff—working-class music, even if much of the rest of jazz has done some social climbing.

It is blues-based music with gospel tinges that connected strongly with audiences in small clubs in black neighborhoods around the northeast (big organ-jazz towns: Buffalo, Philadelphia, Baltimore, Newark, and—less so—uptown Manhattan), the Midwest, and a little bit on the West Coast. It has never lost its functionality, and it has never been expressive enough to become a black art for tourists; you can't move around much behind the eight-hundred-pound Hammond B-3 organ, use it figuratively as a weapon, or express sexual prowess with it, and few organists sing. So it stayed in its own box, benefiting from outsiders' patronage only indirectly and after a long wait, when the sampling technology of international dance-floor music in the late 1980s and 1990s borrowed some of its grooves.

As a subgenre, it is formalized to an extent that can be matched only by the first fifteen years of bebop. Organ-and-tenor records (with a few exceptions, such as those made by Larry Young) sound a certain way, and those limitations must be endured; the music contains no ethic of pushing the envelope, looking to the future, or however you want to express the modernist idea. Jazz critics started having a terrible time with these albums early on, soon after Jimmy Smith became popular. (There's a memorable *American Splendor* cartoon strip by Harvey Pekar in which the author, who was a regular *Downbeat* jazz critic in the 1970s, portrays himself opening his mail and, finding the umpteenth album for review by Jimmy McGriff or Jack McDuff or whomever, explodes: "Another tenor and organ record! I'm sick of bein' the garbageman of their staff!")

"Baby Face" Willette—he made only two albums for Blue Note, and his present whereabouts are unknown—came from a church background, playing to his father's congregation in Little Rock. He was also a pianist and toured with endless numbers of R&B performers: Johnny Otis, Big Jay McNeely, King Kolax, Roy Brown, Guitar Slim—a constant treadmill of working and crisscrossing the country.

Perhaps this gave him a certain amount of wisdom by his late twenties. Whatever the reason, he made *Face to Face* a few months after arriving in New York, and it has a driving quality that sets it apart from the hordes of similar albums Blue Note was making at the time.

Willette played great organ bass lines, and he paced himself, finding one area of great swelling intensity per song. The stock chord sequence in tenor-and-organ music was, of course, the blues form. But most such numbers were cheery, light, and perfunctory sounding. On *Face to Face,* there are a number of different kinds of blues, some dark and deep.

"Goin' Down" is the slowest and deepest, with doubled-up triplets in Willette's organ and Grant Green's guitar radiating a dire feeling. Willette's two solos are masterful examples of the classic organ style, with long notes and repeated and accelerated phrases. Fred Jackson plays a solo with an absolute minimum number of notes, and some of them are played so quietly that you can barely register them; he salts the improvising with squeals and reed-pops. Even better is the band's version of "Whatever Lola Wants," from the musical *Damn Yankees.* For nearly a whole chorus, Willette keeps a single left-hand note down as he implies the chord changes with his right hand; thus he finds his way to the unbearably tense sonic swell, which is the point of all organ-jazz performances.

The point about *Face to Face* is that through little ways—a concise solo here, a loathness to play glib eighth-note patterns there, a certain rhythmic propulsion overall—it transcends cliché. And at the same time it is very much representative of a great and durable tradition within jazz.

62. DUKE ELLINGTON:

Money Jungle

(BLUE NOTE 7-46398-2)

Duke Ellington, piano; Charles Mingus, bass; Max Roach, drums.

Recorded 1962

A failure or a success? George Wein, in his liner notes for this trio date, might have been more honest than he intended when he described the lineup as "a triumvirate, not a trio." The all-star grouping had a confrontational, anarchic looseness about it. All play well, though according to an ethic of danger and confrontation more than sympathy.

As for the new jazz of the 1960s, Ellington once delivered a priceless remark. Asked whether he was interested in making an "avant-garde" recording, Ellington wondered why it was necessary to go back in time that far. *Money Jungle* is the closest Ellington came to the anxious feeling of the new black jazz of the 1960s. But it is primarily a blues album and unique in its ingredients.

Ellington was, in a rare moment, between contracts; this was a one-shot recording for Blue Note. Mingus had typically fallen behind schedule in writing music for a twenty-seven-piece orchestral concert at New York's Town Hall, which was to take place two months later, and he had been tetchy, talking about retiring. Max Roach had come into his most forthright stage, conjoining art and politics. He was rewriting the role of the jazz musician as a seer, a hectorer, a griot, and here he was with one of the greatest "mere" entertainers in jazz. (Ellington's politics were the politics of surviving gracefully, the sort that enabled him to fire a sideman so smoothly that the sideman didn't feel it.)

The atmosphere at the session was a little tender: Mingus didn't like Roach's accompaniment—which might have been unusual for Ellington but certainly not terra incognita for Mingus—and respectfully threatened to cut it short, only to be talked down by Ellington's shrewd blandishments.

The music has its feelings on the surface. Ellington rises to the occasion, becoming a nasty blues player. Roach uses a peaks-and-valleys attack in his drumming—a pronounced lope, rather than an evenly spread swing. In "Wig Wise," a driving, abrupt, boogie blues, the B-section grows frenetic, with Roach stoking the cymbals and Mingus filling the space with outrageously bubbling pizzicato. Mingus fights with his strings, plucking them and producing loud, snapping glissandos. (Here you see the seeds of William Parker's melodic-rhythmic bass style in the following generation.) In "Money Jungle" and "Switch Blade," Mingus adopts a guitarlike role, hammering blue notes, making them percussive, sticky, noisy, bratty. And here is the meanest "Caravan" I have heard; Ellington sounds gleeful in doing a little damage to the tune. As it turned out, he didn't need a smooth rhythm section to sound good.

But it's not all noir anxiety. Two of Ellington's best ballads make the album one of the most weirdly dynamic in jazz: the bewitching, fully chorded, pentatonic-scale "Fleurette Africaine," with Mingus's steady stream of plucked, high-register commentary weaving around Ellington's lovely chords, and a solo-piano version of "Solitude." The album, even remastered, has below-average sound, and the piano isn't as good as it could have been, so "Solitude," with its longish introduction, is a bit marred. Still, positioned at the end of the album, it is almost a necessary palate cleanser, to get the taste of ashes out of your mouth.

63. THELONIOUS MONK:

Monk Alone: The Complete Columbia Solo Studio Recordings, 1962–1968

(COLUMBIA LEGACY 65495, 2 CDS)

Thelonious Monk, solo piano.

Recorded 1962–1968

There is a common prejudice that Thelonious Monk repeated himself so much after the 1950s as to render most of his work thereafter superficial. This is a point often contested by producers and others who have vested interests in his Columbia recordings (those made after 1962) and not made particularly well by anyone else.

I don't intend to take up that discussion in whole—only in part. The fact is that in his solo playing, there is a vast difference between Monk's best recording of the pre-Columbia era, *Thelonious Alone in San Francisco,* and this collection, *Monk Alone.* Both are first-class; but I think Monk went deeper into the demands of solo playing in the 1960s. And Monk's solo playing is an important field unto itself, with its own rhythmic conception, its own pushes and pulls and dramatic silences; it is a different music from what he played with his bands.

Thelonious Alone in San Francisco opens with "Blue Monk," a blues that was one of his concert favorites, taken at swinging midtempo; it's a reference to the most mainstream of himself. The album feels like a homecoming—it is inviting, upbeat, cohesive music, some of the most agreeable music in jazz. In *Monk Alone,* a collection of solo recitals studded with great love-song standards that begins only three years later, we hear a lurching pathos unrivaled until the soul-bleeding music of Albert Ayler and John Coltrane. Take your pick.

Monk was so original that he successfully eluded categorization all his life while becoming a major figure—which is plenty hard, given that there is a small industry of critics, record producers, publicists, educators, and students given to defining what era and subgenre any given composer really wanted to join. He was obviously not a bebopper. The bebop process of playing a kind of cynical, jet-age line over well-known Tin Pan Alley chord changes didn't interest him; he was adamant about using the original melody. Fast tempos didn't interest him much either, after the beginning of his career. He was an original throwback, as Ayler was, as Mingus was. The modern-jazz draperies (funny hats, dark glasses, holy-fool act) obscured a player who prized the swing-piano tradition of James P. Johnson and who often wrote original songs that alluded dreamily to a comfortable southern homeland—a 1920s convention shared by everyone from Louis Armstrong to the most marginal and shallow novelty-song composers, such as Rube Bloom.

Monk carried these markings with him into the 1960s as his solo playing grew slower and more fractured. Jason Moran, one of the many young pianists who still worship at his altar, has talked of the excitement he felt as a teenager in the late eighties, hearing Monk for the first time; he detected what he heard as hip-hop rhythm in Monk's left hand, and that's in evidence here. The first track on *Monk Alone,* a 1962 "Body and Soul," is a perfect illustration of this: a lurching, staccato, stride-bass figure transforms the performance.

There are less aggressive, more decorous recordings here, such as "Sweet and Lovely" and "These Foolish Things," and even other takes of "Body and Soul" from the same time. But they are all charged with a new showmanship. Monk was certainly a leg-puller; those who knew him say he used strangeness as an act. (See the film documentary *Straight, No Chaser* for a concise education in Monk's stagecraft.)

And the act—long silences at unresolved moments of the songs, tempo warpings, an aggressive touch that suddenly downshifts into quietude without any transition—was being boosted at this point for the benefit of his new fans. (Columbia helped his visibility a great deal, and he was even on the cover of *Time* in 1964.) But these aren't false performances; if anything, they're more real and poignant. It's hard to listen to the richness of *Monk Alone* all at once. Still, its high level of canniness and constant strategizing—he's *thinking* his way through every bar of this deliberate music—did a service for the tradition of solo piano in jazz.

64. STAN GETZ AND JOÃO GILBERTO:

Getz/Gilberto

(VERVE 314-521-414-2)

Stan Getz, tenor saxophone; João Gilberto, guitar, vocals; Antonio Carlos Jobim, piano; Tommy Williams, bass; Milton Banana, drums; Astrud Gilberto, vocals.

Recorded 1963

This was not Brazilian music's first major inroad into the American consciousness: that honor belongs to Stan Getz and Charlie Byrd's *Jazz Samba* and to the sound track of the film *Black Orpheus,* released in 1959. But this is the album with "The Girl from Ipanema," an object possessed by so many of our parents, the music that millions of kids growing up in the sixties and seventies understood as a latent dream about the eroticism of Brazil and about the worldliness of jazz musicians.

If Stan Getz had not discovered bossa nova and João Gilberto had not ever collaborated with an American jazz musician, both careers would have turned out differently. They would have remained musicians' musicians; they would have had their cults. But perhaps not significantly more than that.

Jazz and bossa nova don't come from anything like the same origin, but they appeal to remarkably similar crowds. In Brazil, bossa nova was first the music of fan-club gatherings and salon performances; it was for young people who turned away from the garishness of popular culture. It was tender, almost feminine; for the men who sung and played it, bossa nova introduced a new kind of masculinity. It was the sensitive, poetically hurt masculinity of Lester Young, which became the masculinity of Chet Baker, which became the masculinity of João Gilberto. (*Chet Baker Sings* came out in 1954; João Gilberto had a nervous breakdown in 1955 and resurfaced two years later singing in a nasal, vibratoless whisper. Perhaps to throw his admirers off the trail, he credited Frank Rosolino, the trombonist of the Stan Kenton band, for coming up with the instrumental tone he sought to replicate as a singer. But let's give credit where credit is due.)

Jazz, in the mid-fifties, had become big on college campuses; especially after Dave Brubeck's appearance on the cover of *Time* in 1954, more Americans were more likely to associate it with an Oxford-shirted twenty-two-year-old in Providence than with, say, middle-class blacks in the industrial Midwest.

You won't find a jazz critic with many kind words to say about Astrud Gilberto's singing on "The Girl from Ipanema"—the album's breakout hit single—though I think it's completely palatable for a music that suggests things other than virtuosity. No, she's no Sarah Vaughan or Elizeth Cardoso either. But there was an everywoman quality to her voice that implied the nearness of the girl from Ipanema—that she might be an average girl within reach. Stan Getz's improvisations had purpose, and in certain cases—such as "So Danço Samba"—they swung hard, harder than records to chill by ever merit. Gilberto's guitar playing is as unassailably mysterious as ever. And "Tom" Jobim's single-note piano playing—not to mention the genius of his melodies—gave the album a lasting weight.

As Ruy Castro reported in his book *Bossa Nova*, Stan Getz took his earnings from *Getz/Gilberto* and bought a twenty-three-room mansion in Westchester County, New York, that had belonged to George Gershwin's sister. João Gilberto earned $23,000; Astrud earned $120.

What did we learn from it all? The main thing, I think, is that even in a time when there's a high premium on intellectualism in adult culture, good art with sex appeal can be good art with integrity and sell incredibly well. Almost every jazz singer of note since the 1960s has tried some bossa nova numbers—from Sarah Vaughan to Mark Murphy—and it's almost always a kind of indulgence, material about the abstract concept of "relaxing," which doesn't hold water after the fact. Record companies have never stopped trying to capitalize on the jazz/bossa nova crossover, though only a slim number of these fusions have been very meaningful.

65. DEXTER GORDON:

Our Man in Paris

(BLUE NOTE 7-46394-2)

Dexter Gordon, tenor saxophone; Bud Powell, piano; Pierre Michelot, bass; Kenny Clarke, drums.

Recorded 1963

The career of Dexter Gordon (1923–1990) stretched out in fits and starts, dipping and surging, going AWOL and coming back in force for a fresh round of jazzman-back-from-the-dead media coverage. Just as in his solos, it took until the end of his life to make any kind of sense of it.

After nearly a decade of jail time for drug arrests, Gordon—the preeminent bebopper on the tenor saxophone—was signed to Blue Note, and the resulting albums confirmed the linking position in jazz history that his previous work had only suggested: Gordon, more than anyone else, had learned the lessons of Lester Young (behind-the-beat melodic phrasing) and Charlie Parker (the bebop harmonic language) and collated them into his own rawboned saxophone voice, which pointed the way to the future. His was the voice that John Coltrane came from, and thus the voice that most tenor players of the past fifty years had come from—Jimmy Heath, Sonny Rollins, Joe Henderson, and on and on. Not that he was alone: Von Freeman, Gordon's lesser-known contemporary from Chicago, has worked with a similar aesthetic. But Gordon traveled farther, and his influence was greater.

All seven Blue Note albums of this period (1961–1965) are excellent, but *Our Man in Paris* has a special distinction. Recorded with Bud Powell and Kenny Clarke—which is to say, the man who invented bebop piano and the man who invented bebop drums—Gordon makes what might be the last of the real-thing, nonnostalgic bebop records. (In France, after all, where all four musicians had been living, bebop was still the celebrated form of new jazz.) It closed an era nicely.

Gordon the player has a mystery about him. He's long-winded, and his improvisations sound weighed down, but he's still wily; he was the perfect cross of fox and hedgehog. By this point, he sounded as if he wasn't meant for the fast, light business of bebop. When he's at brisk tempos, he picks double-time phrases when the mood strikes him, never sounding at pains to demonstrate his brilliance; when he's feeling earthy, he shows the links between bebop and R&B more strongly than did Parker. And his time is a good deal less precise than any of the other top saxophonists of the day. Whereas Parker's playing could be laser-like, pinpointed in a certain pitch and tone, Gordon is perpetually wandering up and down and sideways. His horn and his sound were well suited to hollering long tones and wild, showman's vibrato on the blues—the kind of gestures that made kids pound the stage while saxophone honkers in revue bands bent over backward and played the horn over their heads. And so his long solo in "Scrapple from the Apple" explores repetition devices—honks, scraping sounds, blues riffs—as well as a beautiful restlessness about the register.

There is a special class of records that have an offhanded grace, that sound like they're not fighting for the special real estate of masterpiece culture. This is one—a midnight toss-off blowing session par excellence, with Gordon really improvising at length on each tune—and Powell and Clarke have much to do with it. Gone is the drag-racing keyboardist of the late forties; this Powell is an accompanist, mellow, dark, with only hints of greatness in some of his chord voicings and the continuous molasses of his right-hand logic. Clarke, only forty-nine, sounds like a great aging lion. So there is a heaviness, a thick-fingered feeling about the record—but with bebop, as it turns out, that's a delightful quality.

66. JOHN COLTRANE QUARTET:

Crescent

(IMPULSE! IMPD-200)

John Coltrane, tenor saxophone; McCoy Tyner, piano; Jimmy Garrison, bass; Elvin Jones, drums.

Recorded 1964

In the spring of 1964, Coltrane was heading into major changes—half a year away from *A Love Supreme*, a little more than a year away from *Ascension* with its two-drummer, five-saxophonist, free-jazz wrecking crew, and the similarly dire urgency of *Meditations*. Midway through a year of impressive recording for Bob Thiele at Impulse! Coltrane made his last piece of mainstream jazz in *Crescent*, organizing a record around three ballads, one bright up-tempo piece, and one unconventional (even for Coltrane) drum concerto.

Switching record labels to Impulse! in 1961, he had let down the guard of technical prowess that had flooded his Atlantic recordings—a nearly academic adeptness at harmonic improvising, which is both the greatest strength and the weakness of a record like *Giant Steps*. (I'm picking an unwinnable fight, but I rarely return to *Giant Steps*, good as it is, unless I'm looking for something formal.) On Impulse! he recorded in a variety of settings—on *Africa/Brass, Live at the Village Vanguard, Ballads,* and *John Coltrane and Johnny Hartman*—before landing at *Crescent*, the calm before the storm.

Even the great Coltrane explored extremes that can be turnoffs in nonanalytical listening: of religion, of mysticism, of free playing. *Crescent* does not contain the most impressive solos by any member of the John Coltrane Quartet; but in a span of six years with more cornerstone statements than most bands have listenable albums, it occupies the greatest part of that group's center. Its mood is shy and sensuous, far from the fire-and-brimstone, I-can-see-for-miles quality that he stuck with for his subsequent and final three years. I wouldn't hesitate to call *Crescent* soul music—more so, in a way, than most of the entire subgenre of good-timey organ-and-tenor records.

It was here that bassist Jimmy Garrison and drummer Elvin Jones found their own swing, hard and cutting, yet dramatically slower than typical tempos of the previous decade and dotted with Jones's cross-rhythms. Coltrane's solo section in *Crescent* after McCoy Tyner drops out is some of his simplest but best improvising, holding on to small, distilled patterns as he works through the chord changes. It was a new kind of ballad playing, one that didn't connote physical love in the same way as before. Calling it a statement of spirituality or selflessness is much too easy. It was simply fresh, original musicianship. "Lonnie's Lament"—covered in later years by, among others, Billy Bang (in a wonderful version from the violinist's *Valve No. 10*)—is a truly great jazz ballad from the second half of the century, and there are not many on that list. And the saxophone-bass-drums trio track "The Drum Thing," in its serenity, openness, and unorthodox methodology of largely staying away from cymbals, seems to set up Coltrane for later pure-rhythm excursions like the ones on *Interstellar Space* (below).

67. JOHN COLTRANE QUARTET:

A Love Supreme

(IMPULSE!/UNIVERSAL 051155-2)

John Coltrane, tenor saxophone; McCoy Tyner, piano; Paul Chambers, bass; Elvin Jones, drums.

Recorded 1964

In the five years before recording his defining work, John Coltrane had been indicating that he wanted to get away from two things. One was harmonic exercises, which formed the backbone of the *Giant Steps* period; they now intrigued him less. The other was that he wanted to stop playing the same tunes ad nauseam. The recordings from his European tour of 1963 reflect this problem: he already has an oceanic imagination as an improviser, but his quartet keeps playing the same numbers.

A Love Supreme was his way out, a cohering long-form work written in progressive segments built on short pentatonic themes. Much of the music was modal and intended as an offering to God.

But which god? Any and all. In a pluralistic country like America, it has become hard not to hear Coltrane's modal music—in which an improviser, relieved of having to move through chord changes, becomes free to explore—as a vector for a personal religious search. This is not to say that all modal music had the same impact as *A Love Supreme*. (*Kind of Blue*, one of the other masterpieces of the modal style, has no religious or social meaning; it's just music.) But Coltrane's music had exotic tinctures: the modes themselves; McCoy Tyner's piano fourths; the third-related chord movement you often hear in Coltrane's composition; the slight sharpness of Coltrane's tone; Elvin Jones's polyrhythmic drumming. It all connotes an ancient world outside of (but perhaps parallel to) American society; and when you add poems to God, this is a record with a higher calling, before records with a higher calling had become one more marketing cliché.

Structured as it is, *A Love Supreme* also shows in a meat-and-potatoes way what the Coltrane quartet was up to right then, mostly through its third track, "Pursuance," a blues theme that serves as the basis for extensive solos by all members. It's the part you could most imagine being played at a performance.

"Psalm," the suite's closing section, is based on Coltrane's own religious poem, which was included with the liner notes to the album. The musical rhetoric of his playing is that of a sermon in a black American Pentecostal church, building in intensity, cresting on notes corresponding to stressed words and phrases in the poem. Earlier in 1964, Coltrane had also worked from his own poems for several pieces on *Crescent*; setting words to music may have focused his composing.

A Love Supreme sold well, and fame brought the opportunity for generosity; Coltrane had the power to bring new artists to the Impulse! label, including Marion Brown, Archie Shepp, and Pharoah Sanders. Who knows how these things happen, but somehow the album's mood—its grief, its seriousness, its rootedness in black American expression, and its leaning toward the wisdom of much older art— would mirror the national mood into an anxious, newly wise period (post-Kennedy, post-King, post-Malcolm, Vietnam) more perfectly than any other American music.

Andrew Hill

68. ANDREW HILL:

Point of Departure

(BLUE NOTE 7243-4-99007-2-1)

Andrew Hill, piano; Kenny Dorham, trumpet; Eric Dolphy, alto saxophone, flute, bass clarinet; Joe Henderson, tenor saxophone; Richard Davis, bass; Tony Williams, drums.

Recorded 1964

The loosening effect that Ornette Coleman and Cecil Taylor had on jazz took a few years to work its way into the foundation. But by 1964—seven years after Taylor's recorded debut, six years after Coleman's—jazz really had changed, and until about 1967 the best musicians of the postbop era were catching up with the new modernism, becoming deeply involved in the challenge of composition that was pushing structure and harmony into different places.

The best of these experiments took place in Rudy Van Gelder's studio in Hackensack, New Jersey, and were recorded for Blue Note Records. For this short and fertile period, Andrew Hill's *Point of Departure* is a primary text. As with so many of the best records, its success is in large part because of the musicians Hill chose. Kenny Dorham is the only one who verges on being out of place. (He didn't like to play awkwardly or experiment with sound and texture the way the others did.) The others were astonishing musicians.

Hill, who came from Chicago and worked in mainstream jazz and R&B before 1962, was and is far from a virtuosic pianist. His notes are staccato and stubby, like Monk's would have been if he had little touch; he keeps a supply of short melodic-rhythmic motifs and often uses them. But the monochromatic nature of his improvising is mirrored by the monochromatic nature of his composition, and between them there is a unity; as performer and composer, he seems to be the same honest person.

The pieces on *Point of Departure* don't flow and develop, and they don't have a lot of built-in contrast; there's no crescendo or denouement in the expected places, and they don't make a journey, traveling from a home key to an away key and back. They tend to be organized into two units of the same number of measures or even, in the case of "Flight 19," as one constantly repeating unit. What Hill devised, though, were ingenious ways to work with static harmony. The tunes have intriguingly dark melodies, but on much of the material, when the players find the right scale to work from, they can just let it rip through their solo without having to worry about chord changes.

That proves a perfect situation for the showy, restless Eric Dolphy, who cuts "Refuge" to ribbons with sharp, exciting flurries (even though most of them had been worked out in his earlier playing) and plays a tremendously moving bass-clarinet solo on "Dedication." It works for Joe Henderson, too, whose solos are dark and wary, with original melodic motifs. Dorham lands on some impressive patches—it sounds at those moments as if he were slotting in practiced material—but ultimately sounds frustrated and repetitive. Tony Williams's essayistic soloing throughout is so good that he's really beyond comprehension.

And so it proceeds, through the rest of a consistent, unique recording

and its beautifully colored, strangely uneloquent music. The early sixties was also the time of Andy Warhol and *Last Year at Marienbad*;
blank-faced repetition was in, and jazz had its share of it.

Hill's is a coherent vision. I have written of one of his solo concerts
that it was like looking from above at a landscape but not seeing any
familiar landmarks. And I have written of one of his quartet concerts—
it was a very different setup and altogether different music—that it was
like reading prose without punctuation or capital letters. It wasn't until
later that I realized that those two similes amount to the same thing.

69. WAYNE SHORTER:

Speak No Evil

(BLUE NOTE 7243-4-99001-2-7)

*Wayne Shorter, tenor saxophone; Freddie Hubbard, trumpet; Herbie Han-
cock, piano; Ron Carter, bass; Elvin Jones, drums.*

Recorded 1964

Wayne Shorter, at this moment, is the greatest living small-group jazz
composer, which might not sound like much of a distinction—or at
least a less flashy one than, say, greatest tenor saxophonist. But it
means a great deal, because in the 1950s and 1960s jazz was full of
players who could write fantastically memorable lines, and now there
are very, very few.

Even the most respected bandleaders of the last decade or two seem
to be rooting around in other areas—instrumentation, timbral and textural mixtures, collective improvisation, polyrhythms, improvised
form, America's pop and the music of foreign cultures, or jazz repertory. It's as if the paradigm has shifted, and the battle to write a durable
melody and chord sequence has become dated. But I don't remember
getting that memo, and neither does anyone else.

By 1964, Shorter had been a member of Art Blakey's Jazz Messengers for five years; he had made two records for Vee Jay, Blakey-band

spin-off albums; and he was about to start working for Miles Davis. In eight months, he recorded three albums, offering the first taste of a gnomic compositional style that was to haunt jazz forevermore. His songs are best heard in the mid-to-late Miles Davis band, but never mind: Davis's albums are rare flowers; this album is grass seed. Just about everybody playing jazz born in the 1950s and after accepts it as a foundation.

Its obvious strength is that here, a postbop group sound (AABA song structure, Elvin Jones's swinging drumming, Freddie Hubbard's bravura-blues trumpet playing) can accommodate plenty of mystery. Without playing lots of notes or forcing the issues of dissonance, polytonality, or free rhythm, Shorter found his way to his own kind of new thing. Shorter spent a lot of time with John Coltrane in the late fifties, and his tenor-saxophone sound connects to Coltrane's in its dryness, heaviness, and seriousness.

Occasionally, this album yields real Coltrane flashbacks when Herbie Hancock plays McCoy Tyner–style fourths to accompany Shorter's solos. But Shorter plays far fewer notes than Coltrane, and they are more remote; they're also more bound to the mood and arc of his composition than was usually the case with Coltrane.

That's not to say that all the music here follows familiar guidelines. The lovely ballad "Infant Eyes"—which has melodic similarities to both Mal Waldron's "Soul Eyes" and Coltrane's "Naima"—has a twenty-seven-bar theme, divided into three nine-bar sections; that's pretty strange.

During this period, Shorter composed almost similarly to the way Count Basie improvised—which is to say, he self-edited severely. He took what was already an epigrammatic line and chopped it down even further, so you're left with a few odd but precisely arranged notes; they sound, in a way, improvised.

70. MILES DAVIS:

The Complete Live at the Plugged Nickel 1965

(COLUMBIA LEGACY 66955, 8 CDS)

Highlights from the Plugged Nickel

(COLUMBIA LEGACY 67377)

*Miles Davis, trumpet; Wayne Shorter, tenor saxophone; Herbie Hancock,
piano; Ron Carter, bass; Tony Williams, drums.*

Recorded 1965

Columbia Records made a major investment in Miles Davis, releasing
a few of his records each year during the 1960s (and even up to 1975).
Everything done by his 1960s quintet—the Shorter-Hancock-Carter-
Williams band—has been influential, but for those who didn't see him
play live during that period these albums were particularly influential
for their compositions (mostly those by Davis, Shorter, and Hancock).

Oh, everybody likes live music—it's the real thing—but there are
powerful biases against it where serious jazz performers (and their cus-
todians at record labels) are concerned. It's a European-music holdover
and also a money issue. Composition is more important than improvisation. Publishable composition is more "proper"; it establishes a
legacy; it also generates money.

But there is a truth in common practice, in how any jazz sounds
when it's presented in an informal context. Miles Davis's second quintet, intact with consistent personnel from 1964 to 1967, quickly established a group sound in performance that became the absolute
standard at the time and even now. It was quite a turnabout from the
sound of Davis's previous quintet, which had represented the apex of
hard bop, formal music. The essence of this new band was structured
looseness, and the members found their own devices to work in a consistent state of high musical volatility. Form was being improvised on
the fly. The band had lots of short arrangements that could be cued at
any given time; soloists could also play for as long as they wanted. A
great deal of things could happen.

The Miles Davis Quintet came to play for two weeks at the Plugged Nickel in Chicago over Christmas and New Year's 1965. It had made only one record, *E.S.P.*, with the new lineup including Shorter; the band didn't have much new material, and anyway Davis had traditionally played mostly standards on the road. The song lists for these sets were heavy on the material he had recorded with his previous quintet in the late 1950s—songs such as "If I Were a Bell," "Stella by Starlight," "Walkin'," "Four," "Autumn Leaves," "Milestones," and "My Funny Valentine."

This, apparently, was the reason that Columbia, though it recorded the band for the entire two weeks, didn't release the live music in any form until 1976. The major selling point for Davis, one of the few jazz artists whose records sold much after the Beatles came to America, was that he pointed jazz in new directions, as listeners gathered instantly from hearing *E.S.P.* To confuse the public by showing them that he still liked to play older songs would be counterproductive marketing.

How ironic, then, that it's *Plugged Nickel*—with the rabbity shifts in dynamics, the deconstruction of durable old melodies, the tempo shifting, the reharmonizing performed on the fly—that you hear in an overwhelming majority of jazz groups in 2002. This document—take your choice whether you want the single-disc reduction or the six-disc recordings of two whole nights and six whole sets—is the story of the new mainstream jazz. It appeared on disc, remastered and repackaged, in 1995, and this time it was taken for what it was.

Its lesson is that material, more or less, is neutral. Not so neutral that Davis wouldn't have preferences, favorite melodies, appropriate material for his own sound, technique, and sensibility, but neutral enough that it is not at all the glory of the composers that you hear in "Stella by Starlight" on disc four or "Autumn Leaves" on disc six. Instead, it is the glory of Davis's short, cracked lines, rising up out of silence and returning there again, his unmoored trills, his long notes; of Shorter's runic phrases (as a musician said to me once, "Wayne can play one note and change the entire color and temperature of the room"), wandering away from the tonal center stated by Carter's confident, anchoring bass lines; of Hancock's rhythmically sure arabesques and harmonic sophistication; of Williams's polyrhythms and cymbal work.

Qualities of pure sound, as opposed to melodic variation, became increasingly important to Davis and his band members. The improvisations wander, but there is a tension throughout. Davis specialized in making templates and then moving on as soon as they became fixed styles. How we need him now to change the rules, when this particular template still dictates to us so imperiously.

71. HERBIE HANCOCK:

Maiden Voyage

(BLUE NOTE 7-2349-53312-7)

Herbie Hancock, piano; Freddie Hubbard, trumpet; George Coleman, tenor saxophone; Ron Carter, bass; Tony Williams, drums.

Recorded 1965

In 1965, Miles Davis's music was undergoing a change, and the prime agents of its change were three of the five musicians featured here. It was a volatile period and tremendously fertile; the only impulse unifying the front-running new artists was a sense of fracture, as if jazz had to be cracked, shaken up, rearranged.

Maiden Voyage is an interesting artifact from this in-between stage. The two horns were Freddie Hubbard and George Coleman, and they rooted the record in a new exploratory sound, more heavily patterned and more romantic than, say, Dolphy or Shorter. It's a record that could have been quite different if you had slotted in two different horn players, even other likely candidates; musicians who functioned in the same orbit (and who regularly appeared on Blue Note albums) could be astonishingly varied from one to the other in those days.

Hancock's tunes—conceived as an interconnected suite about ships or water or dolphins or something—were attractive little frames, but what distinguishes the album is the individual playing, particularly that of Hubbard and Hancock; this is their record. Hubbard, I think, is scarcely heard better; he is a battler here, even on the serene "Maiden

Voyage," where he made the wise decision to play loudly and run rippling vertical (i.e., chord-based not melody-based) variations, preventing the tune from drowning in its own prettiness. During "The Eye of the Hurricane," a minute in, after Ron Carter's bass patterns pull free from the minor blues structure of the tune, Hubbard makes rapid runs of thirty-secondth notes, creating his own tonality, and blasts long buzzed notes—the sort of technique that Dave Douglas is known for in 2002.

Maiden Voyage is a chill-out record and a chilly one; it's got early-sixties ennui all over it. Hancock was interested in stasis, in finding chords that could fit over an entire chord progression; it was the next stop after strict modalism. This album is iconic in its use of chords and its harmonic motion; the unresolving suspended chords alone in "Maiden Voyage" and the strange, winding harmonic journey of "Dolphin Dance" are some of the most referred-to benchmarks in jazz since 1960.

The album is influential for setting standards in arrangement (though that could just as well be credited to the 1965 Davis band), in harmony, and in mood. But I have never warmed to it—partially because as good as Hancock is, I find a facile pop element in his soft, searching touch, and I find that under Hancock's stewardship the record became an experiment in harmony when the more interesting of the shifts in the jazz of the period were rhythmic—specifically Tony Williams's rhythmic innovations.

Hancock has an interesting gift for turning around and doing something that isn't expected of him, though he is still confused by attractions of the marketplace in ways that many of his contemporaries seem to have gotten over. (He doesn't seem to get dance music, as revered as he is by the founders of Detroit techno music.) He hasn't made a great, cohesive jazz album in a long time. But several years ago, touring behind his *Gershwin's World* album, he threw over the concept of the record (Gershwin's melodies) and instead concentrated almost exclusively on—what do you know?—Gershwin's rhythm.

72. MOACIR SANTOS:

Coisas

(FORMA, UNRELEASED ON CD)

Moacir Santos, piano, baritone saxophone; Julio Barbosa, João Gerônimo Menezes, trumpet; Dulcilando Pereira, Jorge Ferreira da Silva, alto saxophone; Luiz Bezerra, tenor saxophone; Geraldo Medeiros, baritone saxophone; Edmundo Maciel, trombone; Armando Pallas, bass trombone; Nicolino Cópia, flute; Chaim Lewak, piano; Claudio das Neves, vibraphone; Geraldo Vespar, acoustic guitar; Gabriel Bezerra, bass; Wilson das Neves, drums; Elias Ferreira, percussion; Giorgio Bariola, Peter Bautsberg, Watson Clis, cellos.

Recorded 1965

Cults of rediscovered artists grow quickly and sometimes without much warning; in the 1990s, they have sprouted so rapidly that among the reissues there has hardly been room to appreciate a new young player with something to say. (Who needs Luciana Souza, whose context and range of interests are perhaps not worn on her sleeve, when you've got Phil Ranelin, frozen in time, a perfect snapshot of 1970s black consciousness? Or something like that.)

So I am surprised that there isn't much of a cult around the Brazilian jazz composer and arranger Moacir Santos. Born poor in the northeastern state of Pernambuco, Santos became an itinerant musician, playing around other states in the north, Bahia and Ceará. Toward the end of the 1940s, he moved to Rio de Janeiro, to work in the studios of Radio Nacional, where staff arrangers were needed. But he saw that popular music was art and vice versa, and he studied the big-band composers as well as took lessons with Joachim Koelreutter, the Austrian composer who was lured to Brazil in the 1950s during the age of modernism and taught a whole generation of Brazilian music makers.

I've found little information about what Santos was listening to around the time he made *Coisas,* which was the period right before he moved to Los Angeles (where he still lives) to teach and work on film sound tracks. But it sounds like it was a mixture of two influences: the brass-conscious arrangers who were comfortable with West Coast jazz as well as samba—say, Bob Brookmeyer or Gary McFarland—and the new, small-group arrangements heard on so many Blue Note albums of the time, the spacious, intriguing-instrumentation sound of Eric Dolphy's *Out to Lunch,* say. (If you administered a blindfold test, you'd have people guessing that the vibraphonist on "Coisa No. 2," Claudio das Neves, was Bobby Hutcherson—it's the way the dry, clanky chords are deployed in the arrangement.) He was attuned to American currents; he also sensed what was in the air.

The tracks are simply called "Coisas" ("Things") and numbered one through ten; for some reason, they're presented out of order. On each track, it's the structure and timbre that first seizes you: it doesn't sound based in a genre. The melody of "Coisa No. 1" is carried by baritone saxophone, with sparse counterpoint from muted trumpet and trombone; the rhythm section is a samba setup, with big and small animal-skin drums and an acoustic guitar. The bass lines are minimal, mostly there to help accent the bass drum.

Then it's the melodies, which are concise, bold things, moving through very nonobvious chord choices. "Coisa No. 5" shows that his gift for concision and piquancy was not unlike Wayne Shorter's. How the music unfolds! At first it comes on strong, with tuba accenting a military-sounding waltz; then, after the introduction, the song changes to a more flowing six-eight, with trombone taking the melody, tuba and guitar giving counterpoint. In the second chorus, after the trombone, a flute improvisation takes over until the bridge (juxtaposition was Santos's stock-in-trade), and then Luiz Bezerra's Getz-like tenor saxophone takes over.

The next song, hinging on a two-chord figure and recorded simply with piano and hand drums, at first sounds like one of Ellington's stripped-down miniatures from his 1953 *Piano Reflections.* The fuller band does eventually slide in, with vibraphone and a brass section, again with those spare Afro-Brazilian drums. (That there are very few cymbals on this album is a constant source of wonder for American ears attuned to jazz drumming.) The weight and density of the music changes from track to track; there's an organ (uncredited, and probably played by Santos) on numbers six and ten; there's a small string section on number eight. Different soloists come to light; you don't hear all the soloists play what they know on each track.

"Coisa No. 5," otherwise known as "Nanã," was picked up by the circle of jazz and MPB (Musica Popular Brasilera, or Brazilian pop) composers in Santos's orbit and turned into a hit; more than one hundred versions have been recorded, most of them using lyrics written by Mario Telles. Even before *Coisas* was released in 1965, "Nanã" was recorded by the important Brazilian jazz and pop bands of the day: Os Cobras, Edison Machado's ensemble, and Mario Castro-Neves's, too.

Santos did, in fact, record in the States; he made three albums for Blue Note in the 1970s. But they are long deleted, and even in Japan, the land where jazz reissues are plentiful, there's little interest in rereleasing them.

So there you have it: a foreign jazz arranger with an exploratory and musically sound mid-sixties bent; associations with the loungey bossa nova figures (Castro-Neves, Carlos Lyra, Roberto Menescal, Baden Powell); black-genius stature; obscurity. Why is this man not famous? And why is this CD still unavailable?

73. ARCHIE SHEPP:

Fire Music

(IMPULSE!/UNIVERSAL 051158-2)

Archie Shepp, tenor saxophone, recitation; Marion Brown, alto saxophone; Ted Curson, Virgil Jones, trumpet; Joseph Orange, Ashley Fennell, trombone; Reggie Johnson, David Izenson, bass; Joe Chambers, J. C. Moses, Roger Blank, drums; Fred Pirtle, baritone saxophone.

Recorded 1965

The tenor saxophonist Archie Shepp was John Coltrane's gift to America's broader consciousness: Coltrane managed to get him signed to the new independent label Impulse! where he was the star on the roster. Shepp was promotable—a firebrand, one of the loudest voices of the "new thing" (or, in the proper rendering of mid-sixties bang-zoom marketing, the New Thing!) in jazz.

This new thing came along at right around the same time bossa nova reached America ("bossa nova" means, roughly, "new wrinkle," or, OK, "new thing"), and it had the same combination of new sonic palette and new sociopolitical content. Except where bossa nova whispered, with the cool anxiety of a new generation, in its refutation of the previous generation's bolero, the new thing slid around and howled in refutation of . . . what, exactly? Not Ellington, who remained loved even by the most vehemently political jazz artists; maybe Armstrong, at least as far as his seemingly accommodating stance toward white-bread American patronage; certainly the mid-fifties popular acceptance of white jazz heroes—Brubeck, Getz, Herman, Baker. But when, since the 1930s, had there not been popular white jazz heroes?

As its targets were vague, it took on the targets of other movements. The civil rights movement already had a soul-music sound track in Curtis Mayfield and Sam Cooke, and it needed a commensurate one in jazz. A collection of musicians and writers rushed in to fill that position—the prominent musician being Shepp, the prominent writer being LeRoi Jones. But "jazz" was a suspect term, redolent of blacks singing for their supper, of a black music defined and criticized and patronized and marketed by whites. What they devised was a new black aesthetic disposition that could roll with equal applicability between music, poetry, art, and theater. Certain figures spent equal time in each: the singer Jeanne Lee, for example, for a time in the 1960s and 1970s was as much a theatrical performer and poet as she was a jazz vocalist.

Fire Music is rarely politically explicit, except in the one track on which there are words. Shepp had a resounding baritone speaking voice and excellent diction, and few jazz-poetry matchups have been more effectively executed than this album's "Malcolm, Malcolm, Semper Malcolm." ("We are murdered / in amphitheaters / on the podium / of the Audubon Theater / Philadelphia, 1945: Malcolm! / My people! / Dear God, Malcolm!")

The music on the album is all elbows, and it's glorious. Its arrangements had plenty of free-improvisation pockets, but these are compositions with discrete sections, and Shepp had consistently fresh ideas about chord voicing. He was into uncertain sounds, which partially informs his explanation of why he chose to cover "The Girl from Ipanema": it was the minor seventh in the last chord of the verse, he said, that got to him, and he worked in those minor-seventh chords all over the album. The unusual instrumentation—a small band with two saxophones, two trumpets, and two trombones—shows imagination at work, and that full load of horns often remains in play together. The music is exciting, with tempo changes and shifts between thoughtfully revolving chords and racing pulses with flyaway improvisations.

But there is a delicacy here, too, at its most poignant in the two consecutive tracks that closed the original album. (The CD reissue repeats one piece, "Hambone," in a live version.) Ellington's "Prelude to a Kiss" begins poetically, with the horns, in their shaky intonation, murmuring a procession of background chords for a half measure each, underneath Shepp's guttural, slippery tenor saxophone. When the saxophone breaks away from its brass background, Shepp is brilliant with limited means, which still means brilliant. Improvising on the melody in little bursts of ideas, he cops Ben Webster's bedroom subtones, giving the solo that plush feel of the forties; then he's bratty, perverse, inserting a kid's taunting cry ("nah-nah-nah-nah-NAH-nah" at 3:45) into a purported Great Love Song.

"The Girl from Ipanema" is no less an achievement, with a wholly new bridge full of wild counterpoint, trombone and bass doubling the same line. The ensemble bustle of the introductory chorus winds up to shoot Shepp out of the starting gate again for a six-minute solo, and it's one I'll love forever, with an increasingly cranky improvising logic and buzzing tone. "Ipanema" is sort of pop art, as Shepp told Nat Hentoff in the album's liner notes, and this is a pop-art solo. The atavistic 1940s demeanor peeking through here and there makes it larger than life, and then it shocks you with its glaring colors, flirting with bad taste. Shepp seems both respectful of and thoroughly disgusted with the American commercial culture that seized on the song as a sound track to sophistication. Though he didn't have a thorough command of the instrument by older standards and was a true-blue follower of Ornette Coleman's laws of shifting tonality, he openly loved the tenor-saxophone tradition; like Coleman Hawkins and Lester Young, he used the instrument to make himself an actor.

74. ALBERT AYLER:

Live in Greenwich Village:
The Complete Impulse Recordings

(IMPULSE! IMPD-2-273, 2 CDS)

Albert Ayler, tenor saxophone; Donald Ayler, trumpet; George Steele, trombone; Michel Sampson, violin; Joel Freedman, cello; William Folwell, Henry Grimes, Alan Silva, bass; Beaver Harris, Sunny Murray, drums.

Recorded 1965–1967

Actually, it's not complete: this is Impulse!'s way of telling you that it will not rerelease *New Grass* and *Music Is the Healing Force of the Universe,* Ayler's depressing last statements before his body was found in the East River (tied to a jukebox, according to one unproved but poetic urban legend)—unless a biopic about Ayler starring Denzel Washington happens to be made. (Stranger things have happened.)

But unless you want to go to the ESP-Disk records that Ayler made in 1964—startling documents with woolly sound—this is your best chance to understand Albert Ayler, the saxophonist who grasped something fundamental about the folk roots of jazz and played it at the very top of his capacity.

The great homegrown conceptualists (I don't mean academics) rarely go to jazz anymore—there's much more room for them in what's defined as rock or dance-floor music or world music. Ayler was perhaps the last one to invade jazz and make a great statement on the highest levels—which is to say he released records on Impulse!, an important label after John Coltrane landed there. Despite prejudice among older listeners that he was a fraud or a chaos merchant, he was reviewed numerous times during his lifetime in *The New York Times*. He became an established musician against which other musicians were measured.

Using melodies built on major triads—reveille, Protestant hymns, holiness-church chants—he repeated and repeated and repeated, until there was no more to say. His style of arrangement was when-in-doubt-recap; his brother, trumpeter Donald Ayler, was there for him to go back to square one with when the going got rough. John Coltrane's fascination with Ayler, which formed such Coltrane works as *Ascension* and portions of *Live in Japan,* is an example of a gifted jazz musician on a death mission: surely, he knew that this style of playing would hit a wall soon. Yet he was so captivated by it that he grabbed it and worked it.

The double disc *Live in Greenwich Village* comprises two original LPs, *Albert Ayler in Greenwich Village* and *Albert Ayler: The Village Concerts.* They are both concert recordings, and they're seriously different.

The first disc is Ayler's jazz quintet, pushed to extremes. Sunny Murray, with his snare drum, knocks on the door like an unwelcome visitor; bassists Silva and Folwell sit on the tonic like mother bears protecting their families; Donald and Albert Ayler play and replay the melodies as if there's no time left to lose. The second disc, two years later, contains some of the best third-stream jazz ever recorded, though the only added stringed instrument is Michel Sampson's violin; there is a pronounced difference in the mix, at the expense of the drummer Beaver Harris, and more solo space is given to Sampson and cellist Joel Freedman. (Let's give it up for Freedman: he is as good a sideman as Ayler ever had.)

There are no arrangements for strings; this is a semi-hoedown, with Freedman and Sampson double-stopping and open-stringing as if jazz chords didn't exist. What you hear is the wide-open spaces, the natural capabilities of instruments. But calling it primitivism reduces it unfairly, because Ayler had a sound that was capacious, tender, vicious, knowing. The key changes, as naive as they are (there's no modulation per se—just blam! and you're in another place), have a basic power; the two basses shore up all the moves, bowing along with the strings when the key stays in place.

Ayler's use of American folk forms is unsurpassed but echoed, in ways, by musicians such as Jimmy Giuffre, Cassandra Wilson, and Nina Simone. Jazz has never made enough of its pre–Tin Pan Alley North American roots, its rural origins, which extend back to ring shouts. Ayler exulted in them. Free music got a good deal more complicated after this, but I'm not sure it got more powerful; this music is rooted in a truthful rendering of a culture, and it has meaning, a satorilike, brick-to-the-head meaning. This is last-stop music (the term "post-Ayler" is part of the basic discussion about jazz), a style that must change irrevocably before the next thing comes along. It's as bold, strange, and recognizable as anything in American art.

75. DUKE ELLINGTON:

The Far East Suite—Special Mix

(RCA/BLUEBIRD 66551–2)

Duke Ellington, piano; Cootie Williams, William "Cat" Anderson, trumpet; Mercer Ellington, Herbie Jones, trumpet, flügelhorn; Lawrence Brown, Buster Cooper, Chuck Connors, trombone; Jimmy Hamilton, clarinet, tenor saxophone; Johnny Hodges, alto saxophone; Russell Procope, alto saxophone, clarinet; Paul Gonsalves, tenor saxophone; Harry Carney, baritone saxophone; John Lamb, bass; Rufus Jones, drums.

Recorded 1966

In 1963, Ellington and his band embarked on a State Department–backed tour through the Near and Middle East: Afghanistan, India, China, Iran, Turkey, Egypt, Greece. The following year, the band toured Japan. Ellington and his composer-arranger partner Billy Strayhorn made use of their journeys in their composing, as they made use of any memorable stimulus.

But you shouldn't hold Ellington to literal standards in these pieces. "Doing a parallel to the East has its problems," he acknowledged. "From my perspective, I think I have to be careful not to be influenced too strongly by the music we heard, because there is a great sameness about it, beginning in the Arabic countries and going through India all the way to Ceylon. There are many different kinds of drums, of course, and many strange instruments, and in India and Ceylon they have about ten scales, but the moment you become academic about it you are going to fall into the trap of copying other people who have tried to give a reflection of the music."

An academic approach may have been a trap, yes, but a popular version of "foreign" music would have been a trap, too. This was the era, don't forget, of armchair exoticism in music. Not just Miles Davis and Gil Evans's *Sketches of Spain* but mood albums—music for bullfighting, for tiki lounges, and so on. Plenty of suburban dens had a copy of Olatunji's *Drums of Passion*. So Ellington was right to feel apprehensive before tackling the East as a musical subject—though one wonders if he needed to worry about where his own mind would lead him, since his other tone parallels (that lovely term!) tended to be extremely loose interpretations of what he purported to describe.

This is Ellington/Strayhorn music, with very little of specifically eastern character: the minor scales in parts of "Tourist Point of View," "Blue Pepper," and "Amad" are what any western TV composer might borrow for a snake-charming sequence. It would be crazy to hang Ellington on this. It doesn't matter. A great composer/arranger, with a great band at his disposal—and it still was great, with Gonsalves, Hodges, Hamilton, Carney, and Williams hanging in there—can use anything to his advantage.

The tone colors in these arrangements rank with Ellington and Strayhorn's finest, and Ellington lets the band rip, capitalizing on all its greatest felicities. Gonsalves's tenor saxophone smokily lines out the melody in "Tourist Point of View," with twin clarinets playing high organ chords. An eleven-note birdsong melody played by Jimmy Hamilton provides the melodic backbone for "Bluebird of Delhi," shuttled through various reharmonizations with powerful brass and reeds shoring up the bottom end; the piece is perfectly symmetric, beginning and ending with the same piping line. The luxurious "Isfahan" is one of the greatest concerti Ellington ever wrote for Johnny Hodges's smearing glissandos. Harry Carney, at his romantic best, dominates "Amad" as he did "Sophisticated Lady." "Amad" is a simple riff number with Ellington's percussive piano leading the way into rhythmic heat and harmonic complexity.

"Ad Lib on Nippon," a suite in itself, rises to a rocking blues crescendo out of chamberesque beginnings and a spiky, wide-interval melody, changing after five and a half minutes into a new creation, one of the most moving solo-piano melodies in Ellington's catalog. As with "The Single Petal of a Rose," say, or "I Like the Sunrise," this makes you understand that Ellington had a point when he turned up his nose at the word "jazz." Music like his third strain of "Ad Lib on Nippon" can't be condescended to; it's not part of any utilitarian genre.

76. ROSCOE MITCHELL SEXTET:

Sound

(DELMARK 408)

Roscoe Mitchell, alto saxophone, clarinet, recorder, et al.; Lester Bowie, trumpet, flügelhorn, harmonica; Lester Lashley, trombone, cello; Maurice McIntyre, tenor saxophone; Malachi Favors, bass; Alvin Fielder, percussion.

Recorded 1966

In her 1977 book *As Serious as Your Life: The Story of the New Jazz,* critic Valerie Wilmer theorized that the difference between the avant-garde jazz in Chicago and that in New York was a reflection of architecture—in New York, tall buildings, tight corners, hemmed-in areas; in Chicago, space, light, openness.

During the summer of 1966, John Coltrane, the model for the New York avant-garde, recorded *Live in Japan,* a landmark of terrifying stamina. It was louder and harder than anything that had come before, mixing harmonic obsession with grim-eyed assault. At the same time, Roscoe Mitchell, in Chicago, made *Sound,* a very different sort of record. It was nimble, thoughtful, and funny; it pointed the new jazz in an entirely different direction, one that embraced small gestures and eluded the pull of Coltrane's great smothering mysticism.

It was also a direct reflection of the fact that jazz had finally entered into a modernism that correlated with the modernism of visual art. Arthur Danto has written that the story of modernism in painting could be a reverse version of the story of painting as a fine art up to the mid-nineteenth century, like a film run backward. All the techniques of

---

accurate figurative representation—paint handling, perspective, and so on—were dismantled, until by the early 1950s you ended up with an examination of the materials themselves. The question "How can I get paint to make a sunset look like a sunset?" turned into "What is paint?" Likewise, the traditional forms built up to refinement in jazz—ragtime, stride, swing, bebop, Latin forms—were suddenly not what the music was about. The new music was about itself, its own weights and textures and densities.

Chicago was bound to put its own stamp on the new music. It already had its own tradition of mulishly independent-minded players rooted in the forties and fifties bebop generation, and it was free of the every-man-for-himself competitiveness of New York. The bandleader and pianist Sun Ra had subtly infiltrated the city's jazz underground, creating his own experimental subculture. But even he had left for New York by 1963, and nightclubs in Chicago were dying out in the early sixties. There was no place to play.

But the pianist Muhal Richard Abrams was agitating for a self-determining group to create its own concerts in members' houses, in art galleries, and in churches. The group was known as the AACM (Association for the Advancement of Creative Musicians); it's based in New York now, as is Abrams. The organization doesn't do much anymore beyond produce sporadic concerts, but the name is still associated with jazz that works against the music-school model; it prizes texture and timbre and unusual instrumental combinations above harmonic movement, rhythm-section cohesion, swing, and blues. It wouldn't qualify as jazz but for the important fact that it was what jazz musicians were doing.

Sound, featuring at its core three-fifths of the group that would later become the Art Ensemble of Chicago, was the first and best of the LPs from the early years of the AACM. The record didn't have much immediate impact except on a coterie of aficionados. But its lessons were disseminated through the decades by various offstreams, including the musicians around Yale University in the 1970s—the trumpeter and AACM member Leo Smith, the pianist Anthony Davis (composer of the jazz opera *X*), and the trombonist George Lewis—and the circle of New York experimental improvisers in the early 1980s, including John Zorn, Butch Morris, and Eugene Chadbourne.

Mitchell's saxophone playing on the album didn't try to overwhelm with speed or volume but reveled in featherweight tones, descant chuckles over earthy melodies, self-contained shrieks, and whispers. He didn't position himself as point man in the ensemble (see Henry Threadgill's *Just the Facts and Pass the Bucket,* below, for another example of a sixties-era Chicago musician who has interesting ideas about what a bandleader does), and the music was antivirtuosic.

Lightly tapped cymbals take precedence over drums; in the record's "Little Suite," solos slow down to single utterances broken up by stretches of silence. The musicians play harmonicas, flutes, whistles, bulb horns, mouthpieces, and a sloshing can of water suspended by a rope. (The album's black-and-white target-design cover was cheap but official, like constructivism or pop art; the recording sounded documentary, like a Folkways album.) But the madness was all method.

Mitchell, then as now, was a structural thinker: his music follows from well-conceived ideas. His sextet had been rehearsing nearly every day for months; the form they gave to even the most abstract parts of the record shows that they knew exactly what they wanted to do. Part of the reason that both "Ornette" and "The Little Suite" make such an impression upon first hearing is that Mitchell was smart enough to have these scrappy, ragtag, slightly weedy but very lovable pieces state strong motifs, depart from them, and then return to them at the end. And the twenty-one-minute track "Sound," a kind of empirical but not unamusing instrumental dissertation on kissing, sucking, sighing in the high registers, and so on, had something else: dignity, breadth of vision. During some of the long solo-instrument improvisations, a tiny bell pings at intervals, discreetly asking you to refocus.

Sound was the first step toward breaking the stranglehold New York had on the new jazz. It led to the creation of the Art Ensemble of Chicago, which, in turn, gained renown in Europe, kindling a European avant-garde jazz scene. The album was a succès d'estime: it sold about five thousand LP copies from 1967 to its final deletion in 1990, a surprisingly low number for a fairly famous record, and yet a better seller than any of the other early AACM records.

It was out of print on vinyl in 1990, and Delmark brought out a CD version only in 1996. Perhaps that gap worked against its influence, but a great deal of musicians raided its lessons, learned them internally, and moved on, scattering them like seeds. Today, you don't hear so much of the original AACM's influence in jazz; many of the leaders from the first wave, including Mitchell, have university posts and don't often play clubs. (Not so surprising: the star soloist leading a small band, which is what the touring jazz circuit demands, is a model the AACM never had much interest in furthering.) But *Sound* holds up as a smart and prophetic little manifesto. In its own way it was moral and political—all effective art is—but it broke away from the look-within-and-find-yourself gravity of Coltrane and his followers, bringing the focus back to the realm of aesthetics.

77. JOHN COLTRANE:

Interstellar Space

(IMPULSE! 314-543-415-2)

John Coltrane, tenor saxophone, bells; Rashied Ali, drums.

Recorded 1967

The last studio recording of John Coltrane was a whole album of saxophone-and-drums duets—something he'd done before with both Arthur Taylor and Elvin Jones, but only for one piece at a time. *Interstellar Space* wasn't necessarily meant to be a final statement, but it functions that way.

Technically, the final statement was a live recording from two months later, often bootlegged and released officially in 2001 as *The Olatunji Concert*. But by 1967 Coltrane had become adept in the studio and exercised great control over the recording process; his albums were sure to have a concentrated power, whereas his concerts became increasingly diffuse and pile-driving affairs, keening rackets roping together more last-minute guests than made sense.

Though it has long had a reputation as the John Coltrane album you'll never be ready to deal with, *Interstellar Space* returns to the sense of form that pervaded his albums of the late 1950s and early

1960s, such as *Giant Steps* and *Coltrane Jazz,* and actually provides a bridge between that period and his classic free-jazz period of *Ascension, Om,* and *Kulu Se Mama.*

The format of *Interstellar Space,* for all its intimidating reputation as an explosion of chaos, is actually rather astringently planned. At the beginning of each piece, Coltrane shakes little bells, and Ali begins a coloristic pattern; Coltrane then states the guiding melody fragment and begins to explore. At the end, the bells return.

His playing is intense, lusty, and sometimes smeared with harsh, abrasive noise, but it is not scattershot. He finds areas of exploration and methodically roots around in them. Four minutes into "Venus," he finds a pivot point in the middle register, oscillating back and forth from it toward dark low notes that work their way up the horn. Two minutes and twelve seconds into "Jupiter," Coltrane starts gushing descending scales, almost making them sound as if they're overlapping; he starts altering these with shrieks a minute later. Then around the five-minute mark he finally returns to the three-note theme, repeated and bounced around between octaves; when he's finished, as always, he shakes the bells again—as much a signal to Ali that he's finished as to the listener.

Coltrane didn't tell Ali much about what to do, other than that he would be going in and out of time, and Ali plays a kind of free drumming that has no tempo at all; it's a concatenation of rolls, fast single hits on the hi-hat, snare, and bass drum, and punctuations of sound. He is not reckless; if anything, he is respectful, and there's a rather smooth refinement in his playing.

The fascinating thing about Coltrane's controversial period beginning in 1965—he had already been controversial since *Live at the Village Vanguard* in 1961, but this was a controversy based on new, younger band mates and the generation-gap shock he caused—is that it didn't sever ties with the old Coltrane. "Saturn," for instance, is a rather obvious return to the swing feel of his mid-sixties quartet; the melody, and the six-four in Ali's rhythm, sounds like a reference to "Impressions."

There have been several different phases and strata of free jazz. First there was the music of Ornette Coleman and Cecil Taylor, which at least until the mid-1960s wasn't really free at all; they were playing tunes. Then there was Albert Ayler, who was also playing tunes but inimitably; the harmonic variation was narrow, and he co-opted a kind of pop-art official reality, writing pieces that sounded like national anthems, reveille, English folk songs, or clocktower melodies. It wasn't meant to spawn imitators; his own limitations would make copying him too obvious. And then there was Coltrane, who really gave posterity something to copy: he based his freedom on wide harmonic mobility, and it was disciplined. There was nothing prankish or pop about it.

Free jazz as it has carried on until today—David S. Ware, Peter Brötzmann, Assif Tsahar, Charles Gayle, and so on—comes from the music Coltrane made in his last two years. But the duo format of *Interstellar Space* was especially prescient. I once asked Borah Bergman, the pianist, why so many free-jazz musicians played in duos. He thought about *Interstellar Space,* and he thought about different motivations of players from completely different schools, until he got completely muddled. Then, a few days later, he faxed me a one-word answer: "economics." It's true that it is cheaper to travel and easier to break even as a duo than as part of a larger group. But the free-jazz duo as a viable artistic format with a history and a standard of excellence began here.

78. McCOY TYNER:

The Real McCoy

(BLUE NOTE 46512-2)

McCoy Tyner, piano; Joe Henderson, tenor saxophone; Ron Carter, bass; Elvin Jones, drums.

Recorded 1967

Within days of this album's creation, John Coltrane performed at a fund-raising event in New York City, and the surviving tape from that night was to become the posthumous *Olatunji Concert.* Measuring the distance between that and this, the greatest of Tyner's own albums, is instructive. It's vast. Coltrane, pressing against the limits of what he could do in music and perhaps aware of his own mortality, screamed through the horn, desperate to find the area beyond his field. (In another time, he might have gone into conceptual art.) But Tyner, still chewing over the formal qualities of what the Coltrane quartet had been playing in 1964, made the better album. He was helped immeasurably in this by Joe Henderson; though all five tunes on *The Real McCoy* are by Tyner, and Ron Carter and Elvin Jones contribute greatly to the music's deep center of gravity, you have to consider Henderson's contribution to it.

The history of Blue Note Records separates into easily distinct parts, and Henderson linked two of them. There were the initial recordings of boogie-woogie pianists and New Orleans musicians in the late 1930s. Then there was bop in the late 1940s and early 1950s, the time of Thelonious Monk and Bud Powell. In the late 1950s and early 1960s, there was hard bop (Art Blakey, Horace Silver, Sonny Clark, Hank Mobley) and soul-jazz (Jimmy Smith, Stanley Turrentine). Starting in 1964, there was something else: a four-year stretch of intensely volatile music that wasn't quite fish or fowl. It lay between traditionally patterned and free jazz; there was still a strong blues and gospel component in some of it, but the darker, more dissonant, and expressive playing both built in a more expansive structured tonality and grew outside tonality altogether.

Alfred Lion at Blue Note somehow charted his label's course so that it would remain as much in the middle of the old and new traditions as possible. What resulted was a fascinating play of vanguardism against roots, a constantly changing mainstream, like the idea of America's living constitution. *The Real McCoy* is in many ways a typical album of its time; it's not a significant marker of one particular style. It may have been three years behind the weather vane in 1967, but everyone, give or take a Miles Davis, was three years behind Coltrane at the end. Coltrane laid templates that left room for expansion and quickly moved on from them; you couldn't do better with the swing and energy suggested by mid-period Coltrane music than this. And this album, second tier though it may be, perfectly represents the mainstream of small-group jazz from the mid-sixties at least to the mid-nineties.

Henderson, an Ohioan, was discharged from the army in 1962 and headed for New York; he made his recording debut in 1963 on Kenny Dorham's *Una Mas,* one of the classic Blue Note records of the time. He was entering jazz at a fertile moment, when a few ambitious, challenging albums, such as *My Favorite Things* and *Kind of Blue,* had actually broken through to a wide audience; a new kind of self-possessed intellectualism was widespread in black music, and the factions between experimental and traditional hadn't yet become hardened. As a Blue Note session regular, Henderson found himself playing solos on Lee Morgan's *The Sidewinder,* an album full of bluesy, hard-bop tunes, and Andrew Hill's *Point of Departure* (above), with its opaque, knotted harmonies and rhythmic convolutions, within the same four-month stretch. He played more roadhouse riffs on the former, more abstract thematic improvising on the latter, and sounded perfectly in context doing each.

Arriving quickly, Henderson put down his mark fast. He was the great saxophone-playing linker of bop and free jazz, even more than Coltrane. He had a tonal range similar to Coltrane's in its guttural urgency, ranging in this album's "Passion Dance" from a classic, dapper tenor richness to a pinched, shrieking sound. Yet it was his own sound, with the grease of R&B players; he connected notes with a rubbery, portamento slide. He took his time; he sounded more joyful than Coltrane, as if he had less to lose. His sound was less self-conscious, happy to be a work in progress.

Tyner, on the other hand, through his seven-year stint with the Coltrane band (he and Elvin Jones had both bowed out of the group before this album was made, complaining that they couldn't hear each other in the din), had established the sound of jazz piano in the 1960s. Its hammering power, and its constant use of fourth chords in the static landscape of modal music, was the dominant sound of jazz piano. But *The Real McCoy* gets beyond that, too. The ballad "Search for Peace" has lighter colors, more chordal movement, and it doesn't use fourths except in a small sequence of Tyner's solo; "Blues on the Corner" balances perfectly between a bright, workaday hard-bop line and dire Coltrane music.

79. JAKI BYARD:

The Jaki Byard Experience

(PRESTIGE/FANTASY 1913-2)

Jaki Byard, piano; Rahsaan Roland Kirk, tenor saxophone, clarinet, whistle, manzello, kirkbam; Richard Davis, bass; Alan Dawson, drums.

Recorded 1968

Jaki Byard was a talked-about young musician in Boston in the 1940s, but it wasn't until the 1960s that he really found his decade. He was a natural combiner—of styles, of eras, of sensibilities—and the trickster-ish nature of that decade suited him. Like James P. Johnson, one of his idols—whose "Yamekraw" he condensed into a short excerpt on his album *Hi-Fly*—he saw jazz as a beginnings-to-future continuum, and there wasn't enough fun in it for him if he couldn't make stride and ragtime shake hands with avant-gardism.

His recordings demand some attention and some love; you have to meet them halfway. His string of albums for Prestige, produced by Don Schlitten, are a gold mine of repertory and original approaches to jazz, but they're often marred by bad pianos and not-so-great sound quality. Still, *The Jaki Byard Experience* might be the most valuable for putting him in more context, including as it does the contributions of Rahsaan Roland Kirk.

Both Byard and Roland Kirk, as he was then still known, were playing with Charles Mingus. And both might be considered along with Mingus as study-minded rabble-rousers—musicians who came by their subversions naturally but had too much practice and study in them to jump on the bandwagon of free jazz. Kirk was a combiner, too, and this album shows it: on "Teach Me Tonight" he plays lovely, spacious blues choruses on the tenor with old-fashioned vibrato; on a roustabout version of Thelonious Monk's "Evidence" he rushes the beat with impressive streams of sixteenth and thirty-secondth notes. But it's on "Evidence" in which Byard's solo, immediately following Kirk's, shows the greater wisdom of experience.

Kirk jumps into circular breathing after stating Monk's melody, and by the end of the first chorus his wind is starting to oscillate between weak and overstrong. It's an exciting solo, but it essentially goes through a decorous bebop first chorus as a formality and then, right on the first downstroke of the second chorus, goes crazy, saving its highest firepower for the bridge and final A-section of the third chorus. Byard, on the other hand, works in equal amounts of spaciousness and note flinging in the first chorus; lands on a useful idée fixe (a blues scale hammered top-to-bottom in chords) in the second, ending the second with Monkish rhythm; in the third, he pours in the notes but becomes decorous again in its bridge and ends with a pronounced trill. Essentially, both musicians are using a similar comportment, but Byard handles his with provocative tension and release, while Kirk, after the introduction, is all tension.

Not to denigrate Kirk, a great artist, but his overloading power comes so close to stealing this record that one must pay attention to Byard's canniness. "Evidence," with all its modern wallop, is followed by Eubie Blake's "Memories of You," in which Byard plays an absolutely first-rate solo at slow tempo in stride rhythm, full of lurching accents and no-left-hand divagations—a take on Tatum in which a newer sensibility peeks out.

This is an album full of New York piano history, with its Bud Powell, its Tatum, its Monk, its Blake. You can look elsewhere for the influence of European modernist composition on Byard (like the great suite "European Episodes" on his *Out Front!* album). But Byard, who was nearing eighty when he was murdered at home in 1999 (the trail has gone cold, and the motive is still a mystery), was shaping up to be the paterfamilias of old-into-new musicians—surely of Jason Moran, Marty Ehrlich, and Michael Moore, who were among his students, but of Marcus Roberts, too, who hasn't mentioned Byard's influence.

80. MILES DAVIS:

Get Up with It

(COLUMBIA LEGACY C2K 63970, 2 CDS)

Miles Davis, trumpet, electric piano, organ; Dave Liebman, Sonny Fortune, flute; Steve Grossman, Carlos Garnett, soprano saxophone; Pete Cosey, Reggie Lucas, John McLaughlin, Dominique Gaumont, guitar; Michael Henderson, electric bass; Cedric Lawson, Keith Jarrett, electric piano; Herbie Hancock, clavinet; Khalil Balakrishna, electric sitar; Billy Cobham, Al Foster, Bernard Purdie, drums; Mtume, Airto Moreira, percussion; Badal Roy, tabla; Wade Marcus, brass arrangement; Billy Jackson, rhythm arrangement.

Recorded 1970–1974

By this time, Davis wasn't using tenor or alto saxophone. He himself was not playing trumpet for long stretches. He was making records with Teo Macero as producer, and from the time of 1969's *In a Silent Way* Macero had become interested in postproduction tape splicing, making larger canvases out of short pieces, making short pieces out of long jams.

In the early 1970s, Davis's record making was very different from his performances: live, he arranged the improvisation with brutal efficacy, bringing out sections of the band, letting musicians start up vamps with no preparation but a key and a rhythm, and sometimes not even that. There was plenty of real-time shaping going on. In the studio, he laid down music in three-hour bursts, then called an end to the session without the musicians having the slightest idea about how what they'd done might be used.

This album, recorded in chunks over four years, is a capstone on a wild period. All the other albums of the early-seventies electric period, before Davis's six-year silence beginning in 1975, represent more or less a single sound; they're monolithic. But this is an album of extremes. "He Loved Him Madly," thirty-two minutes long and inspired by a Christmas card Davis received from Duke Ellington, is still the subject of debate: had *anything* at all been planned for the track? (Mtume, the percussionist, says no; the guitarist Dominique Gaumont says yes, a melodic line was rehearsed.) It doesn't matter; this is a rare example of music that sounds like breathing, like nature. It has a tender, slow drum groove, and organ parts made by Davis that are usually clusters; Dave Liebman's flute playing has such a heavy application of reverb that it sounds like he might be down a well. It is nearly motionless, and its length can make you wonder what on earth Davis was doing. A close listening reveals the tape edits; the contributions of musicians drift in and out. But it has an atmosphere, a kind of erotic lethargy, that's special in music.

Far to the other end of the spectrum, there's "Rated X"—a fast seven minutes, thudding and dense, with funk that's so thick it barely breathes. Guitars and keyboards stay on one chord each through wah-wah pedals; Davis's organ is a constant, and the rest of the band appears and disappears, cut off mercilessly to create gaps at moments of unbearable intensity, as when Davis presses a forearm on a pile of organ notes. It's filthy, frightening music. Davis alienated many people with it. And its legacy keeps lingering, through the work of bands such as Tortoise and Radiohead. In the way it was made and the way it was fooled with afterward—not to mention the larger, philosophical ideas of songs that he was broaching—there were tools that rock bands could really mine and are only in recent years beginning to deal with.

Disc two is slightly less interesting for the inclusion of "Red China Blues," a standard blues redeemed (possibly) by Davis's wah-wah trumpet. (It's puzzling why it was included; the album gives you a clue that it isn't exactly an A-item, with the credits to Wade Marcus for "brass arrangement" and Billy Jackson for "rhythm arrangement"— not areas Davis particularly needed help with.) But it has another strong thirty-minute track, "Calypso Frelimo," as well as the churning "Mtume" and "Billy Preston," the only funk track on the album more inspired by the American vernacular than by European avant-gardism.

Karlheinz Stockhausen, the German avant-garde composer, is said to be hovering over *Get Up with It,* via his influence on Paul Buckmaster, an English cellist and composer who gave Miles aesthetic guidance during this period. But aside from some hard edits and the collision of electronics and acoustic instruments, Stockhausen didn't make music that sounded remotely like this.

Get Up with It is several steps beyond Davis's famous *Bitches Brew* (1970), even several steps beyond the strange but conceptually unified *On the Corner* (1972). It's not a sellout for rock audiences; it's not a sellout for anybody, particularly. The total abstraction of funk—done by musicians who really were from funk, like the bassist Michael Henderson and the guitarist Pete Cosey—was one of Davis's greatest ideas, and *Get Up with It* presents ideas that must be chewed over for a long time before they're understood. For the Miles Davis enthusiast, and for anyone interested in the intersection of jazz with the vanguard of electric music, the album is always just sitting there, glowering at you; it must be dealt with in sections, bit by bit, over time.

81. MAHAVISHNU ORCHESTRA:

The Inner Mounting Flame

(COLUMBIA LEGACY 65523)

John McLaughlin, guitar; Jerry Goodman, violin; Jan Hammer, piano; Rick Laird, bass; Billy Cobham, drums.

Recorded 1971

John McLaughlin moved fast upon relocating to America from England in 1969. He joined the band Lifetime, led by Tony Williams, Miles Davis's former drummer. Williams had been the youngest member in the group and the one most open to the new rock of the 1960s; Lifetime still bears a blitzkrieg power. Verve, which released its initial album, seemed not to know how to record such distortion, and its dirty sound quality seemed fitting, as if the tape had been scorched by the music.

McLaughlin was a new kind of player in jazz. His experience in England was split between working with rock people such as Graham Bond and Eric Clapton and working himself into Ronnie Scott's new music, which was still based in a resolutely jazz aesthetic. Starting in

Lifetime, he played a solid-body guitar, with none of the resonating, natural tone of jazz guitarists in the past (except maybe for Sonny Sharrock, who will always be an oddity). In the chronology of jazz-rock, Gary Burton's *Duster,* from 1967, featuring a young Larry Coryell on guitar, probably comes first. Miles Davis's *In a Silent Way,* from 1969, was the next significant step, though still sonically rather soft. Lifetime's first album, *Emergency!,* was recorded several months before Davis's *Bitches Brew,* the work that paved a marketplace for jazz-rock.

On *The Inner Mounting Flame,* the first album by McLaughlin's own band, the guitarist has an unrepentantly hard-rock sound, pushed up to a screaming-tubes level at which a note could be sustained for ten seconds, but he manipulated it with the fleet rhythmic vitality of a bullish jazz player. And he also got more dirt in his chord sound than did, say, Led Zeppelin's Jimmy Page. I've always been puzzled by the use of Jerry Goodman on violin in this group; what exactly did the instrument add? Maybe a folk element, a more universal element, connecting it to the driving sound of eastern European folkloric string music (certainly not to fiddle playing in American country music). But Jan Hammer's electric keyboard, in the total sound mass, was necessary; ever since Herbie Hancock started using it with Davis in 1967, the mentholated, distortable sound of the Fender Rhodes was the signature timbre of the new music. And Billy Cobham, the rhythm-rushing drummer, was another connection to Davis, having played on the trumpeter's sessions prior to recording with Mahavishnu.

The song material here isn't the single-chord vamps that McLaughlin had been playing to such good effect with Williams and Miles Davis (on *In a Silent Way, Jack Johnson, Bitches Brew,* and *Big Fun*). The new music is fast, busy, mathematical, downshifting at times into the familiar, like the rocking blues figure in "The Dance of Maya." But "A Lotus on Irish Streams," with speed-demon Spanish-guitar improvisation leading toward a slow piano-guitar-violin rhapsody, is something else altogether—the organic-hippie side of a frightening-monster music. This element (again, with the exception of Sonny Sharrock) would always go hand in hand with jazz-rock. The model was being set, and it would play itself out in a lot of different ways: into other jazz-fusion with Weather Report and Return to Forever; into rock with groups such as Kansas and the Charlie Daniels Band; even into heavy metal thirty years later with bands such as Candiria and Dillinger Escape Plan.

82. EDDIE PALMIERI AND HIS ORCHESTRA:

Vamonos Pa'l Monte

(TICO 1225)

Eddie Palmieri, piano, keyboards; Charlie Palmieri, organ; Ismael Quintana, vocal; Bob Vianco, guitar; Jose Rodriguez, trombone; Alfredo Armenteros, Victor Paz, Charles Camilleri, trumpet; Pete Yellin, tenor saxophone; Ronnie Cuber, baritone saxophone; Nick Marrero, timbales, bongo; Eladio Perez, conga; Arturo Franquiz, clave, chorus; Monchito Muñoz, bomba; Santos Colon, Justo Betancourt, Marcelino Guerra, Yayo El Indio, Elliot Ramero, Mario Muñoz, chorus.

Recorded 1971

For four decades, Eddie Palmieri has been refashioning Latin music. And though bred-in-the-bone innovators often aren't the best weather vanes for what's popular in a music, sometimes—compare Miles Davis—they are.

Palmieri's first popular band, Conjunto La Perfecta—formed in 1961—brought the sound of trombones into a *charanga*-band front line, which had traditionally been flutes and violins, based on the courtly *danza* tradition of Cuban music. Why did he do this? Because in the early 1960s *charanga* was starting to look like an anachronism and because Palmieri had paid sporadic but close attention to jazz, studying pianists as diverse as Art Tatum, Bill Evans, Dick Twardzik, and McCoy Tyner. Yet beyond this structural innovation, his music performed as an Afro-Cuban popular music; rhythmically, it hadn't changed, and Conjunto La Perfecta was for all intents and purposes a dance orchestra.

Ten years later, everything was different. New York salsa exploded in the late sixties and became immensely popular; with popularity comes decadence, innovation, subversion. And jazz-fusion appealed to Latin musicians; it depended on virtuosity and pleasure and was innately (by its incorporation of million-selling elements) a popular art. (Going to a salsa club on a good night—even now, long after the high days of salsa—is the closest one can come to experiencing what the atmosphere for jazz might have been like in the 1930s, when it was a complex and popular art that was responded to by dancing.)

By 1971, the time of *Vamonos Pa'l Monte,* the climate was right for Palmieri to follow the lead of experimental jazz and experimental rock and incorporate freer structures into his music; it was possible to make albums that weren't really for dancing anymore. *Vamonos Pa'l Monte* is a kind of jazz-fusion album, but in the vein of Miles Davis's *Bitches Brew* rather than, say, a Mahavishnu Orchestra album. It's not just an eruption of chops; it's spacey in stretches and uses strange, counterintuitive mix and production techniques, with plenty of echo.

A tune like "Caminando," driven by a mambo rhythm and Palmieri's distorted electric piano, reflects not just the cute, compact, poplike melodies of hard-bop jazz but also the new fuzzed-out Latin funk of the group War. And at the same time the music keeps returning to traditional elements—the basic setup of a *sonero* singer (Ismael Quintana) improvising against a vocal chorus in "La Libertad Logico"; the double-trombone chases of the sort made popular by Willie Colon in the late sixties; the customary orchestral rhythms built from timbals, bongo, and conga; the cyclical *guajeo* piano lines common to Cuban music and salsa.

Essentially, Palmieri was easing new elements into salsa without accomplishing the full split from tradition that European culture dictates as the meaning of innovation. More than thirty years later, he's still working at this gradual process of adding and subtracting; the only audience he has estranged is the hard-core dancers, who are always the most fickle and judgmental listeners.

83. EARL HINES:

Earl Hines Plays Duke Ellington

(NEW WORLD 8031-2, 2 CDS)

Earl Hines, solo piano.

Recorded 1971–1975

Jazz musicians didn't start beholding and celebrating their own collective achievement in the 1980s. The first wave of homage-tribute-analysis arrived in the 1960s.

Many of these album and concert projects were about Thelonious Monk. Why Monk? Because he had always been attractively independent and unbound by subgenre or cliché; because his work—solo, quartet, and big band—encapsulated much of the endeavor of jazz since it had become an art form shared by all kinds of Americans; because he created nuggets of melody, harmony, and rhythm (often all in the same small sequences of music) that jazz musicians wanted keenly to expand on; because at that time he suggested the past and the future of the music and had found a new, hard-won success after 1962.

The next candidate for study was obviously Ellington. He, too, was still alive, still creating art of high quality (the *New Orleans Suite* and *Sacred Concerts* are not to be condescended to), and his aesthetic palette was vast; musicians could approach him from many different angles and still make something of value. (He was, after all, a father to many of those angles.)

Earl Hines and Duke Ellington were shaped by many of the same forces—most notably the New York stride-piano tradition—and came to the fore as important figures at about the same time, in the late 1920s. Hines had a few inventions: he hybridized the role of the left hand, making it both a timekeeper and a melody shaper; and he was able to mirror the new arialike strength in soloing that Louis Armstrong had proposed as a trumpet player. In doing so, he was able to create improvisations that weren't necessarily based on the song's themes; they were original material. And Hines, who had wanted to become a classical concert pianist in his youth, had the technique to pull off this new soloist role.

But in Hines's career, outside of his ill-timed modernist big band (largely unrecorded because of musicians' union bans in the 1940s), he was prized as a soloist more than as a composer or arranger. By the 1960s, he was down on his luck, as many great jazz musicians were, and his method of creating a comeback was largely as a solo pianist.

Through the agency of friends and producers, he recorded solo-piano albums that dealt with a number of individual composers. (Surely Stanley Dance, his great champion through the final years, thought of Art Tatum's legacy, enhanced so greatly in the end by the monumental series of solo-piano recordings that Norman Granz persuaded him to make.) *Earl Hines Plays Duke Ellington* was among the last, recorded as two LPs across four years. It presents twenty transformative versions, and it's as good an example of the jazz process as anything out there.

Hines was a florid pianist, one who liked—for example—to offset a strong bass-clef rhythm (boogie-woogie, stride, or something of his own devising) with mobile tremolos in the right hand. There was always a range and a balance going on, on micro and macro levels; none of his work is dry. He could also be an eccentric player, in ways that surely grew out of his early experience in the competitive, stylized world of the independent New York piano tickler. (For early evidence of that tendency, consider his 1940 "Child of a Disordered Brain.") In approaching Ellington music, he was going to be as balanced as he could: this was music he respected, and therefore he would have to let the compositions shine through while stamping out his own ingots.

He created his own structure as he went along. When he recast the accents of a melody—as he does in "Don't Get Around Much Anymore"—he does so only after stating it in the way it was made famous; having done so, he makes something of it, building on his own idea. He abstracts chord changes and makes new material out of them or blasts down the runway for a while on a single chord. (Hear the last three minutes of "Don't Get Around Much Anymore," or "C Jam Blues.") When you've pegged him as a crowd-pleasing pianist who keeps tempos steady, he veers off and double-times or plays rubato. ("I'm Beginning to See the Light" condenses these changes within a relatively short track, ending in dire, out-of-rhythm French-impressionist chords.)

These performances are quite elaborate: the original three-minute hits are routinely stretched out to six minutes, and "Black Butterfly" is a pièce-de-résistance 10:42. "Black Butterfly" proceeds slowly, and after the initial melodic statement, before the solo choruses begin in earnest, there's a jagged pause in the right hand, rare for Hines. You become aware that you're settling in for a ride. After a minute of sweet, slow, decorous playing, the next chorus (forecasted by three stirring, staccato introductory chords) jangles the nerves, his hands working independently. The next one arrives slyly, medium tranquil, and double-timed, with ingenious variation in the right hand. And so on, arriving at a landing in a slow approach. (There is another forte, fractured sequence, giving way to drawing-room quiescence over the last two minutes—it could be the work of two entirely different musicians.) As a whole, it is masterful.

So Hines doesn't blast the original away from the beginning, as Tatum did; and he doesn't leave you feeling replete after two songs. He improvises in melody and harmony, and he improvises in form.

84. JULIUS HEMPHILL:

Dogon A.D.

(MBARI, LP ONLY)

Julius Hemphill, alto saxophone, flute; Abdul Wadud, cello; Baikaida Yaseen, trumpet; Phillip Wilson, drums.

Recorded 1972

This album hasn't been in print on CD for a decade. Do I have an agenda in including it? Yes, I have an agenda.

The jazz musicians of the early 1970s had to make a very conscious decision to go into jazz. The money was ridiculously bad—there was no market for jazz at the time—whereas the touring R&B groups, in which you could make a better living, were still plentiful. But idealism is powerful enough to make money a secondary issue, and the range of expression available in jazz was growing; many different kinds of artists could now get involved.

The AACM in Chicago was extending technique and composition, as was the BAG (Black Artists Group) in Saint Louis, a musicians' collective that included Julius Hemphill. In New York, where many of these musicians moved in the early seventies, a new self-sufficient, self-promotional scene was developing downtown, in unregulated artists' lofts. It would continue through the early eighties, a galaxy unto itself, documented by tiny labels and low-budget filmmakers. Long, free-form jams were its bricks and mortar. Its breakout stars were Arthur Blythe and David Murray; its supergroup was to be the World Saxophone Quartet, which included Hemphill; its spirit continues today in the circle of musicians around the bassist William Parker and his annual Vision Festival.

But this is perhaps the first great document of the New York loft scene, the first great structural statement of a new era. Hemphill was interested in long, patient explorations, but he wasn't an incantational droner. He had a keen imagination and a wicked sense of humor. He was from Texas and sounded authentic playing the blues; he had spent some time in funk bands as well. But he was an artist, an original thinker, and was fascinated, essentially, by new kinds of American vernacular chamber music. That was the idea behind the World Saxophone Quartet; but the idea goes back further.

Dogon A.D., which Hemphill put out on his own Mbari label before anyone had ever heard of him, is a dry, pretty, wide-open-spaces record. Its instrumentation is lean, as if to refute the density that experimental jazz had been accruing. The music searches, but never impetuously; all these players were self-possessed and remained so through their careers. Instead of a bass player, the quartet included cellist Abdul Wadud, who functions here as a lead instrument, bowing and plucking equally, playing guitarlike chords, lining out melodies. All musicians rarely play together at once. Two or three establish backbonelike rhythmic or melodic cycles (such as *Dogon A.D.*'s funk in an eleven-beat rhythm, or the cello vamps in "The Painter"), and the quiet improvisations accompanying them serve as commentary. There are only three tracks, but each needs all the time that it is given.

It is a beautiful and unpretentious album, and this low-key beauty needed to return to American free jazz, which was losing sight of its own aims, becoming engulfed in radical politics, disoriented by the deaths of Albert Ayler and John Coltrane.

Hemphill died in 1995, after much artistic expansion: he provided most of the best music for the World Saxophone Quartet; he wrote an opera, as well as music to accompany Bill T. Jones's dance company and also some classical-music pieces; and he perfected a saxophone sextet that played his own increasingly gorgeous compositions, a kind of R&B rethought from the ground up, with beautiful, sliding harmonies.

85. PAT METHENY:

Bright Size Life

(ECM 1073)

Pat Metheny, guitar; Jaco Pastorius, bass; Bob Moses, drums.

Recorded 1975

Since the 1970s, Pat Metheny's music has cut across the field of serious adult popular music in the same way that Brazilian popular music has and for good reason: they are intertwined. *Bright Size Life,* Metheny's first album—a remarkably strong statement for a twenty-one-year-old and one that's quite resilient more than twenty-five years later—has a silver-hued openness, a sensuality, that some might designate as American. (Some of his unusual guitar tunings and open harmonies can bring to mind Americanist musicians such as John Fahey or Leo Kottke.) But in its context, it's much more connected to the romanticism of Milton Nascimento's first three albums between 1969 and 1973, early Ivan Lins material, and the work of Toninho Horta, a composer and guitarist who had worked with Nascimento.

In jazz, the emphasis on song had decreased enormously since the 1940s. Bebop turned the music's preeminent convention toward new harmonies and variations on well-worn changes. Various kinds of jazz in the 1950s and 1960s prized qualities that lay on the intellectual side: texture, repetition, density, multipart form, rhythmic and melodic looseness, "classical" instrumentation. Serious ballad writing had disappeared, for the most part, and the dominant language for jazz guitarists was blues (via Wes Montgomery) and, in smatterings, bebop (via Kenny Burrell); if Jim Hall paved the way for a number of possible redirections, Metheny seized the opportunity and ran. He brought back ballads, writing poignant, romantic songs—on *Bright Size Life*, just about every song falls into that category—with impressive harmony; his solos were notey.

But the solos' learned, ferociously schooled quality made them the property of jazz; his application of echo and digital delay to a jazz guitarist's classic dry tone created a liquid sound that became hugely influential in the jazz language. Systematically, Metheny built a school, or at least a platform for others with different backgrounds (such as Bill Frisell) to perch on. The guitar became an important part of jazz. If there are cultlike aspects to the guitar scene now centering around the Berklee School of Music in Boston, it is a large cult with its own language.

Metheny's career has been broad. What you might not hear through his exact technique is a deep love for Ornette Coleman, and Metheny has found several ways to penetrate the mysteries of Coleman's small-group language—first among them hiring Coleman and his sidemen Dewey Redman and Charlie Haden. He's worked with the deepest of jazz drummers, Roy Haynes and Jack DeJohnette, and the most beat rushing of jazz-fusion rhythm sections. He's toyed with solo-guitar music as pure abstract noise (*Zero Tolerance for Silence*) and performed duets with the most entrenched of avant-garde guitarists, Derek Bailey. There's a rare dualism here—the narrow, academic, chess-club concentration of the Boston guitar school and Metheny's natural disposition toward making music that sounds popular.

In his own nonconfrontational way, Metheny has been forceful about jazz as an evolutionary language, which can and should change beyond recognition. "My contention has always been that jazz is, and I hope will always be, a form of folk music, but a very, very serious and sophisticated folk music, almost a scientific folk music, " he said in his keynote address to the IAJE (International Association of Jazz Educators) convention in 2001. "I am talking about the tradition of musicians using every aspect, all the materials, all the sounds and moves and vibes and spirits of their time in a musical way. The attempts to make jazz something more like classical music, like baroque music for instance, with a defined set of rules and regulations and boundaries and qualities that must be present and observed and respected at all times, have always made me uncomfortable."

That a musician of such stature, with more or less the largest core following in jazz, should be saying this marked an interesting development in the tradition-versus-experimentation dialogue. Since *Offramp* (1991), some of Metheny's music has been formatted as pop-jazz, played in the smooth-jazz radio format; he has certainly made commercial choices in his career. But the core of his being remains rather intellectual, coming out of an almost European art-music predilection for originality.

86. EVAN PARKER:

Monoceros

(CHRONOSCOPE CPE2004-2)

Evan Parker, solo soprano saxophone.

Recorded 1978

In describing Evan Parker's music, sooner or later you're going to use a circle metaphor—a wheel, a mandala, a spiral.

Since 1965 or thereabouts, he's been rigorously attached to a narrowly focused kind of soprano-saxophone language, one more or less of his own devising. In it, the normal jazz improviser's code of conversational broken phrases is discarded in favor of long, continuous statements; Parker uses the technique of circular breathing and can blow without pausing for twenty minutes or more. But rather than droning, he gives you bunches of notes that come stippled with ornament, making low tones and high overtones collide, trilling them and rolling them together so closely into line that he sounds as if he's playing two instruments at once.

Typically, he lights upon distinct patterns, generates a fairly small range of harmony, and uses a handful of favorite polyrhythms that he taps out on the keys. It's a system, and it's instantly easy to follow, but it is mysterious, too. His performances launch such a complex barrage on the ears, with such an original use of wind and stamina, that they seem polymorphous: they start as coldly as math and then turn into sex. When I think about Parker in the abstract, I can't imagine getting any more out of his performances than I already have, and so many of his records seem similar. Then I hear a good one, or I see him perform, and I'm surprised by how deeply he's reaching, how profoundly affecting he can be.

Parker is contingently related to jazz—as much as Bob Wills, say. He is an improviser, and he plays in contexts that jazz has claimed (solo and duo improvisation, saxophone-piano-drums trios such as his own with Barry Guy and Tony Oxley, as well as another led by pianist Alex Von Schlippenbach). He is listened to largely by those who listen to jazz. His double- and triple-tonguing techniques, his circular breathing, his fast, cyclical arpeggiation—these are things that he found in jazz early in his education, in Coltrane and Dolphy and John Tchicai, and wanted to expand upon. That he does so at the expense of the rest of jazz's recognizable harmonic and melodic material does also put him in another tradition—that of the European abstract improviser, alongside musicians such as Derek Bailey and the members of the group AMM (Keith Rowe, Eddie Prevost, John Tilbury).

Far from being without idiom or context, the European abstract improvisation scene is hyperidiomatic: it produces unconvincing copycat players (there are many Sonny Stitts to Evan Parker's Charlie Parker), has its own rather hermetic festivals, and has more or less exhausted itself. A new form, electro-acoustic improvisation, in which computers and digital processors interact with acoustic instruments, is threatening to eclipse Parker's original context completely.

Parker, wisely, has already begun working with live processing. But in 1978, the pure, undiluted process of nonsonglike improvisation from scratch was an exciting idea. *Monoceros*—one of Parker's strongest solo albums—was recorded in one take, using direct-to-disc technology, in which the music was transmitted onto a disc without the middle step of tape. This wasted less studio time and forced the improviser to be as perfect as possible, since there was no possibility of going back to a tape and editing it. And indeed there is a supercharged, paratrooper aspect about the whole enterprise.

Parker, who has an interest in science, writes in the liner notes to the reissue of this album that "the saxophone has been for me a rather specialized bio-feedback instrument for studying and expanding my control over my hearing and the motor mechanics of parts of my skeleto-muscular system, and their improved functioning has given me more to think about." It is, in a sense, music for his own purposes; it's the ultimate research music, in that Parker isn't only researching a set of tones as tones, he's researching himself. But it is not a listener-be-damned situation. Because as he alters his own hearing, he alters yours.

87. BETTY CARTER:

The Audience with Betty Carter

(VERVE 835-684-2)

Betty Carter, vocals; John Hicks, piano; Curtis Lundy, bass; Kenny Washington, drums.

Recorded 1979

Betty Carter initially struck jazz critics as too strident. It was the way she leaped inside words, pushing her alto to breathy high notes and swooping down to an exaggerated bottom register, drawing out phrases like a sad sack, almost as if joking—or as if daring to use the emotional range allowable to male singers, which, in fact, she was.

Seeing her was a physical experience: her time spent singing with big bands (she toured with Lionel Hampton in the late 1940s) taught her about projection and interacting with audiences, and by the 1970s her time battling the vagaries of the jazz world—contracts, managers, promoters, musicians who found her too demanding—gave her a stinging authority. Early on, she became interested in arranging and exerting a control over her musicians during performances that wasn't common to jazz singers. Until her death in 1997, she perfected a technique that gave her the role of a bandleader and a musician, not just a singer. She tripped up her players with false starts, set breakneck tempos for the rhythm section to ride from the start of a tune, then suddenly switched up, keeping musicians and audience on guard.

As a singer, she didn't present a popular song in a neat package. As Michael Ondaatje is a line-by-line novelist—which is to say, his larger structures aren't as impressive as the sureness with which he writes a single sentence—Carter was a line-by-line singer. In the standard "Spring Can Really Hang You Up the Most," on *The Audience with Betty Carter,* you can feel the furious mental processing going into the delivery of only a few words at a time. And as she does so, the dynamics of the band vary wildly, according to her directives. It's a hot-lava performance; she takes very little about the song for granted.

For all her insistence on spontaneity and variation—the art material of jazz singing—she knew how to connect with an audience in an eerily personal manner. In one word she could dislodge tears. The idée fixe in her own lyrics, as in "Thirty Years" and "Tight," was the difficulty of maintaining relationships and the luck of having something go right in your life; she made you feel her commitment to the idea that all successes are hard-won, and you were flattered that such an imposing person was working so hard for your benefit.

The Audience with Betty Carter, recorded live in San Francisco, begins with a twenty-five-minute track, "Sounds," full of the improvised form shifting that she'd become known for. It includes a flying-tempo version of "The Trolley Song" (it hits considerably more than 208 beats per minute, the high end of a standard metronome), a "My Favorite Things" with extreme tempos, where she rushes through lyrics in the slow parts and draws them out in the fast parts, and three of her best originals, "Tight," "Fake," and "Open the Door."

Carter ran her own record label for several years, Bet-Car Records, and she released *The Audience with Betty Carter* on her own. Verve wisely bought the rights when it signed Carter at the end of the eighties. It's the best single representation of who she was; she's all here. It could be an album that sums up her career; all that's missing to understand who she was even a decade later is the gravitas her voice and personality acquired in the later years.

She was also known for her policy of always hiring young, unknown musicians in order to train them, put their names out in the world, and help them grow up as men. In this practice, during the last forty years of jazz she's second only to Art Blakey, who used his Jazz Messengers band as a similar proving ground. The musicians who passed through her band in the 1990s are among the best sidemen, if not leaders, today: saxophonist Mark Shim, pianists Cyrus Chestnut and Marc Cary; bassists Tarus Mateen and Dwayne Burno; drummers Clarence Penn and Lewis Nash.

Carter thrived on competition. According to William R. Bauer's biography, *Open the Door,* she created devices to challenge, confuse, and even irritate her musicians through music so that they would strike back by playing harder. And she was sure of herself: "After me there are no more jazz singers," she declared to the drummer Arthur Taylor in 1972 (in an interview collected in Taylor's book *Notes and Tones*). That's remarkably early in her own life to say such a thing, but we may understand it as a challenge that she threw out in the hopes that somebody would prove her wrong. It's almost true: she took the traditional art of jazz singing about as far as it could go, and now the best new singers are coming from rather different traditions altogether, using jazz as one ingredient among many.

88. THE HENRY THREADGILL SEXTET:

Just the Facts and Pass the Bucket

(ABOUT TIME 1005)

Henry Threadgill, flute, clarinet, alto and baritone saxophones; Fred Hopkins, bass; Pheeroan AkLaff, John Betsch, drums; Olu Dara, cornet; Craig Harris, trombone; Deirdre Murray, cello.

Recorded 1983

Plenty of jazz musicians have varied backgrounds in listening and playing. But with Henry Threadgill, because his music *sounds* so varied and so different, it's instructive to know what he remembers listening to. As he told Ted Panken in 1996, that included "Western European classical music, a lot of Polish-American and American-Mexican music, a lot of black gospel music, and what we called 'hillbilly' music, and of course boogie-woogie piano."

Chicago, Threadgill's hometown, was a culturally fertile place in the 1960s. As far as its black population was concerned, it was a southern town in the Midwest; its artists, having transplanted themselves or having come from transplanted families, had a self-determinative streak. The city produced Howlin' Wolf and Muddy Waters; important strains of gospel music, including Thomas Dorsey and Sam Cooke; and some of the most individual-sounding saxophone players in the history of jazz—musicians who almost have to be considered as schools unto themselves, such as Von Freeman, Eddie Harris, and Gene Ammons. Threadgill learned the classical repertoire, as did everyone who was taught classical music in university; he performed with VFW Post bands, playing Dixieland and Sousa marches; he played with a traveling evangelist preacher, Horace Shepherd from Philadelphia. And he became drawn to Muhal Richard Abrams and the Experimental Band, an avant-garde congregation that later became the AACM.

Threadgill, his music expressing a curiousness and quick-wittedness from the start, was a natural for the AACM. But it doesn't seem as if that organization was the central fact in his life, as it does for many of its older members. His music grew its own definition, and by the 1980s, with his sextet, he was writing music that sounded like a Webern string quartet one minute, a roadhouse funk band the next. His adept manipulation of forms as far apart (putatively speaking) as those is a great achievement.

But if the funk claimed his sense of rhythm, the Webern claimed his soul: he believes in ordered music, and improvisations were given short, concise windows in the sextet. It is difficult music to play. *Just the Facts and Pass the Bucket,* the second album by the group, shows Threadgill at the peak of his powers as a composer: "Gateway" still stands as perhaps the single best piece of writing he's done.

The sextet—which had seven members and was later rendered "Sextett"—had two trap-set drummers, which has never, in my experience, been a bad idea. (I'm thinking, mostly, of live experiences: the Grateful Dead, Pere Ubu, the Allman Brothers, Sonny Sharrock, a band Marcus Roberts had for a minute, a band Joe Lovano had for a minute.) It had, in a sense, two bassists, with the heavy-toned Fred Hopkins and

Deirdre Murray playing her cello like an avant-garde Oscar Pettiford, full of rhythmic drive. It had two brass instruments. And Threadgill's role was something like the leader of a Pentecostal gospel group, or like George Clinton's: he isn't the star soloist but the composer/director/focal point.

Which isn't to say that his alto-saxophone solos aren't great in their own way. They're urgent, rhythmically gapped, and they quickly get to shouting. (His flute playing, tending toward full-bodied long notes and quieter textures, has a completely different character.) It's just that the group's concept was paramount, and this music really fulfilled something that jazz listeners were looking for in the 1980s. We'd had Ayler and Coleman and Taylor; we needed the dance impulse back, but we also needed to be befuddled again. We needed to try to figure out where this music was coming from and ask ourselves what jazz is.

89. WYNTON MARSALIS:

Live at Blues Alley

(COLUMBIA G2K-40675)

Wynton Marsalis, trumpet; Marcus Roberts, piano; Robert Leslie Hurst III, bass; Jeff "Tain" Watts, drums.

Recorded 1986

Wynton Marsalis came into jazz right when the stock of the posthippie generation was untested and very high. It seems so long ago: in the early eighties, jazz still had strong associations with a kind of lingering black nationalism, and its New York avant-garde underground was revered enough as to be thought heroic. Those avant-gardists were bucking the odds, working against a rising pop market; nothing could touch Michael Jackson in 1982, but David Murray, Arthur Blythe, and Henry Threadgill were pretty widely seen as the newest guarantors of quality in a tattered, shallow jazz world.

In came Marsalis. First, he functioned as eager musicians do, sitting

Wynton Marsalis

in here and there, forming associations that now seem odd or intriguing. (He was a member of the New York Hot Trumpet Quintet, alongside Lester Bowie, for a short time in the early 1980s.) But quickly he formed his own style, and it did look like a straight arrow's reaction against all the freedom and vagueness in the new jazz. He found success very quickly; three years after moving to New York, he had a deal with Columbia. Since bohemia is another form of high school, Marsalis was treated like a leper, and since money creates powerful allies, those who accused Marsalis of being square were treated in turn like lepers.

By the mid-eighties, Marsalis's small-band concept had jelled. There was some early-sixties Coltrane in it, for its density and its attention to timbre; but it had a different rhythmic feeling, one that was more forthright and wakeful, in which a walking bass and a strong drummer made the songs stand at attention. Marsalis was trying to have a trumpet sound that was as complete as it could be. Its tone was full, producing notes that had a rich center, as opposed to the thinner, spindlier trumpet tones floating around the avant-garde jazz scene. He played an awful lot of notes, and they were true and in rhythm. If anything, his drive to cut through the mist and make a new black American instrumental music of extravagant talent and technique didn't leave much to the imagination. His music was and is very rarely mysterious.

Yet it was quite complicated. The Wynton Marsalis Quartet didn't play in a one-size-fits-all style; the music wasn't built on a standard, unchanging time signature and the theme-solos-theme format. It was fragmented but explicitly so. Jeff Watts did keep changing the focus of his rhythm, though he was always playing a *rhythm*.

Marsalis's compositions during this period weren't especially memorable; their themes were chromatic and very rhythmic and needed the right kind of band interplay to make them sound good. (In other words, they were difficult to whistle.) A lot of critics complained about Marsalis's lack of faith in abstraction, but his band had a strategy for its own kind of free jazz—the "burnout" style, as Marsalis called it, adapted from mid-sixties Coltrane. It was a method that could be freely applied to a tune or not ("Knozz-Moe-King" is the test case on *Live at Blues Alley,* with four different versions)—Marsalis would make his trumpet whinny and shout but always with a trackable relation to the song's tonal center. Jeff Watts broke up his rhythm, but the accent on the two and four was always implied. He played polyrhythms, but the pulse never sagged. Audiences loved it; it was expressive, and it wasn't obscurantist. Yet if a traveling musician from an earlier generation of jazz were plopped down in the middle of one of these burnout tunes and asked to hang in there, he'd be at sea.

To me, Marsalis's improvisations can sail by without much really sticking, but I don't feel the same way about Marcus Roberts, and this album is a good demonstration of Roberts's talents. Roberts has a wide command: he's a great accompanist, he has a percussive, resonant sound, and he is drawn to weird ideas. In the first version of "Juan," for example, Roberts finds small patterns and becomes stubborn with them, repeating them, changing them here and there, until the individual notes gain greater significance. It's an extramusical thing, a form of hypnotism—something the avant-garde were close to—that just wasn't part of Marsalis's conception.

This is a live showcase for young, athletic players, working hard. There's only one ballad on *Live at Blues Alley*—"Do You Know What It Means to Miss New Orleans?"—and it has a hopeful feeling about it. (Marsalis's music is always bright.) It is also an old southern standard, made famous by Louis Armstrong, and that sort of song, at that time, was never being played—or if it was, it was being done as a sly revisionist job. It was extraordinary to hear Marsalis bring back such music and get inside it to the extent that he does on *Live at Blues Alley*. It could only have come from New Orleans, where the local musicians know and respect their local history, and also where a kind of amiable cuteness enters into the music. These players aren't having an Oedipal war with jazz.

Jazz was getting into a kind of philosophical crisis about what was real and what was not, and Marsalis was interested in the real. To his mind, there were a few decades of lost, woolgathering time in jazz to make up for, and he was hotly ambitious about what he desired to accomplish. By the time of *Black Codes (From the Underground)* in 1985, it was clear that Marsalis would be interesting as a bandleader; *Live at Blues Alley* is the album that capitalizes on that promise, showing what this young crop of musicians (Marsalis was twenty-five at the time) were up to. Hearing it now, ten years after the last of the really embarrassing critical debates about conservatism versus radicalism in jazz, one hears a hot, interactive, influential band, lifting this or that from the 1960s but basically a new flavor, a new entity.

90. CECIL TAYLOR:

For Olim

(SOUL NOTE 1150)

Cecil Taylor, solo piano.

Recorded 1986

One of the infelicitous moments of Ken Burns's *Jazz* television series had to do with Cecil Taylor. It was in the infamous episode ten, treating jazz from 1960 to the present, and it went like this. Nat Hentoff tells a story about how Taylor couldn't find work easily in the 1950s because he was so different, because his music was considered difficult to follow, and how at night he would perform concerts in his loft for an ideal, imaginary audience. Then the show's voice-of-God narrator, Keith David, intones: "Cecil Taylor once said that since *he* prepared for his concerts, the audience should prepare, too." Cut to Branford Marsalis, who—apparently reacting to this decontextualized bon mot—says: "That's total self-indulgent bullshit, as far as I'm concerned."

I'll make a reasonable assumption. What any viewer carried away from this insidiously edited sequence, any viewer who doesn't have Cecil Taylor's work already close to his heart, was an elided version of the above: Cecil Taylor's music is self-indulgent bullshit.

There may be some self-indulgence in what he does, yes. (The quality is known to occur in jazz.) But if you invent an effective musical system, one that can take a long time to reveal itself, you're not being self-indulgent; you're being true to the way your system works.

Cecil Taylor lives for his art (as most jazz players do) and presumes that audiences might be ready to receive him for what he is, which does have something to do with jazz and also doesn't. He is right: he has, in fact, been received for what he is, to an amazing degree. There is a place for him, and it's a place that he more or less invented.

In the initial phase of his career, up until 1961, he was a jazz musician fair and square—though he was destabilizing music by Monk and Ellington as well as various standards with an eruptive, impetuous improvising style, using clusters that didn't necessarily have a harmonic logic, sometimes playing the piano as percussion. Then he formed a trio with saxophonist Jimmy Lyons and a drummer—first Sunny Murray, then Andrew Cyrille—that traveled farther away from jazz, except for basic qualities of improvisation, percussiveness, and dance impulse. He became wickedly effective as a solo performer, and his solo music reached a kind of soulful, lapidary stage by the 1970s; in the 1980s, he was a survivor icon who could write his own ticket, whether that meant his own big-band music, poetry delivered in a scowling chant, or an eleven-CD box set of different improvised groupings recorded at a festival in Berlin devoted entirely to him.

Taylor is fascinating enough that I have been tempted to write about three of his albums here. But I have chosen only one, from his later career, because he had such a long formation. And also because for all the brouhaha about his impact—it became a cliché in jazz books written in the 1980s to have two final chapters, one on Ornette Coleman and the other on Taylor—he did not have the same kind of impact on the jazz-piano tradition that Coleman or Coltrane had on the saxophone, or, more properly, on all instrumentalists who share the lingua franca of jazz.

He helped found an alternate tradition that proved to have all sorts of entryways into jazz as it is commonly practiced. (He influenced all kinds of different players who have developed small-group languages: among them Don Pullen, Chucho Valdés, Irene Schweizer, Marilyn Crispell, Matthew Shipp, Yosuke Yamashita, D. D. Jackson, and Vijay Iyer.) But Taylor himself, at this point, has ended up aesthetically isolated, even given the fact that he has played rather celebrated duet concerts with musicians such as Mary Lou Williams and Max Roach. He still has a trio, but it's not one of consequence; his solo performances are more special. I consider that a point of strength; it's rare to see a musician, any sort of musician, with his determination.

Taylor became famous for long improvisations that proceeded in cell-like structure—not based on an overall repeating chordal cycle but moving from exploration A to exploration B to exploration C. Jazz was his foundation: he absorbed Johnny Hodges and Billie Holiday, Parker and Davis and Coltrane, and the Boston musicians he knew while a student at the New England Conservatory, such as Jaki Byard and Serge Chaloff. Like Tatum, like Keith Jarrett, he makes the piano sing and roar and hiccup. The blues is in there, too—not as in the blues form but as in the blues scale, the blues language. I'm not sure I have heard anyone get more expressive blue gestures out of the piano; Taylor can make piano notes almost bend, as if he's breathing through them.

I call on all these other names because it must be understood that Cecil Taylor does fit into the society of jazz. Yet Taylor moved into a position of being an American artist more than a jazz artist and, even beyond that, an artist who found great applications for his own work in dance (this is a helpful way to understand Taylor—as a kind of improvising dancer using music instead of movement), in literature, in architecture. Recently, when interviewed by the magazine *Signal to Noise,* Taylor took an interesting detour on the notion of "structure"—the word that his detractors have aimed at him through the years, complaining that he doesn't have enough or any. In the interview, instead of discussing the thirty-two-bar song or the blues or the concerto grosso or whatever, Taylor talked about the Spanish bridge engineer Santiago Calatrava. "There's nothing 'free' about any of this," he said. "If you look at the plans for many of [Calatrava's] constructions, they look like animals, or plants. . . . You see, we're dealing with space. And if you look at a bridge, you cannot ignore the spatial, rhythmic connotations, particularly when you look at cable-stay box-girder bridges." "Free" jazz is a faulty notion, since the mind can't really create random sequences. But Taylor takes special issue with being branded as a free-jazz player because he uses *elaborate* structure.

Like bridges, Taylor's lengthy performances bring you from one side to another. *For Olim* was recorded live, and its track selections might seem to anyone but Taylor like simply parts of a long whole. But he is working on ideas—tremelos, harmonies, rhythmic units—that repeat or are reconstituted in various ways as his musical idées fixes keep bubbling up to the surface.

After the long piece—or the four midsize pieces, as Taylor has rendered it—the audience claps, and Taylor finishes with four miniature encore improvisations. If you're someone of short patience or feel yourself constitutionally hostile to what you know about Taylor, start with these. They're like postcards instead of his challenging novellas, and they're packed with startling beauty; he squeezes bravura technique into them, and some of the best pathos outside of Billie Holiday and Lester Young.

For Olim is Taylor on a good night—no more, no less, no marketing concept, no theme. It is a particularly instructive example of Taylor doing what Taylor does.

91. TOMMY FLANAGAN:

Jazz Poet

(TIMELESS SJP 301)

Tommy Flanagan, piano; George Mraz, bass; Kenny Washington, drums.

Recorded 1989

Tommy Flanagan had attained old-master status by the time his solo career took off in the early 1980s, after twenty-five years spent mostly accompanying singers. He wasn't just another high-level pianist, a fluent bebopper, of which there were dozens at the time. He had his own distinct repertoire, a high-craft version of the jazz mainstream, which he played perfectly with a restrained, lapidary touch, as if it were the Platonic form of jazz piano. His sets leaned toward American theater songs chosen carefully for their melodic-harmonic jewels; he also favored Billy Strayhorn and Thad Jones and added a bebop song or two.

Flanagan came from Detroit, which in his youth was such an important center for jazz that it was possible to play in a nationally known band without leaving town. The Blue Bird Inn, where he was long part of the house band that played with visiting stars, was one of the most hallowed jazz clubs in the country, and an extraordinary list of local talent played there: it included the brothers Elvin, Hank, and Thad Jones, playing (respectively) drums, piano, and trumpet; vibraphonist Milt Jackson; pianist Barry Harris; bassist Paul Chambers; guitarist Kenny Burrell; and singer Betty Carter.

Flanagan moved to New York in 1956, the year after Charlie Parker died, and through the filter of his own strengths learned bebop as a distinctly witty, fluid language. He handled its labyrinthine progressions of chords like he was a painter with a fine brush; he had the speed but not the rattling intensity of Bud Powell, another close colleague in New York.

It was clear even then that he stood in the stylistic tradition of Art Tatum and Teddy Wilson. They and he were technical wizards who played sustained single-note lines and who integrated rhythmic and melodic ideas with both left hand and right hand. And also like Tatum and Wilson, Flanagan was a song connoisseur; he wouldn't settle for second-rate material, and he didn't spend much time in the medium of the blues, unless it was a Charlie Parker version of the blues, with plenty of filigree and hardly any gutbucket gestures. Playing bebop, he seemed to refute the notion that it was ever an aggressive music. He didn't lean on the sustain pedal; he wasn't a housewrecker. He just flowed along with his admirable legato, sometimes fast (as in "Mean Streets," on this album), sometimes slow (as in "St. Louis Blues").

With his trio, Flanagan stuck to a formula, but it was a beautiful one, and by the time of *Jazz Poet*, playing with a well-seasoned working band, he really knew how to make a jazz record. His trio created arrangements lined with short improvisations; one player's solo was framed by concise phrases worked out between the other two musicians. A sense of self-restraint permeates all these performances. Solo breaks aren't too long, all ideas are tastefully wrapped up; the melody line never disappears under the leader's improvisations. Flanagan's touch and rhythmic bounce connoted the spontaneity of jazz, and yet the shape of his playing gave evidence that he could see a map of the entire piece.

Keith Jarrett

92. KEITH JARRETT/GARY PEACOCK/ JACK DeJOHNETTE:

Tribute

(ECM 1420/21, 2 CDS)

Keith Jarrett, piano; Gary Peacock, bass; Jack DeJohnette, drums.

Recorded 1989

Through the last two decades, Keith Jarrett's standards trio has been sitting there in the corner like a massive, unimpeachable obelisk; no matter if you love it, ignore it, or throw eggs at it, it has a weight and a persistence. I've often felt something of a cold, angry aura around it, too, but that's an extrapolation from nonmusical things: the block-type-and-solid-color design of the band's records on ECM; Jarrett's baronial pronouncements in interviews, suffused with a put-upon, standard-bearing egotism, as if all other jazz musicians around him are simply asleep to the essential issues of truth and beauty; and the Jarrett cult, which has been fanatic enough to absorb eighteen CDs of standards in as many years.

On the other hand, Jarrett's brand of dedication, which is focused on the art of jazz at its most tender and fragile, rather than on the mundane notion of hauling a band through two decades to please the fans, *is* pretty extraordinary. It's not quite right to say that these three musicians give you your money's worth; they want to give themselves their money's worth. In the performances I've seen, they abhor easy comfort; when they're looking for something but haven't found it, they make it clear.

A big part of that volatility comes from drummer Jack DeJohnette, who is the best colorist in jazz but also, when he wants to be, a severely swinging musician. DeJohnette started his career as a member of the Chicago AACM, so the experimentalism seems hardwired within him; he's as interested in disruption as he is in flow. But the disruptions are often just spurs to some other, more effective ideas. There's a self-critical aspect about this band; if I understand the philosophical subtext of the challenge implicit in Jarrett's standards repertoire, it's something like: *nostalgia represents death, and jazz must represent life; these songs are intimately connected to nostalgia, so how do we separate the standards from the nostalgia?*

Tribute may not be the trio's greatest achievement—that might go to the six-CD *At the Blue Note* set, which I can't in good faith recommend to the average person (there are ninety-nine other albums you need to pay attention to, after all). But it delineates the challenge especially well, not just selecting twelve unkillable standards of American popular song but a particular interpreter of those songs to pay homage to. And though I would never be able to tell you that the rendition here of "Solar" is a nod in the particular direction of Bill Evans or that "Lover Man" is supposed to conjure Lee Konitz (both dedications are made clear on the album's back cover), I can tell you that the connections intrigue me. Jarrett is a music-alone person. Some of his greatest early work, with his American quartet including Dewey Redman, Charlie Haden, and Paul Motian, as well as the gigantesque personal statements of *The Köln Concert* and *Sun Bear Concerts,* established him as a musician who doesn't let professional expectations alter his will. It's always interesting to hear how musicians like this were influenced; for Jarrett to throw out lifeline connections to figures great (John Coltrane, for example, in "It's Easy to Remember") and small (Nancy Wilson, in "Little Girl Blue") is worth cogitation.

The standards trio, at its worst, can bog down in a tepid lyricism that seems to be the opposite of what they're looking for. Jarrett is maniacal about touch and has always been interested in making the piano "sing"—to get around its physicality-once-removed aspects, its hammers-as-prophylactic aspect. Playing someone else's music, he will tease out a fragment of composed melody and toss it around until it changes its shape entirely.

"Lover Man"—the first track, and it's thirteen minutes long—doesn't bode well for this album; it's soft to the point of no return. (Even Konitz has a sensible acidity mixed in with his diaphanous Lester Young sound.) But the set gradually takes flight, and by disc two, starting with a version of "Just in Time" that Jarrett dedicates to Charlie Parker (I don't know about Parker per se, but at least the piece is festooned with fleet bebop phrases), the band is reminding you of its tremendous stature.

What Jarrett repeatedly accomplishes—you might not get it for fifteen minutes straight, but you will get it somewhere on each album he has released—is the mystical moment where a song with a familiar melody becomes transformed; the band finds its window of original insight, clambers in there, and builds something with full-bore group improvisation that you haven't ever heard before. All great individual jazz players have achieved this; Ralph Ellison heard it in Louis Armstrong and described the effect in the early pages of *Invisible Man*: "Instead of the swift and imperceptible flowing of time, you are aware of its nodes, those points where time stands still or from which it leaps ahead. And you slip into the breaks and look around." The Jarrett trio achieves it collectively.

In the next paragraphs, Ellison writes of a dream in which there are levels beneath levels beneath levels. That notion was actually made physical in the Jarrett trio, with the device of fast-on-slow and slow-on-fast tempo layering. That device—as heard in Brad Mehldau's trio, in Greg Osby's and Jason Moran's groups, in Ethan Iverson and Mark Turner—is one of the greatest gifts Jarrett has given to contemporary jazz. It has proved that "freedom" didn't have to mean no song, no structure; in fact, the material, in and of itself, is meaningless. It ain't what you do, it's the way that you do it.

93. DON PULLEN:

Random Thoughts

(BLUE NOTE 7-94347-2)

Don Pullen, piano; James Genus, bass; Lewis Nash, drums.

Recorded 1990

Don Pullen, the pianist, and David Murray, the saxophonist, offered different versions of the same gift: they were able to take the drive and energy of free music from the 1960s and 1970s and redirect it toward a more structural, more swinging jazz that had outgrown the transgressive stage, like adults retaining the optimism and wisdom of the teenager.

Both were virtuosic, in their own ways; they could make music cascade forth from their instruments, like an unstoppable flow, circling higher and wilder. By the 1980s, however, in his solo recordings and in the band he led with the saxophonist George Adams, it was obvious that there was greater tonal logic in Pullen's improvising. When he was picked up by Blue Note at the end of the decade to make his versions of mainstream-jazz albums, his mastery of a mixed idiom, perfect for its time, was even more evident.

New Beginnings was the auspicious title of the first Blue Note record. But the bassist and drummer—Dave Holland and Jack DeJohnette—halted his rebirth a little; they didn't provide the blank slate Pullen needed. Their personalities got in the way. On *Random Thoughts,* Pullen worked with James Genus and Lewis Nash, who were then young and, as is second nature to young mainstream jazz musicians, played cleanly and unobtrusively. This gave Pullen room to show what kind of pianist he was, and the whole affair—even all this time later—has a freshness about it, a hunger, a delight.

Pullen had a technique of rolling his wrists as he improvised—the outside edges of his hands became scarred from it—to create moving tone clusters. Building up from arpeggios, he could create eddies of noise on the keyboard; they were like concise Cecil Taylor outbursts, and they had great muscle behind them. But by the late eighties, he was fusing avant-gardist piano techniques with blues and gospel vamps, tunes written to a crisp rhythm, and above all a new songful sensibility.

Random Thoughts is the summit of that sensibility. He became a bona fide writer of melodies, one of the few that the entire avant-garde-jazz movement produced. They were relatively simple structures, and Pullen was never an overbearing pianist, even when he created banging dissonance; he seemed to find peace with the fact that jazz needn't be overly complicated or overly empty. The ballad "The Dancer," for one example, picks up where Billy Strayhorn left off—you can imagine Ellington-band horns wrapping around it—and Pullen fashions a swinging, lean, perfectly proportioned solo from it. It is an actual performance, as are many of the tracks on the album; he is conscious not only of rhythm and form but of pacing himself, of never running out of rhetorical steam.

Pullen's wilder techniques could come off as too limited. His rhythmic banging in "Endangered Species: African-American Youth" is too much of a good thing. And the cheeriness of this album seems to betray an unwillingness to go deeper into lyricism. But the amount of music Pullen absorbed, personalized, and balanced to become who he was— Bud Powell, Monk, Ellington, Erroll Garner, Cecil Taylor—was wide and well condensed.

94. CASSANDRA WILSON:

Blue Light 'til Dawn

(BLUE NOTE 0777-7-81357-2-2)

Cassandra Wilson, vocals, arrangements; Brandon Ross, steel string guitar, octave guitar, arrangements; Charlie Burnham, violin, mandocello, arrangements; Tony Cedras, accordion; Olu Dara, cornet; Gib Wharton, pedal steel guitar; Don Byron, clarinet; Chris Whitley, guitar, arrangements; Kenny Davis, bass, arrangements; Lonnie Plaxico, bass; Lance Carter, Bill McClellan, drums; Cyro Baptista, percussion, arrangements; Kevin Johnson, Vinx, Jeff Haynes, percussion.

Recorded 1993

Cassandra Wilson

In the 1980s and early 1990s, it was already clear that Cassandra Wilson might amount to something beyond the current scale of the jazz scene. She was part of the M-BASE group (see Steve Coleman and Five Elements's *The Ascension to Light,* below), a circle of musicians based in Brooklyn who were thinking creatively, beyond the limits of 1960s ideology, about what it meant to be young black musicians playing jazz.

Did you (they asked) have to feign distaste for all popular music but classic jazz? In what sense would the Isley Brothers, Sly and the Family Stone, James Brown, or hip-hop exist for you after you "ascended" to this territory? Was it necessary to get wrapped up in the duality of guilty and virtuous pleasures? Couldn't all that pop music you listened to, combined with the discipline of jazz, engender something new?

It did, for each of them, in different ways. Cassandra Wilson, who grew up in Mississippi, where she listened to blues, jazz, and folk music of the James Taylor and Joni Mitchell variety, made curious, modern, intellectual, earthy, and lightly funky records; then she made *Blue*

Skies, a not overdutiful exploration of standards. Her voice was fascinating, partly because it had the husky timbre of a sixty-year-old's and the chops of a woman her age. It descended from Nina Simone's, but without the stridency; there was even some of the mentholated somnolence of the pop singer Sade in it.

But *Blue Light 'til Dawn* was something new. She connected with Craig Street, a little-known producer, and they worked together on assembling unusual instrumentation. Her core musicians assumed arrangement duties. The music sounded as if it were produced by a few people sitting around on a hot day with nothing but acoustic instruments. But there were some unifying rules to the album. Instruments don't state the melody, but circle around it. Wilson herself only states the melody as backhandedly as possible, as part of one long, slow exhalation, with a lot of improvising. The instruments were recorded closely, and there would be no clutter. The more that urban and rural sounds could be combined, the better: Charlie Burnham mixed Stéphane Grappelli licks in with some country-blues fiddle; Brandon Ross put blues figures in a harmonically elaborate folk-music context (of which Joni Mitchell is the avatar). Accordion and pedal steel guitar found a home in this music, and so did very swinging, jazz-drilled rhythm. Saxophones did not.

A few ideas worked like crazy. There is a wise version of Robert Johnson's "Come on in My Kitchen," led by Ross's guitar. Charles Brown and Oscar Moore's "Tell Me You'll Wait for Me," with only voice, bass, and snare drum, is a special performance, giving evidence of Wilson's superiority as a jazz singer. Her own "Redbone" is nothing but a poem over Afro-Cuban rhythm and steel guitar, but her improvisations, and the poem itself (about a light-skinned black woman who likes to drink and fight but also loves God and, the lyrics assure us, will go to heaven), achieved perfection. A version of Van Morrison's "Tupelo Honey," though its only jazz content is in the delayed phrasing of her lyric delivery, is devastatingly beautiful.

Reconsidered, this album seems emblematic of a new, democratized good taste that stole over this country beginning in the early 1990s—the taste made omnipresent by Crate and Barrel, Ikea, Starbucks, cilantro, Miramax's foreign-film department, triple-A radio, Alison Krauss, the *Buena Vista Social Club* album and film, and the Coen brothers' *O Brother, Where Art Thou?* It's a clean, domestic aesthetic that at least pretends to cut across borders of culture and class and has been a real turnaround in marketing to adults. I don't mean to idealize mass-marketing schemes—a new Starbucks looks sure to decimate a nice coffee shop in my neighborhood—but this trend has mixed high-minded idealism and commerce in an impressively concerted effort. Wilson grasped the new high-art populism early, before it was a cliché, and has worked with it ever since.

The ooze of this record helped bring on a new, folkish languor for jazz singing, the very opposite of the alert, interactive group sound that Betty Carter worked so hard to further. It's a healthy counterweight to the traditions of mainstream jazz, and Wilson has already made her mark in history. I am bothered, though, by the fact that her song choices, even nine years later, are all eminent possibilities for the good-taste adult-music samplers that Starbucks makes and plays in its shops. I do feel a little compromised, as if I am buying into a lifestyle, when I enthuse about her now. But I still think she is one of the most original personalities to be involved in jazz in the last generation.

95. STEVE COLEMAN AND FIVE ELEMENTS:

The Ascension to Light

(RCA/BMG FRANCE 74321742192)

Steve Coleman, alto saxophone, clave, Chinese gong, vocals, composer; Gary Thomas, tenor saxophone; Ralph Alessi, Shane Endsley, trumpet; Vijay Iyer, piano; David Gilmore, guitar; Anthony Tidd, bass; Sean Rickman, drums; Gregoire Maret, harmonica; Thomas Goodwin, philosophy; Min Xiao-Fen, pipa; Cassandra Wilson, Sophia Wong, vocals; Valerie Coleman, flute, piccolo; Toyin Spellman, oboe; Mariam Adam, clarinet; Jeff Scott, French horn; Monica Ellis, bassoon.

Recorded 1999

I always find the newer Steve Coleman albums to be the best ones. There is a similarity to the twenty or so records he has made, and I don't often return to early-nineties works like *Rhythm People* or *The Tao of Mad Phat* because I don't find any particular flavors there that haven't been subtly improved on in the new work. But there is a special jump in quality in his albums of the past ten years. His mind, as obscurantist as it can be, has been taking in a lot of material from other cultures lately, and his bright, clear, balanced saxophone playing has been getting ever better.

Starting in the late 1980s, Coleman appeared to be at the forefront of the M-BASE group of Brooklyn-based improvisers. That acronym means Macro-Basic Array of Structured Extemporizations, which means looking at different musical languages and combining them with composition and improvisation. He, more than the rest, desired to make it clear that he wasn't just writing tunes as vehicles for the new soloistic licks but that he was hooking into a greater well of language information. Initially, that well included R&B (for Coleman, the James Brown records of the late 1960s and 1970s are an important key, in their rhythm-section work and in Maceo Parker's saxophone solos), bebop, hip-hop, astrology, and eastern philosophy; it has since grown to include more contemporary and ancient music and thought.

All jazz is a series of systems and languages, but the popular-art side of jazz musicians banishes theory to the background, where it generally belongs. Coleman, however, found that he enjoyed the juncture of popular art and quasi-academicism and supposed that others would enjoy it, too; he never wavered in that supposition, and his explanations—in interviews and liner notes—for why he has done various things have been wary and sometimes even needlessly hostile to those who don't understand him, though they are generally thorough. They're also based in reality. Coleman has not retreated.

By the mid-nineties, he learned about Yoruba culture, traveling to Cuba, Africa, and Brazil, and it energized him; he found out about the religious and ritual meanings of various rhythms and modes of living that have influenced American life directly. His ensembles grew larger, and his music grew denser, sometimes involving Cuban percussionists. But where other musicians would pull ten years of a career from an enlightening brush with another country, Coleman kept moving on, incorporating still more into his music. He has become an important mentor, not only to the members of his own band but in traveling educational workshops; he has been sharing his process with musicians in America, Cuba, and Europe. (Through his workshops, he has helped foster a new avant-garde Cuban music, both there and here; that's quite an accomplishment for an American.) He has made himself increasingly influential and kept the lines open for his own music to change, too.

The Ascension to Light is inspired by ancient thought (surely it's the only album that gives a philosopher a credit—for "philosophy"— among the list of musicians) and has moments of hard, impenetrable music; sometimes the changing-meter funk rhythms can come off as excessively masculine and forbidding. But things change. "Embryo" begins with a lovely saxophone-drums duet and leads to a harmonica improvisation by Gregoire Maret over a repeated bass figure; then the ensemble, with Coleman, trumpeter Ralph Alessi, and the rhythm section, builds up into collective play, anchored in written lines.

"The 42 Assessors" includes a long, baleful recitation from a Kemetic (ancient Egyptian) text, but lovely things sprout from it. Min Xiao-Fen improvises, with both crystal-clear and scratchy tones, on the pipa, the Chinese string instrument; Cassandra Wilson performs remarkable wordless vocal improvisations.

Above all, the music is clean. Coleman has prized smooth tone and rhythm since the beginning; his work has had a certain slickness, never fetishizing authenticity in lack of polish, as does a lot of music outside the mainstream of jazz. (Its tonal centers are well articulated; the intonation of all players is excellent; a great deal of the music is written.) For Coleman, authenticity seems to be a cerebral and constantly moving proposition. Though jazz is the pedagogical grounding for most of the musicians involved in this recording, I think Coleman couldn't care less whether it is jazz or not. Jazz is what jazz musicians do.

96. DAVE HOLLAND QUINTET:

Prime Directive

(ECM 1698 3140547-950-2)

Dave Holland, bass; Chris Potter, soprano, alto, and tenor saxophones; Robin Eubanks, trombone, cowbell; Steve Nelson, vibraphone, marimba; Billy Kilson, drums.

Recorded 1999

The settings seem highly variable in Dave Holland's new quintet: time appears in odd meters or shifts from two-beat rhythms to fours and fives; funk morphs into swing. Short cyclical themes suddenly sprout into longer, harmonized passages that twist off into melodies and twist again into improvisations, from which the soloist suddenly drops out.

But guiding it all is a control that's almost unparalleled in jazz at the moment, as well as a strange kind of modesty. Holland started out, fresh from England, with Miles Davis's electric groups in the early seventies; he then played in Circle, with Chick Corea and Barry Altschul, and organized the impressively lovely semi–free jazz album *Conference of the Birds*. As a player on his own, he's become one of the few first-rank freelancers. But as a bandleader during the last fifteen years or so, he has created a bona fide small-band music, as opposed to a music that loosely associates individual players, and there is a stealthiness about it. I have been dumbstruck by this band live, but it has taken longer for the achievements of the albums to reach me. They are very, very good—quite similar from song to song and even album to album but still records of the highest quality in the past ten years.

The latest version of the quintet, with Billy Kilson and Chris Potter, has a signature sound and rhythmic feeling. That sound may have its roots in the late 1980s, when Holland let himself rub up against the M-BASE players. (See Steve Coleman and Five Elements, *The Ascension to Light*, above.) For a time, he had a quartet with Coleman, and they both displayed a mastery of funk rhythms in a stripped-down jazz context. They let grooves breathe and speak for themselves. (Again, it was a stealthy music, not a bright-burning, overimpressive kind. Ten years

Dave Holland

ago, Steve Lacy mentioned to me that what jazz needs more of is best described by the French word "*pudeur*," which means a sense of privacy, of restraint, even of cool; I don't think he was necessarily talking about the emotional chilliness that European jazz is famous for.)

The themes on *Prime Directive* are often cute, Monk-like curlicues decked out with contrapuntal arrangements. But the group is really defined by vamps, that old device of repetition and gradual build that comes from African music, then the blues, then Ahmad Jamal and Miles Davis and John Coltrane and Latin music; today, it is one of the jazz bandleader's most useful tools, not a diversion or an interlude but the thing itself. It allows for maximum freedom, while holding down the center; it sounds ancient, while letting in all the rhythms and phrase shapes of the moment.

Holland, as bassist and bandleader, is deeply settled into his role as keeper of the vamps. The music swirls around him; he keeps calm, creating a deep, resonating hum, an atmosphere of serenity at the middle of the music.

All members of the band write for it, but the tunes come out sounding terrifically unified; it's a band with roles. In a sense, too, it's an all-percussion band: the five players, including Kilson, Potter, vibraphonist Steve Nelson, and trombonist Robin Eubanks, take turns contributing to the great interlocking rhythmic structures.

The contrasts come with the outbursts of improvisation—especially with Kilson's, which are loud and explosive. But they are solos that always develop shrewdly and feed back into the overriding design. The surprising drawback of a band this well conceptualized is that the concept can override the song; sometimes individual pieces are hard to remember. But it's music vibrating with assurance and self-knowledge, tough and built to last.

97. JOHN LEWIS:

Evolution

(ATLANTIC 82311–2)

John Lewis, solo piano.

Recorded 1999

This album, Lewis's penultimate statement during his lifetime (it was followed by *Evolution II,* a full-band record), was released the same year as Keith Jarrett's solo-piano record, *The Melody at Night, with You.* After six months, according to SoundScan, the firm that tracks retail music sales, it had sold roughly one thirtieth the number of the copies in the States that Jarrett's had. This can be explained by a number of things: ECM's aggressive marketing of the Jarrett disc and the simultaneous withering of Atlantic's jazz department (it died completely in November 2001); Jarrett's more constant performing schedule (Lewis wasn't well enough to tour anymore); and the persistence of the Jarrett cult among players and music students.

But, while there's room for complaint, the imbalance in sales also points to the fact that historical analysis has not been kind to John Lewis. As discussed above with the Modern Jazz Quartet's *Fontessa,* Lewis has regularly been perceived as the stiff element of the MJQ, the one who didn't let Milt Jackson swing enough, and his obsession with European classical forms has been derided as fussy. What's overlooked is the sensuality in his playing, its human qualities.

This is a poignant record. There are some statements that can't be made in youth, and *Evolution* is one of them. Programmed with jazz standards and some of Lewis's own compositions, it captures the burned-off essence of his style—which is full of straightforward elements, major harmonies, and two-note chords—in a context of shifting rhythm. It was recorded at the Tarrytown Music Hall, a concert hall, without an audience, a production technique that favors his light touch and his even legato. There's also something unbearably wistful about imagining the aging John Lewis playing his lovely, soft miniatures in an empty theater. Some of it produces the same goose bumps that a good

---

rendering of Bach's *Partitas* does; it is a good album for the stillness of winter.

Lewis applied as much thought to the arrangement of these songs as he would have if he had been playing with a group, and then he made music that's utterly at peace with itself. A little bit after the model of Baroque preludes, he introduces a concise melodic or rhythmic motif at the beginning of each track, then brings that motif to bear on the tunes and improvisations that follow. When he becomes expansive, it feels like a well-considered choice: there's a thirty-two-bar stretch in his performance of "September Song" that lifts up out of the quiet surroundings. Suddenly he goes into four-four time, uses strides and accents, moves around thicker chords, plays blues figures.

As always, he economizes at the piano, and his laconic style of phrasing and harmony places him in the same tradition as Ellington, Basie, and Monk. That is a tradition of percussive playing, and here Lewis occupies a branch of his own: his sound can be soft to the point of self-effacement. But it's the self-effacement of a very powerful man. In its own gentle way, the recording makes you aware that Lewis's vision was much, much broader than a single record could ever intimate.

98. NEW DIRECTIONS:

New Directions

(BLUE NOTE 7243-5-22978-2-5)

Greg Osby, alto saxophone; Mark Shim, tenor saxophone; Stefon Harris, vibraphone; Jason Moran, piano; Tarus Mateen, bass; Nasheet Waits, drums.

Recorded 1999

The history of Blue Note records in the 1950s and 1960s is both routinely fetishized and dulled. There's no other period of jazz from which the documents are so beautiful: Reid Miles's constructivist album-cover designs, Francis Wolff's tenebrous photographs of musicians in the studio; the intimate, resonating sound created for them by engineer Rudy Van Gelder. And yet when the average group of young jazz musicians these days decides to play an iconic piece associated with the label from that period, like Lee Morgan's "The Sidewinder" or Joe Henderson's "Recorda Me," look out for musical diffidence, the stuff that gives jazz a stodgy name, with no apparent will to update those tough little melodies and small-group arrangements.

What's really impressive about *New Directions*, then—a special band made of players signed to the Blue Note label in the nineties, including Greg Osby, Stefon Harris, Mark Shim, and Jason Moran, who were given the opportunity to record their choice of tunes from Blue Note's history—is how unlabored and efficacious their reworkings of these tunes are.

This is an album that sets the mark for what cool is in jazz in the late 1990s, not only in playing but in conception. Every number is reworked from scratch: where there was a vamp in a piano's bass clef, it has been transferred to a higher register on a different instrument and reharmonized. Where there was a dominant rhythm, like the bossa nova beat in Horace Silver's "Song for My Father," it's been wiped away without a trace. Lingering chords from Harris's vibraphone and Moran's piano, pushing against the time of the rhythm section, add an air of watery irresolution and mystery to the tunes; Osby's and Shim's saxophone lines are clean and darting, and Nasheet Waits maintains a balletic, rising-and-falling stammer on the snare drum and ride cymbal.

For Blue Note to ask its young, iconoclastic wizards of jazz to pull music from the catalog is a rather neat corporate idea, but the paradox of this repertory-centered record is that a truly original group sound is at work. There's such comfort in the musicians' interaction that whatever songs they choose are ultimately unimportant. Still, judicious thought was given to the song list, which ranges from the hits and modern standards by Morgan, Henderson, and Silver, to much lesser known pieces such as Sam Rivers's ballad "Beatrice" (here done as a duet for piano and vibraphone), Wayne Shorter's "Ping Pong," and some beguiling originals by members of the group.

As a postscript to the album, the group performed at the Village Vanguard six months later, and it added one more layer to the paradox, playing sets that mostly stayed away from the Blue Note cover tunes. Instead—if one was looking to interpret the performances beyond the nuts and bolts of the music itself—the sets were commentaries on current uses of the jazz canon. While the high level of group improvisation ensured that the audience didn't know what would come next, there were references abounding to the idea of a trained musician's roots.

Osby at one point appended a scrambled montage of Charlie Parker themes to "The Sidewinder." The group connected "I Didn't Know about You" and "You've Changed" by sandwiching them around Björk's "Joga," improbably enough. Playing Thelonious Monk's "Skippy" (a Blue Note track that didn't make it onto the album), the band seemed unworried about expending energy and changing the tune whenever it wanted to: song-closing crescendos rose in the beginning, middle, and end of the tune.

One of the most pressing themes in jazz at the moment is the balance between a traditional canon (or a repertory, for lack of a better word) and the 1960s lessons of "freedom." These musicians understand how to exploit that balancing act to make a legitimately new jazz.

99. CHARLIE HADEN:

Nocturne

(VERVE 440-013-611-2)

Charlie Haden, bass; Gonzalo Rubalcaba, piano; Ignacio Berroa, drums; Federico Ruiz, violin; Joe Lovano, David Sanchez, tenor saxophone; Pat Metheny, guitar.

Recorded 2000

At least since Jerry Gonzalez and the Fort Apache band recorded *Rumba Para Monk* in 1988, Latin music has been the most consistent source of intelligent concept albums in new jazz. (You could certainly extend that thought to the Afro-Cuban jazz recordings of 1947—it's concept music, after all—but it came before the LP era.) The big idea in *Nocturne* is the Mexican and Cuban bolero, as well as the jazz-tinged bolero-*filin* style of 1940s Cuba. It's both a fancy album, bedecked with gold-brushed guest appearances, and a creditable one, rich in a literacy of the New World's popular music.

If music embodies spoken rhetoric, the Cuban bolero is provocative speech: a ballad that's not torchy so much as a stealthily rising succession of crescendos, which then grow piercing when the singer summons loss or regret. But what Charlie Haden and Gonzalo Rubalcaba do to the bolero on *Nocturne* is to render its entreaties all in lowercase. This is full-scale art music, operating almost entirely on one flat plane of dynamics, never surging into common peaks-and-troughs ballad language. With Ignacio Berroa's brushed drum rhythms backing them from start to finish, the songs build up an almost unbearable tension. You keep expecting it to explode; it never does.

Rubalcaba, who arrived in the United States from Cuba in the late 1980s, made a dramatic entrance, playing jazz standards at blinding speeds and with great power; it was impressive but utterly exhausting and finally boring to listen to. Curiously and to his credit, by the late nineties he had thrown that style aside in favor of slow, nearly still tempos. (The unveiling of this new style first happened on his album *Inner Voyage* in 1998.)

This group is billed as Haden's alone; Haden pulled the album together, but he does not play Cuban-style rhythm, and he takes a fairly reticent role in the music's big picture. The playing shows deep concentration: the rhythm section is as quiet as a mouse until it's time for Haden to step forward with a few thick, woody notes, and Rubalcaba keeps his hands around middle C, etching each serene phrase into the piano with minute precision.

The Cuban and Mexican thirty-two-bar bolero operates in a processional two-four rhythm (as opposed to the Spanish bolero's three-beat); it has only a secondary relationship to jazz. It's certainly not jazz rhythm, and there isn't much improvised interactivity. Still, there is plenty of individual rhythmic identity, from Rubalcaba's forcibly restrained virtuosity, to Joe Lovano's freer sense of swing, to Federico Ruiz's huskier, more rustic take on Stéphane Grappelli, to Haden's bursts of slow, flamenco-style playing.

In its program of beautiful songs are many that jazz enthusiasts won't know: they include "Yo Sin Ti" (Arturo Castro), "No Te Empenes Mas" (Marta Valdes), and "Tres Palabras" (Osvaldo Farres). The change in rhythmic feeling between one track and the next can be tiny, but you may feel compelled to understand how they're slightly different. And so the album sustains itself on its syrup-slow journey.

100. JASON MORAN:

Black Stars

(BLUE NOTE 7243-5-32922-2-5)

Jason Moran, piano; Sam Rivers, tenor and soprano saxophones, flute, piano; Tarus Mateen, bass; Nasheet Waits, drums.

Recorded 2001

Pianist Jason Moran, still under thirty in 2002, has made two of the great small-group albums of the last fifty years since he burst into our consciousness—surprisingly, with no warm-up—as a member of Greg Osby's quartet in 1997. *Facing Left* is the first; *Black Stars*, with his guest Sam Rivers, is the second. There's a refinement going on, even as the influences that Moran chooses to share with us keep widening.

Jazz has had its share of visionary characters who want to position their music in a larger sphere of art making. I'm not talking about the not-uncommon instance of a jazz composer being hired by an opera or dance company; I'm talking about a multimedia vision that comes from the musician and bleeds into everything he puts his hand to. Ornette Coleman is one of those people, with his cross-discipline performances, his travels, his painting, his desire to make everything around him bend to his philosophy of harmolodics. (What is it? Ask him.) Charles Mingus and Julius Hemphill and Steve Lacy are others. Anthony Braxton is one, too, though his talent has splintered into almost complete obfuscation, and he has drawn the curtains of alternative academia around him to such an extent that you can't see the master for the students.

Jason Moran

(Some of the students are not very good musicians, yet they play in his ensembles, which is another problem; the larger the vision, the more help you need to realize it, and the less charted are the waters.)

Jason Moran is in this tradition, though he has a posthippie skepticism and catholicity that jazz needs and that in fact comes naturally to jazz. After all the razing of black stereotypes in culture, it's amazing that it should still be significant when a black musician connects himself to both European high culture and black Americana, but the truth is, outside of Wynton Marsalis, people don't tend to see more than one side of a jazz musician. People are always surprised to find out, say, that Larry Willis, the pianist in Roy Hargrove's quartet, plays the classical-piano repertoire, or that Matthew Shipp practices Bach at home. And, if you're black, Europeanism can also capture you, take you out of your position as an artist making music in the jazz tradition; either by your own volition or by outside opinion, you become an avant-gardist, and you're automatically less involved in the web of jazz as such.

Moran has been keeping his options open. I think he has a prankish streak, but he's smart enough to know that some of the great shocks in jazz are cumulative, traditional or repertorial choices rather than the self-consciously outré. He's also smart enough to know that developing and sticking with a band of excellent, little-recognized musicians is the best thing a bandleader can do.

In his bassist Tarus Mateen and his drummer Nasheet Waits—both of them unknown as recently as the mid-nineties, although Mateen had played with such almost-famous musicians as Rodney Kendrick and Tim Warfield—Moran has found his rock-solid crew. Waits is expert at elongating or contracting phrases as much as Moran requires; on *Black Stars* he follows the pianist so closely in his serpentine improvisations, shoved between bits of composed material, that you wonder whether they're all following rhythm tracks. That would be impossible, though, because the rhythmic sound is so organic. For some, it doesn't swing enough; for me, it's got just the soupçon of hip-hop rhythm (in the dialogue between Waits's snare drum and hi-hat, meted out like a rapper's wordy flow) that can help jazz stay current, without becoming some sort of contrived beatbox-made-flesh situation.

Moran isn't much of a melodic composer (yet); his signature melody is the "Gangsterism" series (on his first album, it was "Gangsterism on Canvas," on his second it was "Gangsterism on Wood," and on *Black Stars* it's "Gangsterism on a River"), and it's a kind of chromatic soul-ballad melody that works fine but doesn't pack a wallop, the way the group's interaction does. "Draw the Light Out," from this album, is mostly an arpeggiated chord run up and down a scale. More often, and especially in performances, Moran and company worry over short melodic fragments, repeating and repeating, sometimes without even a B-section. It doesn't matter: the approach to group interaction is fresh enough, and the way the band changes gears rhythmically and dynamically is the thing.

But he's becoming a referential musician, which is of increasing use to a jazz audience drawing further from the music's past. Moran spent four years studying with Jaki Byard, whose eclecticism and mixture of Harlem with Europe has been a prime influence; he also studied with Andrew Hill, whose harmonies got under his skin. He seems to be exploring Ellington (of course—if Harlem-meets-Europe is on his mind) with "Kinda Dukish" on *Black Stars* and "Wig Wise" on the previous album; it figures both that the compositions are on the obscure side and that they're propulsive, bouncy tunes. Moran is interested in drawing up his own porous canon, one that calls into question all the prevalent ones.

Some of the recordings below are mentioned in the text. Some are not. They are shoring-up discs, for greater historical background.

COLEMAN HAWKINS: *A Retrospective* (Bluebird RCA), 2 CDs, 1929–1963.

BENNIE MOTEN, *1930–1932* (Classics).

FATS WALLER, *Fats Waller 1931–35* (Classics).

CASA LOMA ORCHESTRA, *Casa Loma Stomp* (Hep), 1931–1937.

ROY ELDRIDGE, *Heckler's Hop* (Hep), 1936–1939.

ARTIE SHAW, *Self-Portrait* (RCA Bluebird), 5 CDs, 1936–1954.

SIDNEY BECHET, *1937–1938* (Classics).

JELLY ROLL MORTON, *The Pearls* (Rounder), 1938.

BENNY GOODMAN, JAMES P. JOHNSON, COUNT BASIE, ET AL., *From Spirituals to Swing: The Legendary 1938 & 1939 Carnegie Hall Concerts* (Vanguard), 3 CDs.

ELLA FITZGERALD, *Something to Live For* (Verve), 2 CDs, 1938–1966.

CHARLIE CHRISTIAN, *The Genius of the Electric Guitar* (Columbia), 1939–1941.

ART TATUM, *God Is in the House* (High Note), 1940–1941.

NAT "KING" COLE, *The Vocal Classics 1942–1946* (Capitol).

LESTER YOUNG, *The Complete Aladdin Sessions* (Blue Note), 2 CDs, 1942–1947.

DUKE ELLINGTON, *Black, Brown and Beige* (RCA/BMG), 3 CDs, 1944–1946.

DON BYAS, *Savoy Jam Party* (Savoy), 2 CDs, 1944–1946.

SLIM GAILLARD, *Laughing in Rhythm* (Verve), 1946–1954.

CLAUDE THORNHILL, *The Transcription Performances 1947* (Hep).

WOODY HERMAN, *Keeper of the Flame* (Capitol), 1948–1949.

BUD POWELL, *Jazz Giant* (Verve), 1949–1950.

STAN GETZ, *The Complete Roost Recordings* (Blue Note), 1950–1954.

MACHITO AND HIS AFRO-CUBANS, *Carambola* (Tumbao), 1951.

OSCAR PETERSON, *The Song Is You* (Verve), 1952–1959.

MODERN JAZZ QUARTET, *Django* (Fantasy), 1953–1955.

CHET BAKER, *Let's Get Lost: The Best of Chet Baker Sings* (Capitol), 1953–1956.

ELMO HOPE, *Trio and Quintet* (Blue Note), 1953–1957.

ART BLAKEY AND THE JAZZ MESSENGERS, *A Night at Birdland Vol. 1/Vol. 2* (Blue Note), 1954.

LOUIS ARMSTRONG, *The Great Chicago Concert 1956* (Sony Legacy), 2 CDs.

DINAH WASHINGTON, *The Swingin' Miss D* (Verve), 1956.

GUNTHER SCHULLER, JOHN LEWIS, JIMMY GIUFFRE, J. J. JOHNSON, CHARLES MINGUS, ET AL., *The Birth of the Third Stream* (Columbia), 1956–1957.

THELONIOUS MONK, *Monk's Music* (Fantasy), 1957.

SONNY ROLLINS, *A Night at the Village Vanguard* (Blue Note), 2 CDs, 1957.

SONNY CLARK, *Cool Struttin'* (Blue Note), 1958.

MILES DAVIS, *Milestones* (Columbia), 1958.

MILES DAVIS, *Porgy and Bess* (Columbia), 1958.

CANNONBALL ADDERLEY, *Somethin' Else* (Blue Note), 1958.

JIMMY GIUFFRE TRIO, *The Western Suite* (Atlantic), 1958.

ORNETTE COLEMAN, *Change of the Century* (Atlantic), 1959.

HAROLD LAND, *The Fox* (Fantasy), 1959.

CHARLES MINGUS, *Mingus Ah Um* (Columbia), 1959.

TITO PUENTE, *Revolving Bandstand* (RCA), 1960.

CECIL TAYLOR, *The World of Cecil Taylor* (Candid), 1960.

JOHN COLTRANE, *Live at the Village Vanguard: The Master Takes* (Impulse!), 1961.

LEE KONITZ, *Motion* (Verve), 1961.

JAKI BYARD, *Out Front!* (Fantasy), 1961–1964.

BENNY CARTER, *Further Definitions* (Impulse!), 1961–1966.

PAUL BLEY, *The Complete Footloose* (Savoy), 1962–1963.

GRANT GREEN, *Idle Moments* (Blue Note), 1963.

STEVE LACY–ROSWELL RUDD QUARTET, *School Days* (Hat Art), 1963.

CHARLES MINGUS, *The Black Saint and the Sinner Lady* (Impulse!), 1963.

LEE MORGAN, *The Sidewinder* (Blue Note), 1963.

HORACE SILVER QUINTET, *Song for My Father* (Blue Note), 1963–1964.

HASAAN IBN ALI, *The Legendary Hasaan* (Atlantic), 1964.

ALBERT AYLER, *Spiritual Unity* (ESP), 1964.

ERIC DOLPHY, *Out to Lunch* (Blue Note), 1964.

JOE HENDERSON, *Page One* (Blue Note), 1964.

LUCKY THOMPSON, *Lucky Strikes* (Fantasy), 1964.

BOBBY HUTCHERSON, *Dialogue* (Blue Note), 1965.

WAYNE SHORTER, *Schizophrenia* (Blue Note), 1965.

EDDIE HARRIS, *Greater than the Sum of His Parts* (32 Jazz), 2 CDs, 1965–1968.

FRANK SINATRA, *Sinatra at the Sands with Count Basie & the Orchestra* (Capitol), 1966.

ANTHONY BRAXTON, *For Alto* (Delmark), 1968.

CHICK COREA, *Now He Sings, Now He Sobs* (Blue Note), 1968.

ART ENSEMBLE OF CHICAGO, *People in Sorrow* (Nessa), 1969.

MILES DAVIS, *In a Silent Way* (Sony Legacy), 1969.

MILES DAVIS, *Bitches Brew* (Sony Legacy), 2 CDs, 1969.

ORNETTE COLEMAN, *The Complete Science Fiction Sessions* (Columbia Legacy), 2 CDs, 1969–1971.

SUNNY MURRAY, ARCHIE SHEPP, DAVE BURRELL, SUN RA, ET AL., *Jazzactuel* (Charly), 3 CDs, 1969–1971.

DUKE ELLINGTON, *New Orleans Suite* (Atlantic), 1970.

DUKE ELLINGTON, *The Afro-Eurasian Eclipse* (Fantasy), 1971.

KEITH JARRETT, *Facing You* (ECM), 1971.

DAVE HOLLAND, *Conference of the Birds* (ECM), 1972.

WEATHER REPORT, *I Sing the Body Electric* (Sony Legacy), 1972.

KEITH JARRETT, *Silence* (Impulse!), 1975.

SARAH VAUGHAN, *How Long Has This Been Going On?* (Fantasy), 1978.

AIR, *Air Lore* (RCA), 1979.

WORLD SAXOPHONE QUARTET, *W.S.Q.* (Black Saint), 1980.

RAN BLAKE, *Suffield Gothic* (Soul Note), 1981.

JAMES BLOOD ULMER, *Free Lancing* (Columbia), 1981.

MARTIAL SOLAL, *Bluesine* (Soul Note), 1983.

WYNTON MARSALIS, *Black Codes (From the Underground)* (Columbia), 1985.

DAVID MURRAY, *The Hill* (Black Saint), 1986.

STEVE LACY, *Morning Joy* (Hat Art), 1986.

STEVE LACY TRIO, *The Window* (Soul Note), 1987.

CARMEN McRAE, *Carmen Sings Monk* (RCA), 1988.

CASSANDRA WILSON, *Blue Skies* (JMT), 1988.

JERRY GONZALEZ, *Rumba Para Monk* (Sunnyside), 1988–1989.

RANDY WESTON, *Portraits of Duke Ellington* (Verve), 1989.

CHARLES GAYLE, *Touchin' on Trane* (FMP), 1991.

STAN GETZ/KENNY BARRON, *People Time* (Emarcy/Universal), 1991.

CLUSONE 3, *Soft Lights and Sweet Music* (Hat Art), 1993.

(JOHN ZORN AND) MASADA, *Alef* (Tzadik), 1994.

ANDY BEY, *Ballads, Blues & Bey* (Evidence), 1996.

ABBEY LINCOLN, *Who Used to Dance* (Verve), 1996.

GREG OSBY, *Further Ado* (Blue Note), 1997.

MATTHEW SHIPP "STRING" TRIO, *By the Law of Music* (Hat Art), 1997.

CASSANDRA WILSON, *Traveling Miles* (Blue Note), 1997–1998.

ETHAN IVERSON TRIO, *The Minor Passions* (Fresh Sound), 1999.

MARCUS ROBERTS, *In Honor of Duke* (Columbia), 1999.

DANILO PEREZ, *Motherland* (Verve), 2000.

About the Author

Ben Ratliff was born in New York City in 1968. He has been a jazz and pop critic at *The New York Times* since 1996. He lives in Manhattan with his wife, Kate Reynolds, and their two sons, Henry and Toby.